The Gravity of Sin

The Gravity of Sin

Augustine, Luther and Barth on *homo incurvatus in se*

by
Matt Jenson

t&t clark

Published by T&T Clark
A Continuum imprint
The Tower Building, 11 York Road, London SE1 7NX
80 Maiden Lane, Suite 704, New York, NY 10038

www.continuumbooks.com

British Library Cataloguing-in-Publication Data
A catalogue record for this book is available from the British Library

ISBN 10: 0-567-03137-3 (hardback)
          0-567-03138-1 (paperback)
ISBN 13: 978-0-567-03137-2 (hardback)
          978-0-567-03138-9 (paperback)

Typeset by Free Range Book Design & Production Limited
Printed and bound in Great Britain by Biddles Ltd, Kings Lynn, Norfolk

All we like sheep have gone astray; we have turned every one to his own way; and the Lord hath laid on him the iniquity of us all.
(Isaiah 53:6)

CONTENTS

Acknowledgments   ix
Abbreviations   xi
Introduction   1

Chapter 1
AUGUSTINE'S INWARD TURN: AN AMBIGUOUS BEGINNING   6
  Love Makes the City   6
  The Goodness of the Garden   8
  Participation and Relationality   9
  Civic Foundations: Two Standards and Two Loves   14
  What Happened? The Beginning of Sin   15
  Falsehood   22
  Pride   25
  The Will to Privacy: Isolation and Conflict   29
  Falling into Slavery   32
  The Call to Humility   33
  Augustine's Ambiguous Inwardness in *The Trinity*   37
  Conclusion   43

Chapter 2
LUTHER'S RADICAL AND RELIGIOUS INCURVATURE   47
  Setting the Task   47
  Simul iustus et peccator   49
  Fuel to the Fire: The Persistence of the *fomes*   54
  Copernicus Redux   56
  The Logic of Person and Works   63
  Totus homo: The Postures of Flesh and Spirit   66
  Incurvatus in se as Ignorance: The Critique of Natural Understanding 71
  Using, Enjoying: *Incurvatus in se* as Egoism   79
  Homo religiosus as *homo incurvatus in se*   83
  The Violation of Vocation: Transgressing the Limits of Calling 92
  Conclusion: Augustine *versus* Luther?   95

CHAPTER 3
(HOW) DO WOMEN SIN? DAPHNE HAMPSON AND THE FEMINIST
  CRITIQUE OF LUTHER   98
  Introduction   98
  Hampson's Critique of Luther on Sin, *incurvatus in se* and the Self 99

Hampson's Alternative   105
Transition: Key Questions   114
Problems with a Gendered Approach to Sin   114
Hampson's Account of Sin *per se* and the Controlling Factor
   of Continuity   122
On the Explanatory Sufficiency of *incurvatus in se*   128

Chapter 4
BROADENING THE RANGE OF THE METAPHOR: BARTH'S THREEFOLD
   DESCRIPTION OF SIN   130
Introduction   130
A Brief Apology for Paradigms   131
Sin Christologically Defined   132
Humanity Through a Christological Lens: A Closer Look   145
Sin as Pride: *CD* IV/1   155
Sin as Falsehood: *CD* IV/3   163
Sin as Sloth: *CD* IV/2   168
Hampson and Barth: A Tale of Two Sloths   182
Conclusion   186

CODA   188

Bibliography   193

ACKNOWLEDGMENTS

In what follows, I argue for an understanding of human personhood that sees women and men as constituted by their relationships. So the gentle tip of the hat that comes with the word 'acknowledgment' seems comically understated. I have heard enough stories of people who hide their research from colleagues for fear of filching to be exquisitely grateful for the fireside-warmth of friendship that has accompanied me throughout the last few years on the coast of the icy North Sea. Some of those have been friends nearby, in whose case I have difficulty knowing where their thoughts and intuitions begin and mine end. Only a few of these are Jennifer Anderson, Cindy Burris, Julie Canlis, Tony Clark, Don Collett, Oliver Crisp, Kevin Diller, Josh Edelman, Steve Guthrie, Tee Gatewood, Mark Gignilliat, Keith Hyde, Greg and Kirstin Johnson, Trygve and Kristen Johnson, Jen Kilps, Mickey Klink, Gisela Kreglinger, Darian Lockett, Duffy Lott Gibb, Ivan Khovacs, Dong Yoon Kim, Al Lukaszewski, Jane McArthur, Andy McCoy, Suzanne McDonald, Jeff McSwain, Matt Marohl, Steve Mason, Carl Mosser, Marilee Newell, Stuart Noble, Andrew Rawnsley, Jane Rowland, Ed Russell, Chris Seitz, Dave and Chelle Stearns, Jeff Tippner, Alan Torrance, Ian Werrett, David Wilhite, Cheryl Wissmann, Christiana Worley, Ross Wright and Catriona Yates. The Institute for Theology, Imagination and the Arts is a home for interdisciplinarily aspiring scholars and has been a hothouse for many of the conversations shared with these friends.

Friends who have helped practically and gracefully are Ted Blakley, without whose technical savvy I would have struggled mightily to translate German; Colin Bovaird and Lynda Kinloch, the kindest and wittiest of librarians; Margot Clement, Susan Millar and Debbie Smith, whose administrative and personal graces grease many a wheel in St Mary's College. St Andrews Baptist Church has rooted me in reality and extended to me a family with whom to worship and serve.

One could scarcely ask for a better complement of supervisors than I have found in Trevor Hart and Mark Elliott. Besides depth of insight, breath of experience and a critical generosity in reading, Trevor and Mark have shepherded me through this process with pastoral sensitivity and an eye for the forest during my frequent missteps in the trees. Even more, they have become good friends and will hopefully remain so for life. Alistair McFadyen and Jeremy Begbie examined this when it was in thesis form and have proven thoroughly gracious and encouraging.

Friends far from St Andrews figure in this picture, too. Without a loving kick in the teeth from Steve Wilke, I would likely have never applied. The steady encouragement and conversation of Mark Bilby, Dion Bush, Cameron Doolittle, Alan Jacobs, Bob McHeffey and Carl Toney have slowly suggested that an academic vocation *is* a vocation, a calling, and that I might actually have something valuable to say. A recent band of fresh and good friends has sprung up as I finish writing this at Trinity: A Church of the Nazarene and the Kingdom House in Kansas City. That one could come to love a church, a community and a city this quickly and fully amazes me as much as it delights me. Leaving breaks my heart.

Tom Kraft, Slav Todorov and the good people of T&T Clark have overseen the thesis-to-book process with enthusiasm, flexibility, patience and grace.

Then there is my family. My sister Molly draws me out of myself and has become a precious confidante in recent years. Apart from the financial help of my parents (and the United States government), I would have had to cut the programme short and swim home. Far more, they continue to be my best friends and my safest place. Mom, my ever-ready ear and a writer of splendid economy and pathos. And Dad, grace's incarnation in my life. This is for them.

ABBREVIATIONS

CD   K. Barth, *Church Dogmatics* (Edinburgh: T&T Clark, 1956–75).

LW   American edition of *Luther's Works* (Philadelphia and St Louis, 1955–86).

KD   K. Barth, *Die Kirchliche Dogmatik* (Zürich: TVZ Verlag, 1932–67).

WA   *D. Martin Luthers Werke*. Kritische Gesamtausgabe (Weimar, 1883–).

INTRODUCTION

One of the most striking features of the landscape of the Western mind in the last century was a convergence of ontology in theology and philosophy that produced a view of human personhood, and indeed much (if not all) of reality as fundamentally constituted by its relationships.[1] Indeed, despite the occasional demurral,[2] a broad consensus seems to exist on this point to the extent that one can largely assume its legitimacy.[3] Contemporary Christian theology has returned to Trinitarian reflection, with a number of 'social Trinitarian' theologies and theologians emphasizing the *imago Dei* being a social image of a social God.[4] Even those who are cautious of the potential to render the Trinity tritheistic and who avoid speaking of three personal centres in/as God such as Karl Barth (for Barth, Father, Son and Holy Spirit are divine 'modes of being') can still insist that to image God is to find one's being in relation to and encounter with another.

It is unsurprising, then, that recent theological anthropologies have emphasized continuities between the relationality constitutive of divine and human personhood.[5] Indeed, such a focus on continuity is to be expected in the midst of a recovery of the 'forgotten' Trinity. Yet, as Edward Russell has pointed out, in this Trinitarian retrieval and the broader relational turn, there has been a failure amongst theological anthropologies to account sufficiently for the discontinuities between divine and human personhood and a consequent neglect of the doctrine of sin.[6] Even though human personhood has its

---

1.   Dan Stiver notes a similar confluence in the shared emphasis on a 'holistic, embodied self', something which lends itself to an investigation of the relationships in which the embodied self is always already embedded. See Stiver, *Theology After Ricoeur* (Louisville: Westminster/John Knox Press, 2001), p. 160.

2.   E.g., Harriet A. Harris, 'Should We Say that Personhood is Relational?', *Scottish Journal of Theology* (1998), pp. 214–34.

3.   It is such a consensus which can prompt a subtitle like that found in F. LeRon Shults, *Reforming Theological Anthropology* (Grand Rapids: Eerdmans, 2003).

4.   The wide range of social Trinitarian models includes Boff, *Trinity and Society*; Grenz, *The Social God and the Relational Self: A Trinitarian Theology of the Imago Dei*; LaCugna, *God for Us: The Trinity and Christian Life*; Moltmann, *The Trinity and the Kingdom of God: The Doctrine of God*; Pannenberg, *Systematic Theology*, 3 vols.; Peters, *God as Trinity: Relationality and Temporality in Divine Life*; Volf, *After Our Likeness: The Church as the Image of the Trinity*.

5.   Edward Russell, 'Reconsidering Relational Anthropology', *International Journal of Systematic Theology* 5 (2003), pp. 168–86 (168).

6.   Ibid., pp. 168–9.

own logic apart from the grammar of sin, to speak of *this* or *that* person in *this* world is always already to speak of humanity as sinful, something which has been all too often sidelined in contemporary theological anthropology.

The following pages seek to fill the gap and redress this balance, to argue for a relational construal of sin that builds on the insights garnered from the turn to relationality with an understanding of sin as a violation, perversion and refusal of those relationships.[7] Eberhard Jüngel puts it succinctly, calling sin 'the urge towards relationlessness and dissociation'.[8] And the sinner? 'The sinner is, to put it simply, a person without relations, with no relation to God or to self'.[9] The following chapters will foreground questions of humanity's constitutive relation to God and one another, continually asking after the ways in which our sinning embodies a twisting of these relationships, a radical self-centredness in which we assert an insidious gravitational force, seeking to pull all others into our orbit. We will focus on the metaphor of humanity 'curved in on itself' (*homo incurvatus in se*), as it effectively serves to gather up various strands of a relational understanding of sin and itself deploys a system of entailments which lead to such an understanding.

In *The Body in the Mind*, Mark Johnson argues that 'underlying metaphorical systems give rise to and constrain inferences by virtue of metaphorical entailments'. By 'constraint', Johnson means to say that 'they establish a range of possible patterns of understanding and reasoning. They are like channels in which something can move with a certain limited, relative freedom.'[10] Another way of putting this is to suggest that metaphors are constitutive of certain ways of imagining, and therefore living within, the world. As Johnson notes, their entailments provide a structure within which one can see, question and interpret the world. Indeed, apart from such metaphorical structuring one cannot see the world at all. The 'limited, relative freedom' metaphors provide rules certain questions and interpretations out, but this is not to be seen as an impoverishment as much as a necessary constituent of all human knowing. To understand *this* world in *this* way is to understand it as *not that* world in *that* way. Johnson is clear that such understanding is 'one's way of being in, or having, a world' and therefore 'never merely a matter of holding beliefs'. It is instead 'a matter of one's embodiment' and 'embeddedness'.[11] Metaphorical entailments 'generate definite patterns of inference, perception, and action'. That is, they suggest certain questions (and rule out

---

7.   In speaking of a 'relational' view of sin, I do *not* intend to articulate a 'process' position. Process theology tends to reverse the direction of analogy, such that relationality is defined with reference to human relationships and then analogically extended to the God–human and Trinitarian relationships.

8.   Eberhard Jüngel, *Justification* (trans. Jeffrey F. Cayzer; Edinburgh: T&T Clark, 2001), p. 113.

9.   Eberhard Jüngel, 'The World as Possibility and Actuality', in *Theological Essays* (ed. and trans. J. B. Webster; Edinburgh: T&T Clark, 1989), pp. 95–123 (107).

10.   Mark Johnson, *The Body in the Mind* (Chicago: The University of Chicago Press, 1987), p. 137.

11.   Ibid., p. 137.

others) as well as the places to look for the answers to those questions, certain techniques and hermeneutical approaches and 'a huge system of therapeutic practices' which rest on these.[12]

Applying Johnson's insight to what follows, note that the metaphor of incurvature led directly in the writing of the first chapter to a reconsideration of the propriety of advocating a Christian spirituality of inwardness. The metaphor seemed to entail an understanding of the truly human as an ecstatic being continually drawn out of oneself into fuller relation with others. And insofar as this is a Christian metaphor – that is, one that witnesses to and organizes life around the triune God revealed and given in Christ – such an entailment (ecstatic personhood) would further entail a spirituality that renders Augustine's reflexive model problematic.

More broadly, a different set of questions are asked under a relational model of sin encapsulated in the metaphor of humanity curved in on itself than under models that focus on sin and the sinner in relative isolation from her relationships.[13] Part of this is a simple question of priorities which flow from the entailments of the metaphor of incurvature. It is self-evident (or should be) that one cannot speak of greed without attending to a network of relations of power and possession in which the very category of 'greed' finds its meaning. And yet, defining greed as 'wanting more for me' would seem to serve as a suitable definition for many. Such a definition is woefully inadequate for Christian theology, abstracting as it does from the far more important questions of those from whom we want more in our greed. The point is not so much that insatiable acquisitiveness is sinful (though it is) as it is that greed betrays and enacts a refusal to live with God and others in a relationship constituted by free, self-giving love. A failure to attend to these fundamentally constitutive relationships leads to the formulaic moralism of so much contemporary ethics, theological or otherwise. Ethics is reduced to principles which do not require embodiment in relationships but only application (often of the square peg, round hole variety) in specific settings.[14] Such principles tend to be flat-footed and reactionary.[15]

---

12.   Ibid., p. 136.

13.   Of course, no one speaks of sin in a radically a-relational context. But that sin can be spoken of as primarily an individualistic, private phenomenon and only derivatively as a relational reality is certainly the case.

14.   Not that principles in and of themselves are objectionable. What *is* objectionable is their abstraction from real relationships and re-insertion into contexts without sufficient regard to those relationships.

15.   To take two, brief examples, consider the current disparagement of 'multi-national corporations', which are often deemed simply 'bad' in light of their exploitative practices. Undoubtedly, this is the case for many, maybe most of these corporations. But the questions which should be asked are not whether such a monolithic entity as the 'multi-national corporation' is 'bad' but how businesses can practise generous, empowering practices with their employees, vendors and customers, particularly in developing countries. On the other side of the ideological spectrum, consider the critique of the 'inequity' of affirmative action policies which are said to unfairly privilege the historically disadvantaged. Besides the obvious question of whether 'fairness' is anything like a strict synonym for 'justice' or 'righteousness'

Furthermore, such principalization, coupled with an inattention to the relationships which constitute humanity, can lead to ethical prescriptions which are dangerous by virtue of their contextual independence. As we will see, it is the construal of sin principally rather than relationally that lies at the heart of certain mis-readings and mis-applications to which feminist theologians have called attention. That is, in construing pride as sinful in principle (thus cordoning off all self-assertion as illegitimate), rather than sinful in certain relational contexts, Christian theology has too often underwritten abusive power relationships in its call for a pathological self-denigration under the rubric of 'Christian humility'. But more on this below.

In what follows, I will argue for a relational account of sin in the context of a relational anthropology, an anthropology that will be implicit throughout and explicit at certain points vis-à-vis each theologian. This is, at the same time and again only implicitly, to argue against a substance ontology as well as an existential ontology. The former can all too easily do without the relationships which, I argue, are fundamentally constitutive of human personhood. The latter, in a different way, falls into the same trap, by reducing these relationships to their effects on the self. As Oswald Bayer writes, 'theology can only relate critically to ancient substance-metaphysics or modern subject-metaphysics, because both these forms of metaphysics are unable to admit thinking about an identity grounded in an excentric being or existence persisting in a foreign being'.[16]

More particularly, I will argue that the image of being 'curved in on oneself' is the best paradigm for understanding sin relationally, that it has sufficient explanatory breadth and depth to be of service to contemporary Christian theology.[17] This incurvature is one in which sinful humanity asserts a sort of gravitational pull, seeking to suck all others into its orbit. I look to Augustine as the Christian source for this image in his various references to humanity's turn to itself, though the threads of a relational account of sin are not drawn together with any systematic consequence until Martin

---

(and the related question of whether, if they are *not* synonyms, 'fairness' should be pursued at all), an abstract principle of 'fairness' completely fails in attempts to construct a society in which actual people are cared for and empowered to live as fully functioning members of that society. It ignores the contingencies of *this* person in *this* situation and thereby betrays its inability to speak about what is 'fair' at all.

16.   Oswald Bayer, 'The Modern Narcissus', *Lutheran Quarterly* 9 (1995), pp. 301–13 (310).

17.   The metaphor of being 'bent' or 'curved' can lead in at least two directions. It can speak of a distortion of the self as a result of and an embodiment of sin. But it can also speak of the effects of oppression and violence – that is, the social consequences of sin. So both sinner and sinned against are bent over by sin. While we will focus on the former aspect of the metaphor, the latter will gain prominence in our discussion in Chapters 3 and 4 of the insidious character of oppression, which bends the oppressed over while at the same time implicating the oppressed in their own oppression. For a moving discussion of this second sense of being 'bent', see Elisabeth Moltmann-Wendel and Jürgen Moltmann, *God – His and Hers* (trans. John Bowden; New York: Crossroad, 1991), pp. 57–62. They speak of the healing power of Jesus and of those who invite and empower others to stand up straight.

Luther's description of *homo incurvatus in se* in his commentary on Romans. Luther radicalizes Augustine's conception by applying this relational view of sin to the *totus homo* and by emphasizing its appearance, above all, in *homo religiosus*. The Western tradition of sin understood paradigmatically as pride has been recently called into question by feminist theologians. Daphne Hampson's critique of Luther on this front is considered and critiqued. Though she is right to call attention to the insufficiency of his and Augustine's myopic focus on pride, the question remains whether *incurvatus in se* can operate paradigmatically as an umbrella concept covering a far wider range of sins. Karl Barth's extension of *incurvatus in se* to apply more broadly to pride, sloth and falsehood suggests that incurvature can do just that.

My argument proceeds in two directions. First, it is an argument *towards incurvatus in se* from various features of a relational account of sin, in which I argue that *incurvatus in se* works as a conceptual umbrella under which these features can be gathered. Second, it is an argument *from incurvatus in se* in which I test its applicability and descriptive sufficiency as a paradigm for sin against various sins. Though both directions will be evident throughout what follows, a gradual movement will be sensed from a focus on the first in the chapters on Augustine and Luther to a focus on the second in the chapter on Hampson, concluding with a double focus in the concluding chapter on Barth.

CHAPTER 1

AUGUSTINE'S INWARD TURN: AN AMBIGUOUS BEGINNING

Love Makes the City

Near the end of his life, Augustine of Hippo sent a manuscript of the *City of God* to a layman named Firmus. He sent along a letter in which he outlined the layout of the twenty-two books. If Firmus wished to make five volumes instead of two (the pages would never fit in a single volume), the final three volumes should contain four books each, 'so that four should describe the origin of that City, four its progress, or rather its development, and the four last the ends [*sic*] in store for it'.[1] It is in Books XI–XIV, then, that Augustine speaks of the origin of 'that City' (really, he details both the heavenly and earthly cities). As he draws this discussion to a close and begins to detail civic development, Augustine sums up in what is a telling statement:

> We see then that the two cities were created by two kinds of love [*amores*]: the earthly city was created by self-love [*amor sui*] reaching the point of contempt for God, the Heavenly City by the love of God [*amor Dei*] carried as far as contempt of self. In fact, the earthly city glories in itself, the Heavenly City glories in the Lord. The former looks for glory from men, the latter finds its highest glory in God.[2]

The father of Latin theology could not be any starker in his juxtaposition of the earthly and heavenly cities. Self-love stretches to disdain for God. Love of God is equally scornful of self. Glory is sought from men (and, we are to read, *not* God) or it is sought in God (again, as opposed to being found in men).[3] We might be tempted to nervously laugh off Augustine's string of disjunctions as inflamed rhetoric, were he not so insistent on the fundamental and causal nature of these affections: 'the two cities were created by two kinds of love'.

---

1.   'Arrangement and Contents of the *City of God*' in Augustine, *City of God* (trans. Henry Bettenson; New York: Penguin Books, 1984), p. xxxvi.
2.   Augustine, *City of God*, XIV.xxviii.593.
3.   An immediate apology is necessary for the all-too-frequent use of gender-exclusive language in the following pages. Besides the obvious shortcoming of the English language in its lack of a gender-neutral third-person singular pronoun, Augustine, Luther and, to an extent, Barth display a disappointing (though contextually commonplace) insensitivity to and/or ignorance of the patriarchal cast of their language. Inclusive terms such as 'humanity' will be used where possible, though for the sake of readability the regrettable 'man' and 'men' will also appear.

When Augustine speaks of love making the city, he is collapsing a number of factors into one small word. What 'love' consists in, among other things, is (1) a certain focused attention in (2) a specific direction on (3) an object of desire which intends (4) the good of that object possibly over-against (5) the good of other objects. Love, then, is dynamic and relational, depending on another for its very coherence. The difference between life in the heavenly and earthly cities, between true and false worship, between obedience and sin can be articulated with reference to this complex of willing, attending and loving in a context of particular relationships.

What I will argue in this chapter is that Augustine offers a relational account of sin. Undergirding this is a relational anthropology, seen in his ontology of participation and implicitly throughout our discussion of sin. This is not an exercise in identifying a paradigmatic sin in Augustine's thought. He clearly sees a prideful (if futile) turning from God to self in this role.[4] Rather this is an exploration of a number of strands of Augustine's hamartiology which together form a robustly relational account of sin. If, for Augustine, sin is pride, it is not *merely* pride, but the wilful re-direction of attention and love from God to the human self apart from God which results in alienation from God and the fracturing of human society.[5] Furthermore, as will hopefully become evident in the following chapters, Augustine's various descriptions of sin offer resources for later relational understandings of sin which speak of sinful humanity as *homo incurvatus in se*, humanity curved in on itself. His language of a turn to self shows clear affinities, but more important are the entailments of the metaphor of incurvature that pepper his hamartiology. Thus, while not foregrounding the image of a person curved in on herself, Augustine paves the way for Luther's fuller account by outlining the entailments that follow on the image.[6]

4.   The cause of the angels' misery is 'their turning away from him who supremely is, and their turning towards themselves, who do not exist in that supreme degree. What other name is there for this fault than pride? "The beginning of all sin is pride."' (Augustine, *City of God*, XII.vi.477).

5.   Diane Leclerc critiques Augustine and the Augustinian tradition on the primacy of pride in the doctrine of sin, asserting the multiple and more complex nature of sin and suggesting 'relational idolatry' as an alternative. She does suggest, though, that 'a more complex and multifarious hamartiology' might be found 'in Augustine's *own* texts'. This chapter can be seen as an effort to uncover such a hamartiology and at the same time point to a later organization of this variegated hamartiology under a category which Leclerc rejects, thereby calling into question her rejection of incurvature (a 'theological synonym for pride') as an umbrella structure for sin. See Diane Leclerc, *Singleness of Heart* (London: Scarecrow Press, 2001), pp. 156–61 (quotes on pp. 157, 158). We will return to this mis-identification of incurvature and pride in Chapter 3.

6.   Not that this is the first appearance of the image of incurvature. Nygren notes its appearance in two of Augustine's expositions of the Psalms and in one of his sermons. (Anders Nygren, *Agape and Eros* [trans. Philip S. Watson; New York: Harper & Row, 1969], p. 485 n. 3).

Following an analysis of sin in the *City of God* (chiefly Book XIV, which treats the Fall),[7] we will consider the potential problem of Augustine's characterizing sin as a turn toward self while at the same time staging a number of inward turns (chief amongst which are in the *Confessions* and *The Trinity*) which have been held up as models for spirituality. Does this represent an unresolved tension between competing worldviews, or is there a deeper consistency to Augustine's approach?

The Goodness of the Garden

In discussing sin, Augustine always has in mind God's intentions in creation and the earlier state of Adam and Eve in the goodness of Eden. It will be structurally helpful to look first at how Augustine conceives of prelapsarian human existence in order to understand better the implications of turning from God to self.

Everything God creates is good, Augustine begins in accordance with Genesis 1. God's creation is good, because he is himself 'the Supreme Good'.[8] In paradise:

> [Man] lived in the enjoyment of God, and derived his own goodness from God's goodness...There was no sadness at all, nor any frivolous jollity. But true joy flowed perpetually from God, and towards God there was a blaze of 'love from a pure heart, a good conscience, and a faith that was no pretence'.[9]

Adam and Eve lived richly joyful lives in Eden, loving God with a pure love. Augustine does not envisage this as a static, bland existence, though. He imagines this felicity continuing 'until...the number of the predestined saints was made up', at which time God would grant an even greater happiness than originally given at creation.[10] Augustine has a fundamentally communal picture of the good life established by God in creation. He writes:

---

7.   We have chosen the *City of God* because it is a major late document (412–26/7) in Augustine's corpus which is the closest thing we have to a systematic theology. The *City of God* is both a catechetical tool and a deeply comprehensive vision of reality. What is more, though highly polemical in its overall structure and at specific points, the *City of God* manages to be more than mere polemic and must thus be taken with all seriousness rather than relegated to the status of polemical museum piece on the assumption that polemical works are finally no more than irretrievably occasional works which have no place in constructive Christian theology. Of course, simply because we can spot the rhetorical hyperbole and polemical occasion for a work of Augustine's, or anyone else for that matter, does not give us licence to dismiss it as irrelevant or unreflective. The very manner of doing patristic theology (with such titles as Origen's *Contra Celsum* or Irenaeus' *Adversus Haereses*) points to the fact that theology can be at once polemical and constructive.

8.   Augustine, *City of God*, XIV.v.554.

9.   Ibid. XIV.xxvi.590.

10.   Ibid. XIV.x.567. There is an interesting, if faint, echo here of Irenaeus' doctrine on the imperfection of creation, seen in terms of the growth God intended for creation from the outset.

God chose to make a single individual the starting-point of all mankind...His purpose in this was that the human race should not merely be united in a society by natural likeness, but should also be bound together by a kind of tie of kinship to form a harmonious unity, linked together by the 'bond of peace'.[11]

Note the strength of humanity's social bond. It is not merely a bond of 'natural likeness', according to which people are lumped together by a generic similarity. No, this is much deeper, a 'kind of kinship' that binds men and women into a 'harmonious unity', in which we are linked one to another by the 'bond of peace'. In the harmonious unity, Augustine alludes to the possibility of *dis*similarity, thus establishing difference in the overall structural unity. With the bond of peace we learn that this unity has an ethical component, creating a society in which people live together rightly.[12] This is a vision that dominates the *City of God* from start to finish, and one which is never far from the field of vision. Indeed, a fruitful way of reading the work as a whole would trace Augustine's understanding of this 'harmonious unity', including its source, its inner working, its potential obstacles and its *telos* in the vision of God, a surprisingly *social* vision.[13] Clearly one of Augustine's primary concerns, in Book XIV and throughout the *City of God*, is to assert the fundamentally social nature of the life of both cities.[14]

Participation and Relationality

We turn now to participation, which is Augustine's primary category for articulating humanity's relational constitution. All the good things in this good life together, indeed the life itself, are gifts. Accordingly, at creation man had a proper dependence on God in which his goodness flowed from God's goodness.[15] That this dependence was salutary is emphasized continually by Augustine. When God gave man 'one very short and easy commandment', his 'intention in this command was to impress upon this created being that he was the Lord; and that free service was in that creature's own interest'.[16]

---

11. Ibid. XIV.i.547.

12. For a helpful integration of harmony as metaphysical and moral unity-in-difference, see ibid. XIX.xii.870.

13. See ibid. XXII.xxix.1087: 'perhaps God will be known to us and visible to us in the sense that he will be spiritually perceived by each one of us in each one of us, perceived in one another, perceived by each in himself'. Also ibid. XXII.xxx.1091: 'There *we* shall be still and see; *we* shall see and *we* shall love; *we* shall love and *we* shall praise. Behold what will be, in the end, without end!' (emphasis mine)

14. See ibid. XIX.xvii.879. The real question we have to ask concerns the *character* of each city's sociality. Is it a harmonious, peaceful, worshipful society of persons united in relationship to God and one another, or is it a society of discord, war, private affections and broken relations? In either case, fully divesting oneself of relationships is quite simply impossible.

15. Ibid. XIV.xxvi.590.

16. Ibid. XIV.xv.574. Also see XIV.xxvii.592.

Of course, 'God's instructions demanded obedience', but these are neither arbitrary instructions nor blind obedience, 'seeing that the rational creation has been so made that it is to man's advantage to be in subjection to God, and it is calamitous for him to act according to his own will, and not to obey the will of his Creator'.[17] The creator has structured his creation, has given it a rationality that operates according to his will. This is natural enough to assume of any benevolent creator. Creators seldom create things to work in opposition to their will. Man, being a part of the rational creation, finds things to his advantage when he is in subjection to God and functioning in light of his created rationality. This is not a burdensome task, but one that only comes naturally, as we are speaking here of 'a time when desire was not yet in opposition to the will'.[18]

Augustine speaks of humanity's continual dependence on God as the giver of every good gift (life included) in terms of an adherence to or participation in God. In glossing the serpent's tempting promise in Genesis 3, he writes: 'In fact they would have been better able to be like gods if they had in obedience adhered to the supreme and real ground of their being...For created gods are gods not in their own true nature but by participation in the true God.'[19] Despite attempts to minimize the theme of deification in the patristic era as exotic or simply heterodox,[20] Augustine stands squarely in the mainstream of early church tradition in affirming a form of deification here and in a number of other places in his corpus. The real issue is not whether Augustine affirms deification, but what it looks like in the structure(s) of his thought. Gerald Bonner argues that:

> Augustine's mature understanding of deification is based upon a theological datum and a philosophical concept. The theological datum is, of course, the God-man Jesus Christ, by whom, and by whom alone, we come to the Father...the philosophical conception is that of participation by man in God.[21]

Bonner identifies Augustine's adoption of the Platonic *structure* of participation in God with a kind of spoiling of the Egyptians. Further, while Augustine was first exposed to deification through Neoplatonist philosophy, by the time he came to writing the *City of God* he had rejected a Porphyrian account which saw deification as an end humanly attainable through philosophical effort. In

17.   Ibid. XIV.xii.571.
18.   Ibid. XIV.xii.571.
19.   Ibid. XIV.xiii.573. The Latin reads: *'Dii enim creati non sua veritate, sed Dei veri participatione sunt dii.'*
20.   One example is a recent conference I attended in which deification was referred to as an 'exotic flower' and a secondary theme at best in the Fathers. While such a comment betrays a clear bias and quickly collapses under the weight of evidence, note Gerald Bonner's more irenic point that 'the doctrine taken by itself and without any further definition, is a curious one, and justifies the suspicions of Protestant critics, who feel that it is unchristian' (Gerald Bonner, 'Augustine's Conception of Deification', *Journal of Theological Studies* N.S. 37 [1986], pp. 369–86 [370]).
21.   Ibid., pp. 372–3.

its place, Augustine had posited a far more Christian account, in which we are deified through a divinely initiated participation in God.[22] It is entirely to miss the point to set up the discussion, as D. J. Macqueen does, in terms of *apotheosis* versus *imitatio*. Macqueen offers a false dilemma – being changed into God ('no rational creature can *become* God') and merely being like him (it is 'possible for a creature to *imitate* God').[23] Augustine uses different categories, speaking of the one who is God in himself and those who are gods by participation in the one, true God. These categories allow for a much richer understanding of the always central relationship in which we are transformed as creatures and enter into a life of communion with God.

Returning, then, to the gloss on Genesis 3 above, we note a number of salient points which relate to participation in God:

1) God is the supreme and real ground of our being.
2) It is to our advantage to obediently adhere to him, as this is necessary for us to become like gods. In addition, if he is the ground of our being, our very *life* is to some extent wrapped up in obedient adherence to him.
3) Becoming like gods is a real possibility and is not to be disdained, properly understood.
4) We are never to understand deification as in any way a transgression of the bounds between creator and creature. Even as gods, we are still *created*. Thus, our status as gods refers to our being in some sense 'even more' creaturely, not less creaturely.
5) Godliness is not natural. That is, it is not something that inheres in us apart from God.
6) Since we are *not* gods *in se*, we can only become gods by participation in the true God, a participation which involves adhering to him, particularly to him insofar as he is the ground of our being.

Unfortunately, Augustine says precious little in Book XIV of *City of God* about the mechanics of participation. On one level, that participation is only sketched in a section dealing specifically with sin is not surprising. However, that Augustine can speak directly of deification without reference to Christ is indicative of a wider concern.[24] He is more explicit elsewhere that Christ's participation in our humanity is the sole condition for our participation in

---

22.   Ibid., p. 372.
23.   D. J. Macqueen, '*Contemptus Dei*', *Recherches Augustiniennes* 9 (1973), pp. 227–93 (244).
24.   This may be due not to an insufficient Christology as much as to Augustine's insufficiently calling our attention to what is in fact a central aspect of all of his theology, that is, his Christology. We should keep in mind Brian Daley's observation that Christology is one of the few areas in which 'Augustine seems never to have been drawn into serious debate', sandwiched as he was between Apollinarianism (which was rejected at Constantinople at 381) and Nestorianism (which reached a fever pitch at around the time of Augustine's death in 430) (Brian E. Daley, 'A Humble Mediator', *Word and Spirit* 9 [1987], pp. 100–17 [100]).

his divinity and, hence, in the life of God. The incarnation is a 'short cut to participation in his own divine nature'.[25] In a sermon on Psalm 81 preached at Carthage during the winter of 403–404, he speaks of deification as something which ought not seem incredible in light of the 'more incredible' incarnation of the Son of God.[26] But he still seems at times to use a Christ-of-the-gaps method, whereby Augustine to a great extent knew who God is and what constitutes our relationship to him from his reading the 'books of the Platonists'.[27] It is as if Christ fills out the content of Platonic participation and Platonic understandings of God. But does Christ not radically re-define both participation and the God in whom we participate?[28] Nevertheless, it must be acknowledged that, in reading Augustine's work carefully, one is impressed by his efforts to think more and more scripturally and Christianly over the years.

God intends for his good creation to live in eternal dependence on him, but a dependence which allows for, or rather establishes and sustains, creaturely flourishing. Augustine can call God 'that light which would make man himself a light if he would set his heart on it'.[29] Setting our hearts on 'that light' is akin to adhering to God. As we set our hearts on the light, it illuminates us. We see clearly in this light, and this 'seeing clearly' involves both a well-lit room and corrected vision. That is, we are both brought into the light and, precisely by being in the presence of the light and setting our hearts on it, are ourselves made lights. In the presence of the light and the healing of our sight we begin to see things around us for what they really are. We come to know that we are always already in the midst of relationships, for instance; and we come to see those to whom we relate in the right light. It is precisely

---

25.   See Augustine, *City of God*, IX.xv.360–61: 'The multitude of the blessed is made blessed by participation in the one God...And that Mediator in whom we can participate, and by participation reach our felicity, is the uncreated Word of God, by whom all things were created...God himself, the blessed God who is the giver of blessedness, became partaker of our human nature and thus offered us a short cut to participation in his own divine nature. For in liberating us from mortality and misery...[he brings us] to that Trinity...In the lower world he was the Way of life, as in the world above he is the Life itself.'

26.   See the translation of Augustine's sermon in Augustine Casiday, 'St. Augustine on Deification', *Sobornost* 23 (2001), pp. 23–44 (28).

27.   See Book VII in the *Confessions*.

28.   Two examples of how Christ *does* more radically re-define our participation in God are of note: William Mallard writes that the 'shift in agency from the man participating "upward" to God participating "downward" is quite enough to say a cornerstone of thought has changed for Augustine. A unique "downward" initiative of singular divine agency could not emerge within Augustine's strictly philosophical milieu' (William Mallard, 'The Incarnation in Augustine's Conversion', *Recherches Augustiniennes* 15 [1980], pp. 80–98 [88–89]; cited in David Vincent Meconi, 'The Incarnation and the Role of Participation', *Augustinian Studies* 29 [1998], pp. 61–75). Bonner notes that Augustine uses Platonism in arguing that 'man's being depends upon his participation in God; but Augustine develops this theologically by appealing to Scripture to argue that man's sanctity depends upon his participation in God' (Bonner, 'Augustine's Conception of Deification', p. 379).

29.   Augustine, *City of God*, XIV.xiii.573. See also X.ii.374.

in this renewed vision that we become lights. It is not pushing Augustine too hard at this point to say that, in recognizing (this being a type of *metanoia*) our relationally constituted identities and coming to know those to whom we relate in the right light (God, then others), we become selves. That is, we become fully functioning humans.

What is significant here is the divine extravagance which would make men and women lights. There is no sense that God is in any way threatened, even by the prospect of having 'fellow' lights. This is important to keep in mind, in that there is a way of conceiving of transcendence such that God and creation must always be defined in opposition. Aside from the significant initial dangers of God being only as big as our opposite, there is also the danger of thinking that God and humanity are by definition *required* to stay on either side of the fence. Augustine never wants to ascribe the classical divine attributes (e.g. immortality, divinity) to humans *by nature*, but he *does* want to say that we are granted what is God's *by grace*. Augustine's language is of being, for instance, immortal in oneself versus being immortal by participation. We are never immortal in ourselves, but we are immortal by participation in God,[30] by adhering to God, that is, by grace.[31] In all this, the elect in Christ, while never leaving their side of the fence, are at the same time invited and escorted to the other side of the fence. Of course, Augustine is merely voicing the tradition of the Fathers in these affirmations; but the effect on how we understand transcendence is significant.[32] This distinction between things which are good (or wise or loving, etc.) in themselves versus things which are good by participation is a central rule for negotiating the ontological difference between creator and creation for Augustine. It allows him to make glorious claims on behalf of humanity without blurring the creator–creature distinction or compromising the glory of the creator.[33] And it does this by only ever speaking of humanity *in relation to* the one in whom it participates. Nevertheless, that humanity incessantly resists this participation is patent; and we turn now to an account of the origins and character of that resistance.

30. Kilian McDonnell's remark, that 'God gives in to Adam's original temptation', even granted its playfulness, is wide of the mark precisely because it passes over humanity's sinful desire to be immortal *in se*. See McDonnell, 'Jesus' Baptism in the Jordan', *Theological Studies* 56 (1995), pp. 209–36 (236).

31. Given his use of metaphors like adhering, cleaving, enjoying and contemplating throughout the *City of God* (all of which require a direct object, another), and given his concern to continually uphold the creator–creature distinction, it seems clear that Augustine is not asserting a crude dissolution of the human self in the divine but is rather speaking of a relationship of intimate communion and dependence.

32. We will return to this issue at a number of points, particularly in dialogue with Karl Barth, who wants to define transcendence as God's eternal, self-giving, loving decision to be with, in and for humanity in Christ. Transcendence, God's otherness, is seen in his ability to overcome 'transcendence' by being with us.

33. For one example, see Augustine, *City of God*, XIV.xiii.573: 'For created gods are gods not in their own true nature but by participation in the true God.' David Meconi significantly argues that it is 'participation [which] allows Augustine to maintain two levels of reality.' (Meconi, 'The Incarnation and the Role of Participation', p. 66)

Civic Foundations: Two Standards and Two Loves

Augustine book-ends Book XIV with two characterizations of the two cities. In the opening of the book, he writes:

> There is, in fact, one city of men who choose to live by the standard of the flesh, another of those who choose to live by the standard of the spirit. The citizens of each of these desire their own kind of peace, and when they achieve their aim, that is the kind of peace in which they live.[34]

The two cities, both of which desire some sort of peace, are to be distinguished with reference to the standards by which they live. Augustine is quick, particularly given the broader intellectual climate of his day, to denounce any interpretation of 'flesh' that would lead to a denigration of materiality.[35] He points out that in Gal. 5.19-21, Paul refers to a list of 'works of the flesh' which include works concerned with 'sensual pleasure' as well as 'those which show faults of the mind'.[36] 'Flesh', then, is not equivalent to human physicality, but a synecdoche in which the part represents the whole.[37]

Augustine rejects both Platonist and Manichean anthropologies in light of their inability to call created physicality 'good'.[38] Augustine censures the carnality of a 'cult of the soul' as well as a 'revulsion from the flesh' as attitudes 'prompted by human folly, not by divine truth'. In response, Augustine affirms that the flesh is 'good, in its own kind and on its own level'.[39] In addition to his affirmation of the central Christian tenet of creation – that what God creates is, *by definition*, good – Augustine speaks of a peculiar creaturely goodness ('in its own kind') which is to be viewed in relation to some other realities ('on its own level'). We will return to these in due course.

At the close of Book XIV, in a passage with which we opened this chapter, Augustine puts the distinction even more starkly: 'the two cities were created by two kinds of love: the earthly city was created by self-love reaching the point of contempt for God, the Heavenly City by the love of God carried as far as contempt of self'.[40] In this programmatic passage, Augustine deploys a rhetoric of antithesis to sharpen the point made above: the cities

---

34. Augustine, *City of God*, XIV.i.547.
35. Augustine's full rejection of Manichean dualism, including its notion that an evil counter-deity created matter, which now imprisons sparks of the divine and needs to be escaped, is never far away in Augustine's accounts of anthropology and evil.
36. Ibid. XIV.ii.549.
37. Ibid. XIV.ii.550.
38. *Contra* Alister E. McGrath, *Iustitia Dei* (Cambridge: Cambridge University Press, 2nd edn, 1998), p. 198.
39. Augustine, *City of God*, XIV.v.554. We leave aside the question of whether Augustine's substance dualism is a compelling account of human personhood, as the main point here is Augustine's cordoning off some basic boundaries for subsequent Christian anthropologies. For one, they are to acknowledge the inherent goodness of God's creation. Secondly, and as a consequence, they are not to point to one 'part' of the person as some sort of natural fount of sin.
40. Ibid. XIV.xxviii.593.

are fundamentally differentiated with reference to the objects of their loves. Self-love and love of God are simply incompatible. In fact, they are inversely related. Augustine is speaking of a certain (sinful) type of self-love at this point. He is not dismissing wholesale any concern for oneself but rather critiquing that self-love which would seek its flourishing apart from God.[41] In this sense, the passage reflects Augustine's commitment to an ontology of participation in which creatures find their good in their creator.

What Happened? The Beginning of Sin

In considering humanity in sin, we will start with a rather obvious question: *What happened?* God, who is goodness himself, created nothing but good. He emphatically did *not* create evil, and yet here Augustine finds himself, all too aware of the evils of fifth-century life in northern Africa, seen both amongst churchly people (the Donatist controversy) and in larger society (the invasion of the Vandals).[42] Where do we place the blame? The knee-jerk reaction of intelligent men of Augustine's day, including *both* Platonists and Manichees, would be to blame the body. They might debate on how we got these unhelpful bodies (was there a fall of the soul into a crassly embodied state, as in Plotinus, or did an evil counter-deity create our bodies to entrap the seeds of the divine, as in Mani?), but they would quickly agree that our bodies are things to escape, denigrate, maybe at best to begrudgingly tolerate. While Augustine is decidedly ambiguous at a number of points about the body and related issues (sex being the first that comes to mind), he unequivocally rejects this disparagement of physicality for one simple reason – God created our bodies just as much as he created our minds/souls.[43]

41. Unlike Luther, Augustine can allow for an appropriate self-love. Augustine is not interested in a critique of egoism *per se*, instead he accepts the idea that we all naturally pursue our own flourishing. Indeed, he never questions the reality of humanity's fundamental desire for happiness and a certain kind of concomitant self-love. It is an inescapable category that structures his approach to life in the two cities. He thinks that arguments wrapped up in intentionality, at least in regard to the question of our pursuit of our own welfare, are *faux pas*. The place to challenge is in the path to happiness. In drawing out the common motivation of the two cities, and thus highlighting shared features, Augustine is setting a rhetorical trap. He is preparing to drive the wedge of difference precisely where we have come to recognize commonality. We know that different paths often (though not always) lead to different destinations. One might ask, and rightly so, whether the happiness sought in the earthly city and that sought in the heavenly city are the same happiness. Or are they so different that using the same term for each is sheer equivocation? Presumably, what I intend in seeking my own happiness and what you intend are not identical. Certainly Augustine saw the happiness he desired as not only different from, but contrary to Roman happiness.

42. See Susan Raven, *Rome in Africa* (London: Routledge, 3rd edn, 1993), pp. 190–95.

43. Augustine seems to have adopted the stock mind/soul–body dualist anthropology of his day in a fairly unquestioning manner. At least, he adopted this bi-partite structure and thought in terms of body and soul as two distinct substances. His views on physicality grew more positive over his career, later speaking of the soul's love of the body. See John M. Rist, *Augustine* (Cambridge: Cambridge University Press, 1994), pp. 92–112.

There is one significant difference between the originating sin of Adam and Eve and all subsequent sins in Augustine's discussion. 'After the first sin, we sin involuntarily and are the moral agents of the evil that we do only in the sense that we are ourselves the authors of the condition in which we cannot help but sin.'[44] Thus, sin can be only spoken of as a possibility rather than in some sense a necessity with reference to Adam and Eve (as well as the fallen angels, or at least their leader). That being said, sin subsequent to the fall perfectly mirrors the first sin, except in the later sin's necessity. Of course, many will immediately object that the relative necessity of sin is a morally unacceptable theological claim in the twenty-first century. While this may or may not be the case, it is not a surprising move, but rather a consistent one, given Augustine's commitment to viewing humanity as relationally consti-tuted. Contemporary Christian theology has highlighted the relationality of human existence and even extended this to certain aspects of the doctrine of sin, bringing out the structural and broader relational components of sin.[45] No one seems to be pushing for a reinvigoration of Augustine's sense of inherited guilt and his way of reading the 'in Adam' of Romans 5, however. In an essay evaluating Augustine's scriptural hermeneutics, Richard Trench writes that:

> This chapter [Romans 5] is the rock upon which all Pelagian schemes of theology, which ground themselves on an extenuation of the Fall, on a denial of the significancy of Adam's sin (save in the way of evil example), to any but himself, – which break up the race of mankind into a multitude of isolated atoms, touching, but not really connected with, one another, instead of contemplating it as one great organic whole, – must for ever shiver and come to nothing.[46]

Whatever the merits of Augustine's weighty reading of 'in Adam', we should note how seriously he takes our relational constitution. It is worth quoting him again at this point:

> God chose to make a single individual the starting-point of all mankind...His purpose in this was that the human race should not merely be united in a society by natural likeness, but should also be bound together by a kind of tie of kinship to form a harmonious unity, linked together by the 'bond of peace'.[47]

Relational accounts of theological anthropology and of sin must wrestle with Augustine's profoundly relational point: that all of humanity sinned and is therefore guilty in Adam. For Augustine, this merely serves as the foil for the

44.   William S. Babcock, 'Augustine on Sin and Moral Agency', *The Journal of Religious Ethics* 16 (1988), pp. 28–55 (40).

45.   Walter Wink's series on the powers is one example. Another is Alistair McFadyen, *Bound to Sin* (Cambridge: Cambridge University Press, 2000).

46.   Richard Chenevix Trench, *Exposition of the Sermon on the Mount* (London: Macmillan and Co., 3rd edn, 1869), p. 116.

47.   Augustine, *City of God*, XIV.i.547.

beautiful recapitulation of Christ, in that we are found righteous and innocent in him.[48]

If we ask how things got to be this bad, then, we know at least that it
was an issue of living by the rule of self or by the standard of man. This is
helpful in understanding the contours of fallen existence, but we are still left
with wondering what started it all.[49] If, as we have seen Augustine is eager to
affirm, 'it was not the corruptible flesh that made the soul sinful', what is to
blame? Augustine is quick with an answer: 'it was the sinful soul that made
the flesh corruptible'.[50] And how did the soul itself become sinful? This was
an act of will, initiated by pride.[51]

> For they would not have arrived at the evil act if an evil will [*voluntas mala*] had not
> preceded it. Now, could anything but pride [*superbia*] have been the start of the evil
> will? For 'pride is the start of every kind of sin.' And what is pride except a longing
> for a perverse kind of exaltation? For it is a perverse kind of exaltation to abandon
> [*deserto*] the basis on which the mind should be firmly fixed, and to become, as it
> were, based on oneself, and so remain. This happens when a man is too pleased
> with himself: and a man is self-complacent when he deserts that changeless Good in
> which, rather than in himself, he ought to have found his satisfaction. This desertion
> [*defectus*] is voluntary...the evil act, the transgression of eating the forbidden fruit,
> was committed only when those who did it were already evil.[52]

A sophisticated intertextuality here gives hermeneutical pride of place to Eccl.
10.13 ('pride is the start of every kind of sin'),[53] allowing Augustine to read

---

48.   Augustine's picture was asymmetrical at this point, given his well-known views on
predestination, which leaves room to wonder in what sense Christ's redemption is universal.

49.   This sort of question, which implicitly looks for a cause external to the questioner,
is indicative of the search for a scapegoat that is itself a result of sin. When God questions
Adam and then Eve about their sin, 'their pride seeks to pin the wrong act on another; the
woman's pride blames the serpent, the man's pride blames the woman' (ibid. XIV.xiv.574).

50.   Ibid. XIV.iii.551. Thus, corruptibility is a punishment for sin rather than the sin
(or at least rather than the original sin) itself. Note again, the exoneration of physicality
and the pointed condemnation of the *soul* as the source of sin. See ibid. XIV.iii.550, XIII.
xvii.528–29.

51.   R. A. Markus writes: 'Augustine seems especially determined there [in Book XIV]
to represent sin not in terms of the soul's entanglement in the flesh, but as residing in a
perversity internal to the will itself. Sin is pride rather than sensuality; and sensuality the
consequence and penalty of pride.' (R. A. Markus, 'Pride and the Common Good', in Joseph
C. Schnaubelt and Frederick Van Fleteren (eds.), *Collectanea Augustiniana*, vol. 1: *Augustine:
Second Founder of Faith* (New York: Peter Lang, 1990), pp. 245–59 [251]).

52.   Augustine, *City of God*, XIV.xiii.571–72. Augustine gives a pithy summary of this
in the discussion of Galatians 5 and the 'works of the flesh' mentioned above, writing that
'the fountain-head of all these evils is pride' (ibid. XIV.iii.552).

53.   This is fitting, given as Ecclesiasticus offers the first doctrinally oriented exegesis
of the fall story in ancient literature. Furthermore, its fundamentally conservative outlook
makes it a reliable gauge of orthodox theological teaching in Ben Sira's time. (F. R. Tennant,
The Sources of the Doctrines of the Fall and Original Sin [New York: Schocken Books,
1968], pp. 107, 109).

the first sin (and indeed every additional sin) as paradigmatically prideful.[54] Pride is seen as 'the start of the evil will'. By this, Augustine seems to be saying that pride is the first manifestation of the will's corruption, rather than that it somehow comes before and therefore causally produces an evil will.[55] While unquestionably offering a helpful, imaginative reading of Genesis 3, Augustine presses the text at this point, finding the original sin to lie *behind* and *before* the eating from the tree of the knowledge of good and evil. It is not that evil entered the creation through an evil act, but rather that it entered through an evil will, that of Adam and Eve.[56] Thus, as Babcock has noted, the drama of Genesis 3 in Augustine's reading 'shows us only how human beings, already evil, enacted their first misdeed'.[57] Of course, one could enquire as to the origin of the evil will itself; but here Augustine is agnostic. It is a mystery.[58] Or at least, Augustine believes he has done his job of clearing God from the charge of either deficiently creating or being himself the author of sin. The truly voluntary nature of pride (recalling that Adam and Eve only had truly free wills in their prelapsarian state),[59] and the fact that this is an orientation of will rather than the invasion of some external evil, places the responsibility squarely on the shoulders of Adam and Eve.

Even more, though, asking about the origin of an evil will is asking the wrong question, because it supposes that evil is a substantial reality. Augustine writes:

> The truth is that one should not try to find an efficient cause for a wrong choice. It is not a matter of efficiency, but of deficiency [*non enim est efficiens sed deficiens*]; the evil will itself is not effective but defective…To try to discover the causes of such defection – deficient, not efficient causes – is like trying to see darkness or to hear silence.[60]

---

54.   Interestingly, Augustine could have helpfully employed the previous verse of Ecclesiasticus (10.12) in his discussion of the turn toward self: 'The beginning of human pride is to forsake the Lord; the heart has withdrawn from its Maker'. O'Connell argues that Eccl. 10.9-14 either convinced Augustine or confirmed his conviction that pride is the first sin. See Robert J. O'Connell, 'Augustine's Exegetical Use of Ecclesiasticus 10:9-14', in Frederick Van Fleteren and Joseph C. Schnaubelt (eds.), *Augustine: Biblical Exegete* (Oxford: Peter Lang, 2001), pp. 233–52 (248). Carol Harrison suggests that Plotinus may also have been an influence in the priority of pride, 'expressed as love of self and of one's own powers (including power over others), in antithesis to love of God', referencing a passage at *Enneads* 5.1. See Harrison, *Augustine* (Oxford: Oxford University Press, 2000), pp. 88–9.

55.   After all, as we have just heard from Augustine, 'what is pride except a longing for a perverse kind of exaltation?' Babcock agrees in saying that, 'for Augustine, pride is not the "cause" of the first evil will, but rather its content, taking oneself rather than God as the center and principle of one's existence' (Babcock, 'Augustine on Sin and Moral Agency', p. 52).

56.   Augustine does not treat Eve's succumbing to temptation and Adam's subsequent joining her in eating the fruit as isolated incidents. He is content to treat this sequence of events as a single event.

57.   Babcock, 'Augustine on Sin and Moral Agency', p. 42.

58.   See Augustine, *City of God*, XII.xii.477.

59.   'The choice of the will, then, is genuinely free only when it is not subservient to faults and sins' (ibid. XIV.xi.569).

60.   Ibid. XII.vii.479–80.

Here is Augustine's definition of evil as *privatio boni*, or a privation of good. Simply put, deficiency is not a 'thing' for which we need to account. It is a thing's malfunctioning, which has no independent existence in itself. Augustine's reference to seeing darkness and hearing silence is *à propos*, as these are realities of which we are on one level very aware and yet, upon closer examination, have no existence independent of their positive counterparts. We *do* feel we know what darkness and silence are, as we also feel we know what evil is; but in the end we recognize that they are merely the absence of light and sound. We cannot speak of darkness without reference to light, though we *can* (and here, Augustine is making a penetrating comment on metaphysics, arguing against any form of cosmic dualism) speak of light without reference to darkness. As Charles Mathewes writes, 'this *causa deficiens*, this deficient causality, has its own proper description wholly in what it is not, in its failure to be a good act'.[61] Thus Augustine writes that an evil will:

> Cannot exist except in a nature...Nevertheless good things can exist without the evil, just as the true and supreme God as also all the celestial creation, visible and invisible, exists above this murky air of ours. In contrast, evil things cannot exist without the good, since the natural entities in which evil exists are certainly good, in so far as they are natural.[62]

Augustine never swerved from those aspects of his early theological commitments which were forged against the Manichees, particularly his complete rejection of their metaphysical dualism. Since God has created all things good, anything which is is good. Consequently, any evil is not natural, that is, not according to nature as God created it. Since evil is not natural, Augustine will just as forcefully claim that evil is not, that it has no being *per se*.[63] This will have significant consequences for Augustine's understanding of humanity's fall into sin. He asserts that 'an evil will is not natural but unnatural because it is a defect'.[64] Augustine explains:

---

61.   Charles T. Mathewes, '*Interior intimo meo*', *Journal of Religious Ethics* 27 (1999), pp. 195–221 (205). In exploring how Augustine addresses this issue in angelic sin, Babcock finds this unconvincing, arguing that Augustine is left with either an arbitrary first sin or compelled to the position that the sin was a 'function of God's withholding aid. What [Augustine] could not find was that continuity with the dispositions, inclinations, motivations, aims and intentions of the agent that must be present if an act is to count as the agent's own and therefore as an instance of moral agency.' (Babcock, 'Augustine on Sin and Moral Agency', p. 49). Mathewes counters this line of thinking, arguing that such an approach attempts to locate a real cause for sin and misses a basic point in Augustine's account of ontology and creation: 'To seek a "cause" for sin is to try to render it intelligible, and to render it intelligible is to render it explicable; that would tie it back into the explanatory fabric of the cosmos, the violation of which is what sin quite literally is' (p. 206).
62.   Augustine, *City of God*, XIV.xi.568–69.
63.   Hence Smith's remark: 'What Augustine offers is not an ontology but rather a phenomenology of sin' (James K. A. Smith, *Speech and Theology* [London: Routledge, 2002], p. 121).
64.   Augustine, *City of God*, XIV.xi.568.

> But the first evil act of will [*voluntas*], since it preceded all evil deeds in man, was
> rather a falling away [*defectus*] from the work of God to its own works, rather than
> any substantive act. And the consequent deeds were evil because they follow the will's
> own line, and not God's. And so the will itself was, as it were, the evil tree which bore
> evil fruit, in the shape of those evil deeds; or rather it was the man himself who was
> that tree, in so far as his will was evil.[65]

The evil deeds of the first pair were preceded by an evil act of will which was,
nevertheless, not in itself a *substantive* act but rather a falling away from
God's work to man's works. This choosing involved the exchanging of God's
standards for man's, leading to works of the flesh rather than works of the
spirit. Augustine emphasizes *voluntas* to the point of equating a man's will with
himself (more of the synecdoche of which he is fond). The man is evil himself
as far as his will is evil, and it is this evil orientation of will which is the direct
cause of evil deeds. This much is clear. What are the implications for placing
the origin of evil so squarely in the will? For one, creation is again affirmed as
inherently good. Evil is decidedly contingent; in fact, it is doubly contingent,
reliant for its 'existence' (which is a non-existence) on the good creation
which itself is contingent. A second implication of the centrality of *voluntas*
is that evil is defined relationally rather than substantially. That is, rather
than something which inheres in a person, evil comes to describe a turning
from one person/thing to another.[66] We are evil in giving disproportionate or
inappropriate attention to something or someone. Thus we can be said to be
evil in attending too little to God or other people or in attending too much
to ourselves or other people. Privation, then, as an absence of good, can refer
to an absence of attention, too much attention or the wrong sort of attention
being paid to another. In either case, the absence of good is seen in attention's
inordinate quality.[67] Evil, under this rubric, is not a 'thing' but a description of
the way a person's will is ordered and directed. Keeping in mind Augustine's
near equation of will with personhood,[68] we can describe a person as evil
when that person gives inordinate attention to something or someone. Such
inordinate attention perverts the relationship, as well as both parties in the
relationship, disruptive as it is of the harmony of the creation rightly related
to God.

Returning to our inordinate attention to ourselves, rather than to God,
Augustine writes that our falling away, or *defectus*

65. Ibid. XIV.xi.568.

66. Rowan Williams describes Augustine's 'grammar of evil' in terms of a
'malfunctioning of relations between subjects'. 'Talking about evil is not like talking about
things…it is talking about a *process*, about something that happens to the things that there
are in the universe' (Rowan Williams, 'Insubstantial Evil', in Robert Dodaro and George
Lawless (eds.), *Augustine and His Critics: Essays in Honour of Gerald Bonner* (London:
Routledge, 2000), pp. 105–23 [112, 105]).

67. Cress points out that 'a privation may be indicated either by having too few or too
many parts' (Donald A. Cress, 'Augustine's Privation Account of Evil', *Augustinian Studies*
20 [1989], pp. 109–28 [118]).

68. Willing 'constitutes his very being, making it what it is' (Harrison, *Augustine*, p.
95).

does not consist in defection to things which are evil in themselves; it is the defection in itself that is evil. That is, it is not a falling away to evil natures; the defection is evil in itself, as a defection from him who supremely exists to something of a lower degree of reality; and this is contrary to the order of nature.[69]

The defective falling or turning away ('falling' denotes the lowering of one's sights from the greatest good to a lesser, because contingent, good, while 'turning' emphasizes the re-direction of attention to a new object) is *itself* perverse, Augustine insists. It is emphatically *not* that we are evil as created, as that would contradict Augustine's doctrine of creation. But we become evil (never fully, as no creature can become fully evil and remain a creature) when we choose a radically autonomous path ('the will's own line') in opposition to God ('and not God's'). The assault on created harmony that is evil also entails a frustration of our own perfection.[70] When we live in light of 'the order of nature', we are and are on our way to becoming fully ourselves. Thus Donald Cress suggests that the 'main issue with privation is a thing's ability to achieve its proper level of order and measure, i.e., to progress toward a thing's natural perfection and fulfillment'.[71] We would simply add that the 'natural perfection and fulfillment' of a thing is, in Augustine's schema, always related to its ordering in God's grand harmony. In sum, evil reflects an inordinate love and a misdirected will, a love and will which give undue emphasis to man, setting him up in the place of God. A perversion of our constitutive relationality results, so that in inclining towards ourselves and away from God, we first paint a distorted picture of our relation to God by pretending the relationship does not exist. At the same time, in attempting to extricate ourselves from this prior relationship, we enter into conflict in the human relationships which also make us who we are. We seek to entice or force others to also (to switch the metaphor) move out of God's orbit and into ours. While rarely a self-conscious move, in doing this, we open others to the same fate into which we have handed ourselves – self-isolation and self-denigration. As D. J. Macqueen has written, in addition to being privative, 'perverse self-love is also "separative", inasmuch as it alienates the proud alike from God and neighbour'.[72]

We will turn now to look at three modes of humanity's sinful turn towards self.

---

69.   Augustine, *City of God*, XII.viii.480. Also see XII.vi.478: 'For when the will leaves the higher and turns to the lower, it becomes bad not because the thing to which it turns is bad, but because the turning is itself perverse'.

70.   Rowan Williams connects harmony and the insubstantial character of evil: 'A discord on a musical instrument is not the result of the instrument being interfered with by an external agency *called* discord, it is a function of the workings of what is there, of what constitutes the instrument itself' (Williams, 'Insubstantial Evil', p. 112).

71.   Cress, 'Augustine's Privation Account of Evil', p. 118.

72.   Macqueen, '*Contemptus Dei*', p. 246.

Falsehood

We recall Augustine's striking suggestion that man 'has become like the Devil' by 'living by the rule of self, that is by the rule of man'. Self-rule apart from God is a sort of *imitatio diaboli* and betrays 'a secret itch to acquire the Divine status',[73] attempting to undermine our participation in God by setting us up as persons who are good in themselves rather than by virtue of participating in another.[74] Augustine continues by remarking that the devil whom we imitated 'chose to live by the rule of self when he did not stand fast in the truth, so that the lie that he told was his own lie, not God's'.[75] Living by the rule of self, then, is living a lie, having forsaken the truth in which we once stood. Augustine hints that this is to be grounded christologically, making reference to Christ's claim to be the truth.[76] In abandoning the rule of the one who *is* the truth, in refusing to stand fast in this personal truth (and here again we note the importance of our relational participation in God in Christ for Augustine), we come to live *de facto* 'in' falsehood.[77]

> Not that man himself is falsehood [*mendacium*], since his author and creator is God, who is certainly not the author and creator of falsehood. The fact is that man was created right, on condition that he should live by the standard of his creator, not by his own, carrying out not his own will, but his creator's. Falsehood consists in not living in the way for which he was created.[78]

Falsehood, then, is a life which denies God's creative intentions for us. In living falsely, we continually assert that we are other than who God created us to be. Fundamentally, this amounts to a radical denial of God. He is *not* the creator, we repeat in every self-ruled action.

The obvious point is that this ceaseless denial of God as creator is itself a lie. Augustine picks up on the nuances of human inconsistency in a discussion of the universal desire for happiness. Immediately after stating that falsehood 'consists in not living in the way for which he was created', Augustine writes:

> Man has undoubtedly the will to be happy, even when he pursues happiness by living in a way which makes it impossible of attainment...And hence the falsehood: we commit sin to promote our welfare, and it results instead in our misfortune; or we sin to increase our welfare, and the result is rather to increase our misfortune. What is the reason for this, except that well-being can only come to man from God, not

---

73.   Ibid., p. 243.

74.   We recall Augustine's distinction between things which are good (or wise or loving, etc.) in themselves versus things which are good by participation, which is a central rule for negotiating the ontological difference between creator and creature for Augustine.

75.   Augustine, *City of God*, XIV.iii.552.

76.   Though note that Augustine ascribes this statement to 'God' rather than 'Christ' (ibid. XIV.iv.552).

77.   See ibid. XIV.iv.552.

78.   Ibid. XIV.iv.552.

from himself? And he forsakes God by sinning, and he sins by living by his own standard.[79]

Sin involves us in the greatest of ironies. We want to be happy, yet we pursue happiness along an impossible route. We want to flourish, yet we willingly choose our own destruction. 'And hence the falsehood...' This falsehood, sin, is the will to be happy apart from the only one who can make us happy. In our pursuit of happiness, we reject the living truth who is the only way to happiness.

While certainly illustrative of what we might call 'living a lie', Augustine's point is stronger. Falsehood refers to moral failure, but it also refers to ontological deformity. It will be helpful at this point to bring in a discussion of his idea of the degrees of being in relation to the central theme of evil as *privatio boni*. Augustine writes:

> Yet man did not fall away to the extent of losing all being; but when he had turned towards himself [*inclinatus ad se*] his being was less real than when he adhered to him who exists in a supreme degree. And so, to abandon God and to exist in oneself, that is to please oneself, is not immediately to lose all being; but it is to come nearer to nothingness [*nihilo*].[80]

The image of a sinful turning or inclination towards oneself gathers together a number of threads in Augustine's relational conception of sin, as well as anticipating and bearing a family resemblance to Luther and Barth's description of *homo incurvatus in se*. The form of sin as *inclinatus ad se* perfectly matches the nature of sin so conceived. While the phrase is one entirely devoted to the self, indeed without any explicit reference to any other relations, there is nevertheless an implicit reference to a relationship or relationships from which one has inclined. If I incline *towards* something, the implication is that I had to make a shift in the direction of my attention – that is, I had to turn from one attentional relation in order to incline towards myself. This parallels the irony of sin in which we try to divest ourselves of limiting, defining relationships (beginning with our relation to God, but moving on to include our relations with other people, with history, with the created order, even with ourselves) and found ourselves in ourselves, yet never being able to untangle ourselves from the fundamental relation of dependence on God and others for our very lives.

God exists 'in a supreme degree', Augustine notes in the passage above; and we are most real when adhering to him. We are never as real as he is, of course, as we do not exist in ourselves but only by virtue of him. The inclination towards self is an ontologically downward movement, what is really a *declining* of the level of being offered as one stands in relation to God in favour of a lower level of being. In turning my back on truth and living a

79. Ibid. XIV.iv.552–53.
80. Ibid. XIV.xiii.572–73.

lie, I actually become less of a creature. While this is not immediately to lose all being (and much might be made of the implications of Augustine's use here of 'immediately'), it *is* a venturing towards non-existence, towards the literal undoing of creation. God created out of nothing (*creatio ex nihilo*), and we risk sliding back to nothing in abandoning him. Oliver O'Donovan puts this vividly: 'The rebellious soul finds itself on a greasy pole where the only safe place is the place it has just left, the top'.[81] There is a dynamic potentiality implied in Augustine's degrees-of-being theory. He is quite explicit about our being created 'as a kind of mean between angels and beasts', such that our volitional orientation will result in our attaining to life with the angels or death with the beasts.[82] O'Donovan describes man as standing 'with his feet in the center of the universe, able to stretch upward toward God or to contract back upon himself and fold himself away from God'.[83] With such a dynamic sense of being, Augustine can effectively link the moral and ontological aspects of our existence, such that living poorly by turning away from God and others makes us less ourselves. Indeed, more than merely linking, Augustine identifies the moral and ontological, so that 'to be' is simply 'to be good'.[84] Augustine's metaphysical framework, with its sense of an actual sliding towards nothingness, allows us to sense this more acutely than contemporary society's more existential language which can speak of not being 'real' in a way that evokes a sense of personal hypocrisy and maybe dis-integration, but not an actual diminishing.[85]

81.   Oliver O'Donovan, *The Problem of Self-Love in St. Augustine* (London: Yale University Press, 1980), p. 103. The situation is exacerbated in that our defection from the unchangeable Good to that which is changeable only leads to a further instability (p. 102). Thus, the 'unfortunate soul is carried past her stop and ends up not exactly at nothingness but uncomfortably close to it' (p. 103).

82.   See Augustine, *City of God*, XII.xxii.502.

83.   O'Donovan, *The Problem of Self-Love in St. Augustine*, p. 101. O'Donovan notes further: 'Several times Augustine calls upon this physical picture of the soul's activity, distinguishing between man erect and man bent...In such passages Augustine will usually speak of man's bending downward to the earth beneath him rather than simply to himself; but the two physical metaphors – recoiling upon himself and stooping down to the earth – are part of the same pictorial scheme.'

84.   I am thankful to Trevor Hart for suggesting that this is a matter of *identifying* more than merely drawing the moral and ontological into closer relation.

85.   Though it is interesting at this point to note that one of the significant consequences for Augustine of our sinful inward turn is this movement towards nothingness which is a dis-integration of our ordered selves and worlds. The sin of *inordinatio* leads to further *inordinatio*.

Pride[86]

We return, then, to seeing the inclination towards self as an inordinate exaltation of self, that is, as pride.[87]

> And what is pride [*superbia*] except a longing [*appetitus*] for a perverse kind of exaltation? For it is a perverse kind of exaltation to abandon the basis on which the mind should be firmly fixed, and to become, as it were, based on oneself, and so remain. This happens when a man is too pleased with himself: and a man is self-complacent when he deserts that changeless Good in which, rather than in himself, he ought to have found his satisfaction.[88]

The introduction of the category of 'satisfaction' is illuminating. As we have seen, Augustine is concerned above all with the order of our loves. Satisfaction is the desire that has been quenched and re-kindled in the joy of attaining to its *telos*. Lest we should nudge a category as unsettling as desire to the margins, consider the following words of Augustine: 'The whole life of the good Christian is a holy longing....That is our life, to be exercised by longing'.[89] The very fact that our lives are structured around desire[90] points to a relational anthropology in which the sin of pride is a denial of the very relationships which constitute us. As Hannah Arendt writes: 'Since man is not self-sufficient and therefore always desires something outside himself, the question of who he is can only be resolved by the object of his desire and not, as the Stoics thought, by the suppression of the impulse of desire itself...Strictly speaking, he who does not love and desire at all is a nobody.'[91] This is because, in Robert Meagher's words, 'delight, as [desire's] end, is the

---

86. O'Donovan takes Augustine's emphasis on pride in perverse self-love as 'the Western starting point', noting a 'general contrast between the moral theology of the West and the East' in which 'the latter moves from sensuality to pride, from the temptation of the flesh to the temptation of the spirit, and the former moves in the opposite direction' (O'Donovan, *The Problem of Self-Love in St. Augustine*, p. 105).

87. D. J. Macqueen has conducted exhaustive research into *superbia* in Augustine's thought. See his doctoral thesis, 'The Notion of *Superbia* in the Works of St. Augustine with Special Reference to the *De Civitate Dei*' (University of Toronto, 1958). See also D. J. Macqueen, 'Augustine on *Superbia*', *Mélanges de Science Religieuse* 34 (1977), pp. 193–211; Macqueen, '*Contemptus Dei*'.

88. Augustine, *City of God*, XIV.xiii.571–72.

89. Augustine, *In epistolam Joannis ad Parthos*, tractatus 4.6; cited in Margaret Miles, 'Vision', *Journal of Religion* 6 (1983), pp. 125–42 (134).

90. And, as a result, the 'Augustinian presentation of human sinfulness [is] as a corruption of desire' (Wolfhart Pannenberg, *Anthropology in Theological Perspective*, [trans. Matthew J. O'Connell; Edinburgh: T&T Clark, 1985], p. 91). Anders Nygren locates human sinfulness in the cessation of desire: 'If he ceased to desire, that would mean that he believed himself to possess his "good" in himself, and no longer needed to seek it anywhere else' (Nygren, *Eros und Agape II*, p. 288; cited in John Burnaby, *Amor Dei*, [London: Hodder & Stoughton, 1938], p. 93).

91. Hannah Arendt, *Love and St. Augustine* (London: The University of Chicago Press, 1996), p. 18.

very core of the person'.[92] Rather than being self-satisfied, Augustine's point is that we ought to find our satisfaction in the changeless, and therefore perfect, good, which is God. It only makes sense that the greatest good would afford the greatest satisfaction. The irony is that we have become pleased, fascinated, even charmed, by ourselves. It is difficult to lay out a chronology and argue whether self-complacency or the desertion of God come first. It is probably most helpful to picture these as two perspectives on the same condition, with self-complacency speaking of our self-relation in sin and desertion of God highlighting the broken relation to God. In any case, we note the mutual exclusivity of finding our satisfaction in ourselves versus finding it in 'that changeless Good'.[93]

The same mutual exclusivity applies to basing ourselves on ourselves versus being based on God. Basing ourselves on ourselves is clearly a 'kind of exaltation', in that we become[94] our own ground. We support ourselves with no other props or framework, least of all a creator God. We thus become our own justification. Rather than looking elsewhere in an attempt to explain ourselves, we find in ourselves all that needs to be said. Again, a God in whom we live and move and have our being is rejected. We do all of that *in se*. This is an attempted usurpation of the throne of divinity, in which 'the love of self that runs to the contempt of God is neither egoism nor egocentrism, but "egotheism" – not selfishness but blasphemous rebellion'.[95]

An implication of this radical denial of relationship with God is an equally radical denial of relationship with other people. Here Augustine reminds us of our *imitatio diaboli*, of whom he writes:

> The arrogant angel came, envious because of that pride of his, who had for the same reason turned away [*conversus*] from God to follow his own leading. With the proud disdain of a tyrant he chose to rejoice over his subjects rather than to be a subject himself; and so he fell from the spiritual paradise.[96]

Envy follows pride. Like the devil, we exchange submission to God for being our own leaders and lords. By turning towards ourselves, itself a kind of conversion, we walk away from God to blaze a new trail. In following our own lead, we demand that the people around us do the same (whether or not

---

92.   Robert Meagher (ed.), Augustine, *On the Inner Life of the Mind* (Cambridge: Hackett Publishing Company, 1998), p. 101.

93.   This can never be true satisfaction, of course. Satisfaction, in the *City of God*, is the secure enjoyment of that which we desire. Objects of desire can only be enjoyed, however, in God. He is himself our greatest joy, and all other goods are to and can be enjoyed in him alone. See the discussion of Augustine's distinction between use and enjoyment on pages 79–83 below.

94.   Whether we can ever *actually* become based on ourselves is doubtful. In speaking of this self-grounding, he is speaking 'from below', expressing the vain human attempt at self-grounding.

95.   Burnaby, *Amor Dei*, p. 121.

96.   Augustine, *City of God*, XIV.xi.569.

we explicitly intend to do so), thus becoming our subjects. Meagher notes that a

> frequent theme of Augustine's is that human being cannot escape service (i.e., its own proper place in the order of things) and that all of its attempts at mastery merely alter the conditions of its servitude. Ironically, perhaps, human being is never without its lord. Human being never itself becomes sovereign.[97]

We are not content, as we once were, to walk together in the way of God. Nor are we content to walk in our own way alone. Instead, we are envious of the devotion of others.[98] Risking a psychological extension of this, we might say that, while attempting to ground ourselves, we still seek an additional external justification, which is found in other people slavishly following our perverse lead. Needless to say, this threatens community at its very base, in that we are asserting an alternate base (ourselves) from the one base which, for Augustine, forms a loving community (God).[99]

Self-exaltation is self-deification. We would exalt ourselves to the point of God, which is exactly what we do in re-naming ourselves as ground and basis of our existence. Thus Augustine can speak of 'the self-worship of pride',[100] saying that, since

> man already started to please himself...he was delighted also with the statement, 'You will be like gods.' In fact they would have been better able to be like gods if they had in obedience adhered to the supreme and real ground of their being, if they had not in pride made themselves their own ground. For created gods are gods not in their own true nature but by participation in the true God. But aiming at more, a man is diminished, when he elects to be self-sufficient and defects from the one who is really sufficient for him.[101]

---

97. Meagher (ed.), *On the Inner Life of the Mind*, pp. 198–9.

98. There is a double meaning in our being envious of others' devotion. We want to lord it over others, to receive their devotion in worship. We also are jealous of the purity of their rightly ordered devotion to God. Augustine goes on in his description of the devil: 'After his fall, his ambition was to worm his way, by seductive craftiness, into the consciousness of man, whose unfallen condition he envied, now that he himself had fallen' (*City of God*, XIV. xi.569).

99. Augustine describes the community found only in God: 'the peace of the Heavenly City is a perfectly ordered and perfectly harmonious fellowship in the enjoyment of God, and a mutual fellowship in God; the peace of the whole universe is the tranquility of order' (ibid. XIX.xii.870).

100. Ibid. XIV.xiii.572.

101. Ibid. XIV.xiii.573. Jonathan Edwards makes a similar point, and beautifully: 'Immediately upon the Fall the mind of man shrunk from its primitive greatness and extensiveness into an exceeding diminution and confinedness...shrunk into a little point, circumscribed and closely shut up within itself to the exclusion of others...But God hath in mercy to miserable man contrived in the work of redemption, and by the glorious gospel of his Son, to bring the soul of man out of its confinement...And so Christianity restores an excellent enlargement and extensiveness to the soul' (Jonathan Edwards, 'Charity and Its Fruits', in *The Works of Jonathan Edwards*, vol. 8: *Ethical Writings* [ed. Paul Ramsey; New Haven: Yale University Press, 1989] pp. 252–54).

Augustine's point is that creatures are simply *not* gods by nature, that is, in themselves. Similarly, creatures are *not* grounded in themselves. So, as Augustine points out, any attempt at exaltation is 'perverse' and thoroughly futile. In cutting ourselves off from our true basis in God, we actually cut the ground out from under our feet. Thus, any attempt at self-deification issues in irony. As O'Donovan writes: 'what appears subjectively as aggrandizement is, in objective reality, diminution'.[102] By 'aiming at more', we quite literally become less.[103] There is an inverse relation between our autonomous ambition and our actual achievement. As was noted earlier, it is crucial to keep in mind Augustine's positive appraisal of the notion of deification. It is emphatically not that he recoils at the notion that humanity would be exalted even to a sort of 'god' status. Augustine sees no inherent competition between God and creation, so that God is not threatened in exalting humanity. The creator-creature distinction is maintained in that creatures are never in a place of greater dependence upon God than when they rely for their very deification on God. He gives; we receive. The competition is between God and a creation that desires to be god without God. Thus, competition between God and creation is itself a falsehood (to bring in an earlier category), in that it asserts something which is not truly the case of God and creation but only 'becomes' so in the falsely autonomous pride of humanity's grasping at what is not properly its own.[104] Thus, in sinful self-inclination, our turning is 'at once an act of self-assertion and an act of self-deprivation'.[105] In Augustine's words, self-complacent man 'elects to be self-sufficient' and thus runs from the one who would be sufficient unto deification.

The Will to Privacy: Isolation and Conflict[106]

Augustine's primary comparison in Book XIV is between receiving our good as a gift from God versus claiming to be our own good (being good *in se*).[107]

102. O'Donovan, *The Problem of Self-Love in St. Augustine*, p. 102. Augustine frequently enlists Ecclesiasticus 10; and the sense of pride as an enlargement which leads to or is really a diminishment, coupled with the sense of the disorder and diffusion following on sin is seen in Ecclesiasticus' image of pride as a swelling, bursting and spewing one's insides. On this, see O'Connell, 'Augustine's Exegetical Use of Ecclesiasticus 10:9-14', pp. 234, 248.

103. The diminishment Augustine speaks of is, of course, an ontological as much as a moral reality. Our earlier discussion of falsehood touched on this sense of 'coming nearer to nothingness'.

104. Kathryn Tanner makes this point in reference to the Reformers: 'There is no competition between giving the glory to God and receiving the good in a humanly fulfilling way but there is competition...between a completely autonomous human good and dependence upon God' (Tanner, 're: non-competitiveness and research', personal e-mail message 28 April 2003).

105. Babcock, 'Augustine on Sin and Moral Agency', p. 42.

106. I am thankful to Phil Cary for pointing out to me that the social form of humanity's sinful incurvature includes both isolation *and* conflict.

107. We could also spot this theme in the comparison of *amor Dei* and *amor sui*, or that of being grounded in God *versus* being grounded in self.

Implicit in this comparison, however, is a fundamental point about community. R. A. Markus writes:

> The emphasis in [Augustine's] later writings is on sin as isolation, the retreat of the self from community into privacy, from 'sociable' openness into self-enclosure... the 'sociable' love concerned for the common good as against the 'private' love subordinating the common good to its own power for the sake of dominion...For the hierarchical paradigm of pride Augustine has substituted a social one. 'Suum ["one's own"],' O'Donovan has observed, 'has become an objective, ontological category'.[108]

In an otherwise excellent article, Markus overstates his case in claiming that Augustine substitutes a social paradigm of isolation for his earlier hierarchical paradigm.[109] Augustine does not leave behind his sense that sin is *inordinatio*, which Markus points out expresses 'a classically organized hierarchical cosmology along with the rational morality to correspond'.[110] However, he is right to draw our attention to the theme of isolation in Augustine. With it, he alerts us to another controlling distinction in Augustine's writing, that between public and private.[111]

For Augustine's perspective on sin as isolation and the concomitant public/private distinction, we need to move beyond Book XIV of the *City of God*. It is not absent from Book XIV, but it does remain largely implicit. One exception is in Augustine's discussion of Adam's sinning:

> We cannot believe that the man was led astray to transgress God's law because he believed that the woman spoke the truth, but that he fell in with her suggestions because they were so closely bound in partnership...Adam refused to be separated from his only companion, even if it involved sharing her sin.[112]

108. Markus, 'Pride and the Common Good', p. 251. The citation is from O'Donovan, *The Problem of Self-Love in St. Augustine*, p. 104.

109. Also see R. A. Markus, *Saeculum* (London: Cambridge University Press, 1970), pp. 76–81. Markus admits that Augustine still speaks of order; but he argues that, for Augustine, at least political order is a consequence of the Fall and not natural (pp. 197–210).

110. Markus, 'Pride and the Common Good', p. 248. Interestingly, Markus does point out that *inordinatio* is a feature of even Augustine's latest works. It would seem natural, then, for sin to contain an element of *inordinatio* in the *City of God*, which it does.

111. Note that Markus' tendency to read hierarchical and social paradigms as alternatives in Augustine draws an unnecessary and possibly arbitrary distinction between the two. Even in so clearly a hierarchical thinker as Plotinus (undoubtedly a major source for Augustine's thinking on sin), we find the two as complementary descriptors: 'But we are more truly alive when we turn towards it [i.e., the Absolute or the One], and in this lies our well-being. To be far from it is isolation and diminution.' (*Enneads* 6.9; quoted in W. R. Inge, *The Philosophy of Plotinus* [2 vols; London: Longmans, Green and Co., 1918], vol. 2, p. 138). Of course, the two diverge sharply in their anthropologies. Where Augustine sees sin and death, Plotinus can only admit sickness. See the charitable but pointed discussion of Christian and Plotinian understandings of sin, humanity and salvation in H. Armstrong, 'Salvation, Plotinian and Christian', *The Downside Review* 75 (1957), pp. 126–39. On sin as an extra-Plotinian category, also see Inge, *The Philosophy of Plotinus*, vol. 2, p. 172.

112. Augustine, *City of God*, XIV.ii.570.

Thus in Adam's very desire to preserve relationship, he cripples it. This is not necessarily a *deliberate* assault on relationships. While Adam's taking and eating may have been more consciously contrary to his relation to God (and Augustine and Genesis 3 seem to think this was the case), we could hardly say that Adam intended to play the role of saboteur in his relationship with Eve. If anything, he wanted to play the saviour. But such an inordinate desire for what, finally for Augustine, is a less significant relationship, thus subordinating God to one of his creatures, condemns Adam and Eve's relationship from the start and issues in God's fitting curse later in Genesis 3. Of course, it is not this relationship or even Adam's desire to preserve it that Augustine faults; as always, the fault lies in the perverse direction of the affections, in the turning from God to creation and giving it ultimate pride of place. The austerity of this picture needs to be balanced with Augustine's concern to articulate the fundamentally constructive place of our relation to God. The curse follows not out of the need to satisfy the divine ego but as the only appropriate response to forsaking God. It is as if God were to say, 'This is what life is like when you turn your back on me'.

The isolation of sin is sharply contrasted to humanity's *telos* in the beatific vision. Augustine's description of this vision at the end of the *City of God* is profoundly communal, such that we enjoy God together,[113] and we only enjoy one another as we enjoy one another *in God*. In all this, Augustine implies that in turning from God, we have turned from the only source of true communion with others. Community, then, is only possible in a relationship of participation in God. The converse of this is that relation to God is at one and the same time relation to other people. We cannot have one without the other. Mary Clark, who has argued that 'Augustine is radically a philosopher of community',[114] puts it this way:

> Man is neither an *en-soi* (an inhuman individual) nor a *pour-soi* (a human individual). Of course man-is-in-the-world and he is with-others, but man-is-for-God, yet for a God who creates and loves his world and all persons in it. This is why Augustinian other-worldliness can never be interpreted rightly as anti-world. In the Augustinian context man cannot fulfil his human vocation except by collaborating in the creative work of God. Man cannot really be for-God unless he is for-others. Other men, in the true spirit of St. John's Gospel and St. Paul's vision, mediate God's call to each man, and this is why Augustinian anthropology is a humanism precisely because it is theocentric.[115]

---

113. God 'bound them together in one fellowship, which we call the Holy and Heavenly City, in which God himself is for those spirits the means of their life and their felicity, is, as it were, their common life and food' (ibid. XXII.i.1022). Robert Meagher writes: 'Human blessedness understood as life in the City of God, in contrast to the Greek understanding of blessedness as solitary, apersonal contemplation, is both personal and communal' (Meagher [ed.], *On the Inner Life of the Mind*, p. 285).

114. Mary T. Clark, *Augustinian Personalism* (Villanova, PA: Villanova University Press, 1970), p. 1.

115. Clark, *Augustinian Personalism*, pp. 2–3.

For Augustine, this means that the heavenly city is fundamentally marked by holding everything in common, in much the same way as the early Christians of Acts 2 did.[116] He speaks of:

> The children of grace, the citizens of the free city, the sharers in eternal peace, who form a community where there is no love of a will that is personal and, as we may say, private [*propriae ac privatae*], but a love that rejoices in a good that is at once shared by all and unchanging – a love that makes 'one heart' out of many, a love that is the whole-hearted and harmonious obedience of mutual affection [*id est perfecte concors oboedientia caritatis*].[117]

The idea of a will to privacy and the need for competition in this free city is absurd, according to Augustine. There is no danger in this heavenly city, 'where neither moth nor rust destroys, and where thieves do not break in or steal'.[118] Because everything is secure and joy is guaranteed, a radical unity and mutuality breaks out in which children of grace rejoice in the shared (elsewhere Augustine might say 'public') good and shared goods.[119] These are people who do 'not grudgingly withhold [their] discoveries from another'.[120] Accordingly:

> A man's possession of goodness is in no way diminished by the arrival, or the continuance, of a sharer in it; indeed, goodness is a possession enjoyed more widely by the united affection of partners in that possession in proportion to the harmony that exists among them. In fact, anyone who refuses to enjoy this possession in partnership will not enjoy it at all; and he will find that he possesses it in ampler measure in proportion to his ability to love his partner in it.[121]

The delicious irony of heavenly life is that we *do* possess goodness fully (and all good things, we can assume) by virtue of sharing it with others. Gone are the days when sharing a piece of the pie meant one less piece for me. Sharing a piece of the pie now somehow makes the pie bigger and better-tasting! Note, too, that the joy of possession increases precisely in and by the mutuality of affection, a mutuality which creates and reflects harmony. Motivations change in eternity, too. Where possession was for my sake and bred constant

---

116. The monastic community is a kind of microcosm or anticipation of the heavenly city in this aspect and offers an antidote (if not a complete one) to the isolating pride of humanity. 'Monasticism' in Augustine's thought refers to the oneness of the community in heart and mind rather than the singular isolation of each monk. See Harrison, *Augustine*, pp. 183, 189–90.

117. Augustine, *City of God*, XV.iii.599. Also see *The Trinity*, XII.iii.17.332.

118. Mt. 6.19. Thus O'Donovan: 'For Augustine the idea that one person's individual interests could clash with another's was simply a mistake' (O'Donovan, *The Problem of Self-Love in St. Augustine*, p. 103).

119. Truth is itself a common good, one which *cannot* be held privately. God is the highest of goods, and he is a good who can only be 'held' in the common fellowship of saints.

120. Augustine, *City of God*, XIX.xix.880.

121. Ibid. XV.vi.601.

conflict and competition, the delight I now take in possessing some good is bound up with my loving others in the midst of the possessing. There is a danger in getting caught up here in the old chicken-and-egg dilemma. Which comes first and provides the motivation? My delight in possessing the good, or my loving another? At the eschaton, this simply becomes a non-issue; because possessing the good and loving another both co-exist. Indeed, they constitute one another, such that true possession involves loving through sharing and true loving leads us together to a possession of the good. As D. J. Macqueen writes, for Augustine, love is 'the constitutive bond of society'.[122]

Falling into Slavery

Augustine suggests that God gives humanity the space to live out the consequences of pleasing itself rather than being satisfied in God. There is the sense that, while radical autonomy is never completely possible – we would cease to exist if we were completely cut off from all relation to God – God has allowed our sinful defection from God and towards ourselves to take its course. The results are disastrous.

> He who in his pride had pleased himself was by God's justice handed over to himself. But the result of this was not that he was in every way under his own control, but that he was at odds with himself, and lived a life of harsh and pitiable slavery, instead of the freedom he so ardently desired, a slavery under him with whom he entered into agreement in his sinning.[123]

Again, we see the irony of sin. God's justice hands man over to himself, just as man wanted. But the result is unexpected. The point was for man to be his own king, to have everything pertaining to himself under his own control; but he finds that his grasp for autonomy has led to slavery. He is at odds with himself, having become a nuisance to himself,[124] and is infinitely farther from the freedom he had desired.

The freedom man had sought in turning towards himself is a freedom to be himself on his own terms. He had hoped for a broader range of options in living. Specifically, he had desired his own flourishing apart from God. Rather than opening up a horizon of possibilities, however, man is left unable to do the very things he wants to do. Augustine's description brings to mind Romans 7:

> For man's wretchedness is nothing but his own disobedience to himself, so that because he would not do what he could, he now wills to do what he cannot. For in paradise,

---

122. Macqueen, '*Contemptus Dei*', p. 236.
123. Augustine, *City of God*, XIV.xv.575. Also see XIV.xxiv.589: 'because he did not obey God he could not obey himself'. Augustine is echoing Rom. 1.24-25 here.
124. Augustine, *City of God*, XIV.xv.576.

before his sin, man could not, it is true, do everything; but he could do whatever he wished, just because he did not want to do whatever he could not do.[125]

Augustine offers a portrait of the miserable, because divided, self.[126] He contrasts the slavery of division with the freedom of paradise. Note that the garden's freedom was *not* a freedom for anything and everything. It was, however, a freedom to 'do whatever he wished' (both in terms of man's ability and his being allowed to do what he wished). This was 'a time when desire was not yet in opposition to the will'.[127] Freedom, then, was an integrated loving, willing and doing. Man's freedom entailed his living as God created him to live, because it was right and because he delighted to do so. Because 'the choice of the will...is genuinely free only when it is not subservient to faults and sins',[128] and the pre-eminent sin is an inclining away from God towards oneself, we can say that (radical) autonomy and freedom are *mutually exclusive* terms for Augustine.[129]

The Call to Humility

In contrast to the self-worship of pride, Augustine presents a different kind of worship, one which is humble and looks to a different object, namely God. 'In the Heavenly City, on the other hand, man's only wisdom is the devotion which rightly worships the true God, and looks for its reward in the fellowship of the saints, not only holy men but also holy angels, "so that God may be all in all".'[130] In suggesting that the heavenly city's worship *is* its wisdom, Augustine further underscores the complementarity of God's receiving the worship due him, his being all in all, and our flourishing in his midst. We find a true reward in the wise life of devotion, and this is one found 'in the fellowship of saints'.

The humility of communal worship is the *telos* of the Christian life, itself a picture of the healed humanity. Indeed, it is humility itself which heals the corruption of man after his falling into himself. John Burnaby writes: 'Because

125. Ibid. XIV.xv.575. Compare the Pauline text at Romans 7.15, 19. Despite an earlier reading of Romans 7 as describing a pre-Christian condition, by at least 415, Augustine consistently read it in terms of the Christian's struggle with sin. (Rist, *Augustine*, p. 179).

126. Ibid. XIV.xxiv.589.

127. Ibid. XIV.xii.571.

128. Ibid. XIV.xi.569.

129. When we speak of the mutually exclusive nature of autonomy and freedom for Augustine, we have in mind modern notions of autonomy which really constitute a radical autonomy. Mathewes has argued for a coherent notion of autonomy in Augustine's anthropology, stating that 'the ground of his anthropology is his conviction that at the core of the self is an other, God'. Accordingly, Augustine 'refutes characterizations of his account of divine sovereignty as heteronomous. The account is not heteronomous because there is no self, strictly speaking, apart from, and primordially independent of, God' (Mathewes, 'Interior intimo meo', pp. 216, 211).

130. Augustine, *City of God*, XIV.xxviii.594.

man has fallen through pride, he can be raised again only through humility...
The way of redemption is "first, humility, second, humility, third, humility".'[131]
This is one of Augustine's most salutary points. This relates to our discussion
of the *privatio boni*, for the literal non-existence of evil in and of itself leads
Augustine to the conclusion that 'an evil is eradicated not by the removal of
some natural substance which had accrued to the original, or by the removal
of any part of it, but by the healing and restoration of the original which had
been corrupted and debased'.[132] Augustine's refusal of substantiality to evil
moves him to argue that God redeems humanity not by excising some portion
of it, but by healing it internally. So, God does not destroy humanity and start
over,[133] but chooses instead to heal it. God's faithful commitment to preserving
his creation is emphasized here. Rather than amputation, God prescribes the
medicine of humility. Augustine points to the example of Peter: 'I venture to
say that it is of service to the proud that they should fall into some open and
obvious sin, which can make them dissatisfied with themselves, after they have
already fallen through self-complacency'.[134] Humility involves a reversing of
the process of self-fascination through the self-disgust that comes in falling
into 'open and obvious sin'.

Self-disgust is not the healing of humanity, however, and this is the crucial
point at issue. It is here that we are re-introduced to Christology. It is the
humble Christ, certainly in terms of his moral character, but even more so in
the very condescension of incarnation, who saves us. Rather than requiring
us to ascend to God, God has descended to us in Christ, partaking of our
humanity that we might participate in his divinity. In its recapitulation
of our sin, Christ's humility is a fitting, just, well-ordered response to our
proud, inordinate self-love.[135] David Meconi is helpful here, reminding us of
Augustine's pivotal shift in the direction of participation.

> The Word comes to the lowly and out of their very *limus*, out of their very 'filth,' he
> deigns to build a dwelling (*humilis domus*)...Once inside this lowly dwelling, those
> who wish to enter are lifted upward. Inside this domicile wounds are healed and all
> are nourished by the love of God (*sanans tumorem et nutriens amorem*). But what
> enemy lurks outside this home from which the Word protects us? The enemy is none
> other than ourselves. The Word comes to save us from ourselves: so we may not go on
> further in self-confidence. The humbling of the Word defeats the pride of creation.
>
> Downward participation thus saves prideful humanity from continuing in its own
> self-affirmation. The chasm opened by the pride of Adam is bridged by the humility
> of Christ. This is a chasm nowhere found in Neoplatonism. Does not a good Platonist

131. Burnaby, *Amor Dei*, p. 190.
132. Augustine, *City of God*, XIV.xi.569.
133. Though the case of Noah comes strikingly close to this, God's preserving a remnant
of humanity (in Noah's family) and of 'every kind' (Gen. 6.19) of animal points to God's
commitment to vindicating his creation.
134. Augustine, *City of God*, XIV.xiii.573–74.
135. Augustine clusters the ideas of fittingness, justice and order in his use of metaphors
of harmony. In *The Trinity*, he uses Pythagorean proportionality to speak of a 'harmony of
salvation' (IV.i.5.155). Thus, the unities of beauty, truth and goodness are integrated.

recognize the divine within himself? He is part of the divine...The Christian virtue of humility, then, accords well with the dependence participation implies and the salvation from self Augustine seeks. Christ's abasement...is exactly what restores our relationship to God.[136]

We see here many of the strengths of Augustine's Christology of the humble mediator.[137] The Word has come to make his home among us in a humble downward participation which saves us from having to try yet again to lift ourselves up. This salvation is at the same time a defeat of us in our proud willing to be more than we are. But in defeating those who are their own enemies, the Word exalts us. Before rushing ahead to the glory of exaltation, though, we should return to the Emmanuel. Meconi presents us with Augustine's insistence that it is in the humble home of his assumed humanity that the Word-made-flesh heals us, feeds us on God's love and, yes, exalts us. Of course, there is real exaltation as a result of Christ's humility. We are not merely saved from the poverty of our inclination towards ourselves; we are saved for communion with God and one another in God. Thus, the 'one supreme miracle of salvation' is 'the miracle of Christ's ascension into heaven in the flesh in which he rose from the dead'.[138] The humble incarnation of the Word is followed by, rather is fulfilled in, his *fleshly* ascension to the right hand of the Father, an ascension in which we are included and in which we find 'a short cut to participation in his own divine nature'.[139]

Despite this, an inner tension remains in Augustine's reckoning with the flesh of Christ. On the one hand, there is a clear affirmation of the Word's humility. *The* miracle of salvation is fleshy. Christ is 'not the Mediator in that he is the Word...He is the Mediator in that he is man'.[140] Yet, for all the stress Augustine places on the human Christ in his mediatorial capacity, Christ's humanity seems ultimately instrumental and of only temporary importance. It offers a 'short cut to participation in his own divine nature', but our hope is in the day when his office of mediator will cease and we will participate in the divine life directly.[141]

Coupled with the miraculous humility of Christ is a corresponding humility of humanity. Colin Starnes points out that, despite all Augustine learned from 'the books of the Platonists', their pride meant that 'even their true and certain knowledge could not possibly put him in a proper relation to God if he would not also humble himself by believing in Christ as the way to God'.[142] We

---

136. Meconi, 'The Incarnation and the Role of Participation', pp. 68–9.

137. Note the title of Brian Daley's article on Augustine's Christology: 'A Humble Mediator'.

138. Augustine, *City of God*, XXII.viii.1034.

139. Ibid. IX.xv.361.

140. Ibid. IX.xv.361.

141. That Augustine believes Christ's mediation will cease is clear in *The Trinity*, I.iii.20.80.

142. Colin Starnes, *Augustine's Conversion* (Waterloo, Ontario: Wilfrid Laurier University Press, 1990), p. 183.

are called to submit to a God who humiliates himself by becoming a man, a scandalous call which would jangle in the Platonists' ears. Yet it is just this submission that leads to exaltation.

> In a surprising way, there is something in humility to exalt the mind, and something in exaltation to abase it. It certainly appears somewhat paradoxical that exaltation abases and humility exalts. But devout humility makes the mind subject to what is superior. Nothing is superior to God; and that is why humility exalts the mind by making it subject to God.

Christ's humility is a direct affront to our own efforts at self-establishment, however, because it betrays the lie of our independence. In his preface to *City of God*, Augustine writes:

> I know how great is the effort needed to convince the proud of the power and excellence of humility, an excellence which makes it soar above all the summits of this world, which sway in their temporal instability, overtopping them all with an eminence not arrogated by human pride, but granted by divine grace.[143]

Humility's eminence is the only true eminence and glory, granted as it is by God, the only ground of glory. In its lowliness, it is paradoxically the peak of peaks, a height to which impoverished human pride cannot ascend. There is a formal symmetry and a moral propriety in the fact that 'humility was the necessary condition for submission to this truth [i.e., the truth of the Son of God's condescension to us in the incarnation]'.[144]

In speaking of the humility which is 'highly prized' in contrast to the 'fault of exaltation', Augustine writes:

> This is assuredly the great difference that sunders the two cities of which we are speaking: the one is a community of devout men, the other a company of the irreligious, and each has its own angels attached to it. In one city love of God has been given first place, in the other, love of self.[145]

The heavenly city is characterized by its humility, as is its king.[146] Humility is an appropriate response to God's humble condescension in Christ because it acknowledges that, even in (and, we might add, *precisely* in) his condescension, God is supreme. As supreme, he is to be supremely loved. Exaltation's fault is its ontological glass ceiling. The problem with exaltation is that it can see no higher than humanity. Indeed, the self-exalting man can see no higher than himself.

---

143. Augustine, *City of God*, I.Preface.5. The centrality of humility means that 'a "bishop" who has set his heart on a position of eminence rather than an opportunity for service should realize that he is no bishop' (XIX.xix.880).

144. Ibid. X.xxix.415.

145. Ibid. XIV.xiii.573.

146. Ibid. XIV.xiii.573.

Augustine's Ambiguous Inwardness in The Trinity[147]

There is another problem, however. If, as Augustine argues, sin can be seen as an inclining towards oneself, why would he do just that in looking for God? Of course, Augustine is not so much on a search for an entirely unknown, and hence unfound God as he is looking to suitably locate the *imago Trinitatis*. That being said, Augustine does seem to be seeking to properly locate the tri-une God himself by looking to his created image in his (Augustine's) solitary self to provide an analogy, which is the best way of knowing him.

But why would Augustine look inside himself to find God? He has just set up a relational account of sin in which our misery is a product of our attempt at autonomy. What's more, he has just told us that we are *not* the measure of things. We do not ground ourselves. Our very life, our flourishing and good-ness and wisdom, are all to be found not *in nos* but in participating in the one who is life and has life in himself. In the light of this, Augustine's interior move in *The Trinity* seems a reversion, if not an obvious inconsistency.

Hence the problem of Augustine's ambiguous inwardness. Our sin is our turning towards ourselves. Yet at the same time, some sort of turn towards self is a necessary step in our search for God. At least at first glace, Augustine's inward turn seems both inconsistent and pastorally dangerous.

Before we try to understand Augustine's motivation and method and then offer an evaluation, some ground needs to be cleared. We need to be reason-ably precise in describing his inward turn in *The Trinity*. It is emphatically not what we would today call 'introspection'. *The Trinity* involves little baring of the Augustinian soul or purgative plunging into the depths of the sub-conscious. His treatise has none of the vivid biographical details of the *Confessions*, which itself should not be too quickly dumped into the category of a 'tell-all'. Instead, *The Trinity* is an examination of the apparatus of cogni-tion, a look into how we work internally.

Augustine sets out from the beginning of *The Trinity* to seek God, all the while recognizing that his search is in the context of faith and is itself the context in which God will perform ocular surgery and eventually fit him for the vision of God in the eschaton.[148] Thus, his ascent to the vision of God is heavily qualified. While clearly Plotinian in structure, Augustine fixes his gait toward and gaze on the heavenly city.[149] His ascent is eschatologically oriented

---

147. Note that Augustine finished Book XIV of *City of God* between 418 and 420 and wrote *The Trinity* over a twenty-year stretch, roughly from 400 to 420. Additionally, Augustine seems to have written Book XII of *The Trinity* (where he deals most directly with sin) very close to the same time as he was dealing with sin in *City of God*. See Edmund Hill, 'Introduction', in Augustine, *The Trinity* (Brooklyn, NY: New City Press, 1991), pp. 20, 56.

148. Both the process and the *telos* fit Augustine for vision, being beatific.

149. Denys Turner remarks that, although there is 'very little doubt' that *The Trinity*'s structure had Plotinian roots (Turner points to the three-stage ascent 'away from the things of sense inwards to the soul and upwards to Truth and Beauty'), 'at least as revealing as the similarities are the differences' (Denys Turner, *The Darkness of God* [Cambridge: Cambridge University Press, 1995], p. 76).

and always an ascent of faith.[150] Rather than an intellectual Babel, we have
a humble peregrination towards the heavenly city in which Augustine has set
his hope.

Subversive spirituality?

The second half of *The Trinity* is governed by a motif of ascent. John
Cavadini makes the compelling argument that Augustine's treatise is structured precisely in order to subvert the Plotinian soteriology of ascent. He
argues from epistolary evidence that Augustine's intended audience in *The
Trinity* is those 'few' who have a working knowledge of 'a standard Plotinian
and especially Porphyrian characterization of the "return" of the soul to contemplation or *noesis*'.[151] Indeed, Cavadini calls Books IX–XIV of Augustine's
work 'one of the finest examples of what could be called Neoplatonic ana-
gogy that remains from the antique world'.[152] It is in the mastery of this genre
that Cavadini locates Augustine's ironic inversion. Augustine is engaging in a
polemic, not the speculation so many commentators have described, 'arguing
on behalf of one particular faith and spirituality over against another'.[153] His
thesis is that

> the *De trinitate* uses the Neoplatonic soteriology of ascent only to impress it into the
> service of a thoroughgoing critique of its claim to raise the inductee to the contempla-
> tion of God, a critique which, more generally, becomes a declaration of the futility of
> any attempt to come to any saving knowledge of God apart from Christ.[154]

For our purposes, we need to isolate the notion of *interiority* in this ascent,
in particular because, on the face of things, Augustine seems to retreat to an

---

150.   On the eschatology of ascent, see Edmund Hill's introduction: 'The *De Trinitate*
does not in fact end with XV – it can only end with the beatific vision of God in the world
to come' (Hill, 'Introduction', p. 26). Augustine's motto of *crede ut intelligas* points us to the
fact that one does not move from faith to reason, as if they were, in Edmund Hill's words,
'autonomous spheres of intellectual activity'. For this reason, Hill and John Cavadini both
reject the common reading of *The Trinity*'s structure as being divided into a 'faith' section
and a second 'reason' section. See Hill, 'Introduction', pp. 21–3; John Cavadini, 'Structure
and Intention', *Augustinian Studies* 23 (1992), pp. 103–23 (104, 106).

151.   These 'few' are the same proud 'few' referred to above to whom Augustine will
present his search for the Trinity. Augustine's stated intention at the outset of the treatise is
that 'they may actually come to realize that that supreme goodness does exist which only
the most purified minds can gaze upon, and also that they are themselves unable to gaze
upon it and grasp it for the good reason that the human mind with its weak eyesight cannot
concentrate on so overwhelming a light, unless it has been nursed back to full vigor on *the
justice of faith*' (*The Trinity*, I.i.4.67).

152.   Cavadini, 'Structure and Intention', p. 105.

153.   Cavadini, 'Structure and Intention', p. 110. *The Trinity* 'is not in the first instance
a purely "speculative" work inquiring into the mystery of the Trinity...but finds its context
rather in a polemical dialogue.'

154.   Cavadini, 'Structure and Intention', p. 106.

individualized conception of the self. If this is the case, he would seem to undercut his own relational concerns. Cavadini wants to argue, however, that it is this very notion of inwardness in the Neoplatonic ascent, and much of what it implies, that Augustine is attacking.[155] For Plotinus, the problem of ascent is an epistemological and moral one.[156] The Plotinian fall of the soul into the body and its corollary doctrine of the soul's pre-existence called for a remembering of what was the case (our existence with God as unembodied souls) and a return through ascetic discipline to the One. For Plotinus, this is something which we are able to accomplish by ourselves.[157]

Augustine is far more aware of a *distance* between himself and God, both ontologically and morally. Cavadini underscores the unsuitability of Neoplatonic introspection as a source of knowledge of God as follows: 'The more we persist in contemplating a disfigured image as though it were not disfigured, as though it were, so to speak, an accurate image of God, the more we persist in furthering the disfigurement'.[158] Here we come to the heart of the matter. Introspection that does not recognize and take into account the disfigurement of the *imago Trinitatis* – *even if* it starts out as a search for the Trinity – actually serves to further the disfigurement, because it treats the disfigurement as the real image and proceeds to read a disfigured Trinity from the disfigured image. Simply put, one cannot reliably or effectively learn about the triune God by examining a human who has inclined away from that God.

Is this merely a deconstruction, then? According to Cavadini, Augustine does not simply leave us with a Neoplatonic apparatus that has absorbed Christian content. Rather, the very character of this *noesis* has changed. Christian soteriology is not a clear ascent to contemplation (which cannot but mislead this side of our being made whole), but the way of the humble obedience of faith in the healing redeemer.[159] Faith is 'revealed not merely as a propaedeutic to vision, but as a redirecting of the noetic regard to a decidedly

---

155. Milbank agrees: 'Surely we have here the perfecting of a solipsistic interiority? Yet, in truth, the reverse is the case, because, for Augustine, to know oneself *genuinely* means to know oneself as loving what one should love namely God and one's neighbour as oneself. Hence, not interiority but radical *exteriorisation* is implied, and Augustine, therefore, uses paradoxical formulations which imply that the soul cannot contain itself...The true, imaging soul is a soul crossed out...What must be argued here, against Charles Taylor and others, is that Augustine's use of the vocabulary of "inwardness" is not at all a deepening of Platonic interiority, but something much more like subversion' (John Milbank, 'Sacred Triads', in Robert Dodaro and George Lawless [eds.] *Augustine and His Critics* [London: Routledge, 2000], pp. 77–102 [91]).

156. Scholarship is divided over the extent of Augustine's usage, rejection or transformation of the Platonic doctrine of knowledge as *anamnesis*. It is enough for our purposes to point out that Augustine's eventual rejection of the Plotinian fall of the soul and any sense of the soul's pre-existence issued in a thoroughly distinct understanding of what it means to 'remember God'.

157. Plotinus, *Enneads*, I.vi.9.

158. Cavadini, 'Structure and Intention', p. 108.

159. Ibid., p. 108.

un-noetic realm'.[160] The object of faith is the economy of God's salvific work in Christ, so faith can rightly be said to push the self-absorbed introspection of the Neoplatonic model outward.[161]

Cavadini's thesis is a controversial one, to be sure; but it is a compelling reading of *The Trinity* and deserves at least to stand collegially as a legitimate, if finally unsatisfying reading of the text. He is at his best in exegeting the second point of Augustine's stated intention, his desire to show that proud humanity (which includes all of us, this side of the eschaton) cannot gaze upon God. He is also right to point out the function of *The Trinity* in cultivating a habit of humility in the reader. As we have seen, Augustine was writing to those who resisted Christ's admonition to become as little children; and Augustine would teach all (himself included, as we have seen) to adopt a posture of humility as appropriate (and maybe propaedeutic) to a person of faith. In pointing us to faith and its loving acts, Cavadini brings out Augustine's subversion of an other-worldly, humanly-effected contemplation in favour of a more incarnationally rooted, God-given growth in grace.

Interior intimo meo

All these things being said, in his eagerness to stress the subversive element of *The Trinity*, Cavadini places the weight of his argument entirely on the second point of Augustine's stated intention, missing the first point, in which Augustine expresses his desire that 'they may actually come to realize that that supreme goodness does exist which only the most purified minds can gaze upon'.[162] While Augustine does not seem to be setting out a full-blown rational proof of the triune God's existence (even in his somewhat apologetic stance he is content to articulate the teaching of Scripture from the start), he *is* doing constructive work here. His way of arguing for the existence of this 'supreme goodness' is by frequent reference to the text and theme of Acts 17.27-28: 'that they should seek God, if perhaps they might grope for Him and find Him, though He is not far from each one of us; for in Him we live and move and exist'. God is the context, the atmosphere of created reality, we might say. God is, in the words of the *Confessions*, '*interior intimo meo et superior summo meo*'.[163] That God is closer to him than he is to himself

---

160. Ibid., p. 109.

161. Note that faith's reference to Christ brings both an awareness of the distance between God and humanity and 'a coincident awareness of the love of God which crossed that distance' (ibid., p. 109). Hence, faith's knowledge, by taking into account this 'un-noetic realm', delivers a truer account of the God who is in Christ.

162. Augustine, *The Trinity*, I.i.4.67.

163. Augustine, *Confessions*, III.vi.11. This phrase captures exactly the 'dimensions of neo-Platonist conversion, that while it is a return to the highest reality above the human mind, it is also a confrontation with the deepest reality within it.' (Booth, *Saint Augustine and the Western Tradition of Self-Knowing*, p. 15). Such formal similarity need not imply a material identification, of course. There is also an interesting parallel to be drawn with Rahner and his understanding of God as the ground of being.

is what fascinates Augustine in his discussion of cognition, and he keeps this from collapsing into a pure immanentism by maintaining the second half of the slogan. At times, it seems as if Augustine has taken us on this interior pilgrimage precisely to give the lie to our sinful turn towards ourselves. In sin, we take ourselves to be (and hope to make ourselves) the very ground of our existence, the bedrock of all reality. Along with being our own foundation, we take pride in ourselves, too, as the most important component of reality. But in *The Trinity*, we learn that there is someone who is at once more deeply foundational and far above us in grandeur. All of our efforts at self-estab-lishment, so ardently sought in our *inclinatus ad se*, have failed. As Charles Taylor pithily puts it, 'By going inward, I am drawn upward'.[164]

Thus, while affirming that 'Augustine's basic epistemological move is inward',[165] Charles Mathewes emphatically asserts that Augustine's sense of our

> ineradicable self-presence...entails that the mind is *not* its own self-enclosed reality. Talk about the self's interiority is misleading if we imagine it (as is usual) as a sort of inner private chamber (like a room in a house); interiority is rather a way of conceiv-ing the fact that the self is, at its base, always facing the reality of God. The mind is not in the Cartesian *cogito*'s nowhere...; rather, the self knows itself already, indeed as *always* already, a self in a world...[166]

The point Mathewes makes here is vital. It is a fundamental mistake to read Descartes back into Augustine without heavily qualifying things. Even in Augustine's use of Cartesian *cogito* language (which, of course, is *not* Cartesian language), he is not positing a radically isolated individual who in a very real sense must be said to ground himself. Rather, Augustine is finding God as the ground of our cognition, finding him to *be* our cognition in some sense.[167] Thus, Mathewes is right to point out that Augustine's anthropology is not a solipsistic egoism, for it 'assumes that otherness is already at the base of the self'.[168] This is an argument which finds its culmination in Book XIV

164. Charles Taylor, *Sources of the Self* (Cambridge: Cambridge University Press, 1989), p. 134.

165. Mathewes, '*Interior intimo meo*', p. 196.

166. Mathewes, '*Interior intimo meo*', p. 200. Mathewes makes a similar point in writing that 'an irreducible otherness stands at the heart of subjectivity – the otherness of God' (p. 198).

167. As a consequence of some of these moves, Mathewes sees Augustinian anthropol-ogy as a fruitful way out of troublesome post-Cartesian dualisms (internal/external, mind/body, subject/object).

168. Mathewes, '*Interior intimo meo*', p. 214. Also see p. 212: 'Augustine anchors the self in the created world by placing the Other at the desiring heart of the created self'. And p. 216: 'The ground of his anthropology is his conviction that at the core of the self is an other, God...To go deeply into the mind is to go *beyond* it; to turn inward and descend into the self is simultaneously to reach outward and ascend to God'. According to Lewis Ayres, Augustine's 'primary *cogito* provides not only an awareness of self but of the hierarchy of being' (Lewis Ayres, 'Between Athens and Jerusalem', *Modern Theology* 8 [1992], pp. 53–73 [63]).

when Augustine moves from the mind remembering, loving and willing itself to the mind remember, loving and willing God.[169]

We can conclude, then, that Augustine's inward and upward pilgrimage in *The Trinity* aims at putting man in his place. In this sense, the ascent is a descent, an undoing of the self-exaltation of our turn to self by teaching us (1) that the triune God is not only our redeemer but the very ground of our being (*interior intimo meo*) and (2) that any autonomous attempts to find him apart from his revealing himself and preparing us for the vision are hopeless. Rather than spoiling his relational account of sin in the *City of God*, *The Trinity* reaffirms it. We are led with Augustine to reflect on the pre-reflexive reality that we are relationally constituted to the core.[170] 'Most fundamentally', writes Robert Meagher, 'what is asserted throughout is that human being is a relational creature – its very life consists in its relatedness to itself and to others, which is also Augustine's fundamental assertion regarding the life of God'.[171] God grounds us and moves us through a life of faith-filled, humble obedience, a life which is always ecclesial (Augustine would happily follow Cyprian's *extra ecclesia nulla salus*), a life which leads to the great communal vision of God.

A Vision of a Fleshless God?

Phillip Cary recognizes this, and sees Augustine straining to overcome a Plotinian tendency to turn inward and rest blissfully at home in contemplation of one's own divinity. But the problem is not so much that Augustine portrays an inner self cut off from the rest of the world. It is that the exteriority at the heart of his interiority is yet an exteriority uncomfortable with the flesh of Christ. He can affirm with characteristic brio the indispensability of Christ as the way to God.[172] Indeed, it is precisely a proud rejection of the humble way of the human Christ that kept the Platonists looking at God from afar, seeing 'what the goal is but not how to get there'.[173] Furthermore, Augustine's churchly life and piety force us to back off from wholesale dismissals of his

169. Augustine, *The Trinity*, XIV.iv.15.383.

170. See Turner, *The Darkness of God*, pp. 82–88. Charles Taylor puts the ambiguous nature of what he calls Augustine's 'radical reflexivity' well: 'But for Augustine, it is not reflexivity which is evil; on the contrary, we show most clearly the image of God in our fullest self-presence. Evil is when this reflexivity is enclosed on itself. Healing comes when it is broken open, not in order to be abandoned, but in order to acknowledge its dependence on God' (Taylor, *Sources of the Self*, p. 139).

171. Meagher (ed.), *On the Inner Life of the Mind*, p. 102.

172. Phillip Cary, 'Book Seven: Inner Vision', in Kim Paffenroth and Robert P. Kennedy (eds.), *A Reader's Companion to Augustine's Confessions* (London: Westminster/John Knox Press), pp. 107–26 (123). Cary's argument in this article and the book mentioned below focuses on Augustine's move 'in then up' in *Confessions* VII. This is a structurally similar move to that in *The Trinity* and to a similar dynamic characteristic of Augustine's writings from the start (Cary, 'Inner Vision', p. 118).

173. Augustine, *Confessions*, VII.xx.26.

Christology as merely marginal. The centrality of the Eucharist in his worship and his notion of the *totus Christus* make this clear.

But in the end, Christ remains a glorious *via* rather than the re-definition of Augustine's God.[174] 'The distinctive feature of Christian religion, that God takes on human nature in the person of Christ, does not define what we are ultimately seeking, but rather the way we are to seek it. Our goal is not flesh and blood – not even Christ's flesh and blood – but inward vision.'[175] He looks for the *imago Dei* in himself without sufficient attention paid to Christ, who is himself the *imago Dei* (Col. 1.15). Augustine recognizes that it is only by God's gracious work that he can even begin to see God. Where he fails is in neglecting to look to *Christ* to see God. Instead, the fleshly Christ is merely the way to the 'homeland of peace' he has caught a glimpse of from 'a wooded summit', a land also glimpsed by the Platonists.[176] Augustine quotes a similar statement by Plotinus approvingly in *City of God* which sees the journey to God as one of deification.[177] Of absolutely crucial importance is Augustine's remark noted earlier that Christ's incarnation offers us 'a short cut to participation in his own divine nature'.[178] As we saw earlier, he claims in *The Trinity* that Christ's office as mediator will cease in the eschaton, where we will immediately commune with God. It is hard to escape the conclusion that Christ's flesh, his humanity is merely instrumental rather than nothing other than *who Christ is for us*.[179]

Conclusion

The scholarship surrounding *The Trinity* is dizzying. Consider the three options we have entertained. One (Cavadini) sees *The Trinity* as a subversion of Neoplatonic inwardness. Another (Mathewes) suggests that, in the move

174. 'The power of Augustine's distinctive brand of Christian Platonism is that it is the only form of orthodox theology after Nicaea that offers a powerful alternative to finding the glory of God in the flesh of Jesus Christ. For Augustine the humanity of Christ is indispensable, but it is only the road, not the destination. The destination is defined in Platonist terms, and it is the destination that is the point of the road, not the other way round.' (Cary, 'Inner Vision', pp. 122–3).

175. Cary, 'Inner Vision', p. 122.

176. Augustine, *Confessions*, VII.xxi.27. Also see Cary, 'Inner Vision', p. 107. Basil Studer points out that Augustine sees Christ as both way (*via*) and homeland (*patria*), but he is the former in his humanity and the latter in his divinity. We move 'through Christ as human being to Christ as God' (Basil Studer, *The Grace of Christ and the Grace of God* [trans. Matthew J. O'Connell; Collegeville, MN: The Liturgical Press, 1997], p. 45), and hence both the unity of Christ and the decisiveness of the incarnation for how we are to understand God's identity are threatened.

177. Augustine, *City of God*, IX.xvii.364.

178. Ibid. IX.xv.361.

179. Ultimately, Cary argues, 'Augustine clearly prays and worships and sings to the god of the Platonists, believing that this is no different from the Truth signified by Holy Scripture, to which Jesus Christ is the way' (Cary, 'Inner Vision', p. 123).

'in then up', Augustine locates exteriority *within* the self, calling into question the very legitimacy of dualities of interior and exterior.[180] A third (Cary) argues that, with his inner turn, Augustine forsakes the flesh of Christ, leaving a profoundly unchristian legacy. What are we to conclude about the structure and intention of the work, much less Augustine's spirituality? And how does this bear on the question of a relational account of sin?

It has been our argument throughout this chapter that Augustine articulates a relational understanding of humanity and sin and makes a number of moves which will dovetail and receive more systematic application in later descriptions of *homo incurvatus in se*. So our question with regard to Augustine's move 'in then up' in *The Trinity* (and the *Confessions*) has been whether this represents an inner tension within Augustine's thought. Does he take away with one hand what he gives with the other? With appropriate and significant qualifications, this question must be answered 'yes'. The qualifications come from Cavadini's insight that Augustine rejects any sense of a soteriologically effective inner turn. Further, Augustine locates the *visio Dei* eschatologically, further undermining any false anthropological optimism. Mathewes reminds us that the inner turn uncovers relationality, even exteriority at the heart of the self. This is something Plato and Plotinus cannot offer. So Augustine is clearly not advocating the isolating egoism which characterizes the sinful turn toward self. If anything, he is calling into question the notion that we could ever escape our being-in-relation.

Still (and here Cary is helpful), Augustine's setting up the ascent as a planned failure, while surely a fundamentally *Christian* move in its subversion of Neoplatonic confidence, is not yet *sufficiently* Christian in that, while rebuffing the exuberant claims of Neoplatonist mystics to arrive on their own strength at the vision of God in this life, it does not question their construal of that vision itself. And, while exteriority may abide in interiority, it is a strange exteriority. The 'other' which is always already implicated in the self seems, finally, to be a fleshless God.[181] Further, it seems difficult to sustain the otherness of another who is located inside oneself.[182] Augustine makes only one reference to Col. 1.15 in *The Trinity*, and that without reference to its key description of Christ as the *imago Dei*. Near the end of the treatise, he despairs of a direct vision of God in this life, asking instead after an indirect

180. Milbank combines these first two perspectives in his claim that 'not interiority but radical *exteriorisation* is implied' in a subversion in which Augustine finds otherness within the self (see note 155 above). On this account, in the move 'in then up', Augustine locates exteriority *within*. That is, he locates sociality in the very inner world where we would expect to find an isolated individual. A similar point is made by Michael Hanby (*Augustine and Modernity* [London: Routledge, 2003], p. 58).

181. Recall how important the Platonist recognition of God's incorporeality was to Augustine. See especially *Confessions* VII; Cary, 'Inner Vision', p. 122.

182. '"Outside" is a terribly handy word, if what you love about someone includes the fact that he is quite different from yourself. If our beloved is other than ourselves, should we not be glad to look for him outside our selves?' (Phillip Cary, *Augustine's Invention of the Inner Self* [Oxford: Oxford University Press, 2000], p. 141).

vision in a mirror or image.[183] But even here, the image is strictly the human mind, not Christ. It seems that Augustinian inwardness points us to 'another place to find God than this particular human flesh'.[184]

There is another, more mundane but related danger with Augustine's turn inward. As a model for spirituality, there is little to ensure that one will move beyond the 'in' to the 'then up' dynamic. The danger is that we will get stuck at the lower levels of inwardness, lost like Narcissus in our own reflected gaze. As we have seen, sin is *inordinatio*, a love of lesser goods which involves a forsaking of the greatest good. Augustine is taking a risk in leading us on this interior path, hoping he can hold our attention long enough to bring us to our basic relation to God. One cannot but wonder whether many will not get lost on this first (inward) step and refuse to climb further inward and upward. If treated as a model,[185] Augustine would seem to be insufficiently aware at this point of the powers of sin to draw our attention in a disorienting spiral in on ourselves.

It was just this concern that Luther – a victim of introspective scruples if ever there was one – addressed by rolling out a programme of spirituality governed by a rigorously consistent extrinsicism. Following Staupitz's counsel to look to the wounds of Christ, Luther built a theology of justification and sanctification, but also a renewed sacramental theology which emphasized that which comes to us from outside of us. As Cary notes:

> Orthodox Christian belief in Jesus Christ undermines the motives of inwardness by making it seem much less inevitable that we must find the divine elsewhere than the external world. There is nothing more external than flesh, yet the Catholic Church since the year after Augustine's death has explicitly taught that in Christ's flesh we find the life-giving power of God. Much has been built on this teaching: Eastern Orthodox use of icons, Roman Catholic devotion to the sacraments, and Protestant preaching of the Gospel – all understood as means by which God gives us life from Christ incarnate. Founded thus on the flesh of Christ, Christian piety has long insisted on a kind of 'outward turn'.[186]

In the end, then, the Christian tradition seems to have been convinced that Jesus really does offer the best remedy for sin, the 'medicine of immortality', as many Fathers described the Eucharist. If our sin involves us more than anything in a parasitic love affair with ourselves, what more fitting counter could there be than to look outside ourselves to one who is not ourselves? Despite the legacy of his inward turn, Augustine was himself aware of this; and his call for humility suggests a move in this direction. Nevertheless, while the

---

183. Augustine, *The Trinity*, XV.iii.14–20.

184. Cary, 'Inner Vision', p. 125.

185. Clearly, this is part of the debate. Cavadini's thesis would suggest that this is hardly a model for spirituality. Nevertheless, that many have approached Augustine's inward turn as a paradigm for personal Christian spirituality would seem to be self-evident from the Christian tradition, whether considering works like Teresa of Avila's *Interior Castle* or Bonaventure's *Itinerarium*.

186. Cary, *Augustine's Invention of the Inner Self*, p. 142.

features of a relational understanding of sin were set up by Augustine, he did not follow them through to a sufficiently objectivist, extrinsic and materially mediated account of the Christian life. It will be left to Luther to think this through with consistency in his account of *homo incurvatus in se*.

Chapter 2

LUTHER'S RADICAL AND RELIGIOUS INCURVATURE

Setting the Task

From 3 November 1515 to 7 September 1516, Martin Ludher[1] gave his second full series of lectures (following one on the Psalms) as Professor of Biblical Theology at the University of Wittenberg.[2] He was young (a week shy of 32), but his immersion in the Scriptures and his own existential wranglings (what he called *Anfechtungen*)[3] had led him to a place of theological vigour, precision and creativity, fused with not a little iconoclasm. Gordon Rupp puts it well:

> To turn from the lectures on the Psalms to those on Romans (1515-6) is to recall G. K. Chesterton's remark about H. G. Wells that you could almost hear him growing in the night, so plain is the growth in maturity, independence and coherence in a few months.[4]

It is significant that Rupp locates Luther's greatest growth over those few months in 'a more radical diagnosis of the sin of man, the seat of which, under all disguises and idolatries, is his egoism, lifting itself in rebellion

---

1.   Martin only became 'Luther' in 1518. He was born to Hans and Margaret Luder, which was 'embellished with an "h" to suit the more elegant, academic usage' on his matriculation at the University of Erfurt and only began to spell his name 'Luther' from 1518 (Heiko A. Oberman, *Luther* [trans. Eileen Walliser-Schwartzbart; London: Image Books, 1992], p. 86).

2.   Oberman, *Luther*, pp. 162, 164; Gordon Rupp, *The Righteousness of God* (London: Hodder & Stoughton, 1953), p. 159.

3.   Rupp explains the significance of Luther's choosing 'the word "Anfechtung" with its suggestion of combat rather than "Versuchung" for "temptation."' This is 'an existential word' but *not* one of 'mere subjectivism. The whole meaning of "Anfechtung" for Luther lies in the thought that man has his existence "Coram Deo," and that he is less the active intelligence imposing itself on the stuff of the universe around him, than the subject of an initiative and action from God who employs the whole of man's existence as a means of bringing men to awareness of their need and peril' (Rupp, *The Righteousness of God*, p. 106). On the significance of *Anfechtungen* in the Christian life, note Luther's counsel to 'cheerfully' accept it 'as if it were a holy relic' (*WA* 1:47.46, quoted in Walter von Loewenich, *Martin Luther* [trans. Lawrence W. Denef; Minneapolis: Augsburg Publishing House, 1986], p. 101).

4.   Gordon Rupp, *Luther's Progress* (London: SCM Press, 1951), p. 40.

against God'.[5] In light of this, it might be claimed that Luther's 'discovery' (a regrettable term) was a function of his wrestling with Scripture over the question of sin even more than over the question of the righteousness of God.[6]

It is certainly less than striking to say that Augustine and Luther were very different men. On a superficial level, one could make much of the parallel places they occupy as transition figures – with Augustine claimed at one time as a Father of the church, at another as an early mediaeval theologian, and with Luther straddling the mediaeval and modern eras. But the differences lie in far more than spatio-temporal distance. Augustine wrote *City of God* near the end of his life, and it presents his mature theology in all its brilliant scope. Luther gave his lectures on Romans at the beginning of his academic career, years before he came to prominence. Here we have what is at once a substantial piece of constructive theological exegesis and at the same time a launching pad for further theological reflection (and that of the Reformation). Augustine wrote *City of God* in the midst of the fall of the Roman Empire.[7] Luther lectured on Romans in the midst of the pollution and power of the Roman Church. There are genre differences, too. In Book XIV of *City of God*, Augustine is engaging in philosophical theology in the context of rendering a vision of (Christian) history. Luther, on the other hand, is seeking to faithfully exegete Romans, paying close attention to the Latin of the Vulgate and the Greek texts he had available to him.[8] All of these contextual factors will need to be kept in mind in hearing Luther faithfully on his own terms and in relation to Augustine.

Having seen Augustine's articulation of various strands of a relational anthropology in the previous chapter, we turn in this chapter to Luther's radicalization of these strands and weaving them into the image of *homo incurvatus in se*. Beyond organizing the diverse anthropological and hamartiological insights of the Augustinian tradition under the guiding metaphor of incurvature, Luther radicalizes many of these insights in his consistent application

---

5.   Ibid., p. 40. On this growth and a concomitant break with certain aspects of scholastic hamartiology, see Bernard Lohse, *Martin Luther's Theology* (trans. Roy A. Harrisville; Minneapolis: Fortress Press, 1999), p. 70; Denis R. Janz, *Luther and Late Medieval Thomism* (Waterloo, Ontario: Wilfrid Laurier University Press, 1983), p. 154.

6.   To set the question up in this way is, of course, to offer a false dilemma. Luther's struggles were in relation to sin and righteousness. But what is important is to remember that his concern with the righteousness of God was not an abstract one but rather the anguish of a man who could not find a way around his sin (as scrupulous as he was) to God.

7.   Rome had been sacked by Alaric and the Goths in August of 410.

8.   Luther dictated the interlinear and marginal glosses on Romans in his lectures to his students, who had a copy of the Vulgate text (probably the Basel edition of 1509) with sufficient space to write in the glosses. He also made use of other versions to correct the text at points, as well as the standard *Glossa ordinaria* and *Glossa interlinearis* and a number of patristic and mediaeval commentaries. He was considerably freer with his scholia in the lectures themselves, which he at various times abbreviated, omitted or replaced ('Introduction' in *LW* 25:ix–xi). Luther began using Erasmus' 1516 edition of the Greek New Testament in his lectures on Romans 9 (*LW* 25:81 n. 3).

of them (particularly the *simul iustus et peccator*) to the whole person (*totus homo*) and to the religious person (*homo religiosus*).

Luther has an eye for sin and justification, and our methodology will be guided by these twin concerns. Whereas we focused our attention on the origins of sin in the Genesis narrative in discussing Augustine, looking at the transition from Paradise to Fall, we will take Luther's paradox of *simul iustus et peccator* as a guide throughout this chapter, dialectically moving between the two realities of humanity *coram deo* and *coram hominibus* that are Luther's constant concern in his lectures. For Luther, as for Paul in Romans, consideration of humanity as fallen and redeemed go hand-in-hand. He begins his scholia accordingly: 'The chief purpose of this letter is to break down, to pluck up, and to destroy all wisdom and righteousness of the flesh...this letter is to affirm and state and magnify sin'.[9] It is most appropriate, then, that we turn to Luther's lectures on Paul's epistle of sin to find Luther's portrayal of fallen humanity.[10]

Simul iustus et peccator

Luther uses two analogies when it comes to articulating the life of one who is both righteous and a sinner. The first analogy is of a doctor–patient relationship.

> Thus in ourselves we are sinners, and yet through faith we are righteous by God's imputation...
>
> It is similar to the case of a sick man who believes the doctor who promises him a sure recovery and in the meantime obeys the doctor's order in the hope of the promised recovery and abstains from those things which have been forbidden him, so that he may in no way hinder the promised return to health or increase his sickness until the doctor can fulfill his promise to him. Now is this sick man well? The fact is that he is both sick and well at the same time. He is sick in fact, but he is well because of the sure promise of the doctor, whom he trusts and who has reckoned him as already cured, because he is sure that he will cure him; for he has already begun to cure him and no longer reckons to him a sickness unto death. In the same way Christ, our Samaritan, has brought His half-dead man into the inn to be cared for, and He has begun to heal him, having promised him the most complete cure unto eternal life, and He does not impute his sins, that is, his wicked desires, unto death, but in the meantime in the hope of the promised recovery He prohibits him from doing or omitting things by which his cure might be impeded and his sin, that is, his concupiscence, might be

---

9.   *LW* 25:135.

10.   A certain measure of care must be taken in ascribing systematic significance to any of Luther's works. The Romans lectures come early in his career and before his break with Rome and, while he does not abandon his core commitments, Luther does display growth and even change over his career. His attack on the pride of *homo incurvatus in se* retains its force, but (and this is significant for our argument) later in his career he sees the danger of sloth as well (if not in direct relation to being *incurvatus in se*). On this, see Mary Gaebler, 'Luther on the Self', *Journal of the Society of Christian Ethics* 22 (2002), pp. 115–32 (115, 126) (citing the 1535 Galatians lectures).

increased. Now, is he perfectly righteous? No, for he is at the same time both a sinner and a righteous man; a sinner in fact, but a righteous man by the sure imputation and promise of God that He will continue to deliver him from sin until He has completely cured him. And thus he is entirely healthy in hope, but in fact he is still a sinner; but he has the beginning of righteousness, so that he continues more and more always to seek it, yet he realizes that he is always unrighteous. But now if this sick man should like his sickness and refuse every cure for his disease, will he not die? Certainly, for thus it is with those who follow their lusts in this world. Or if a certain sick man does not see that he is sick but thinks he is well and thus rejects the doctor, this is the kind of operation that wants to be justified and made well by its own works.[11]

Where to begin with such a passage? Probably with the salutary reminder that this is an analogy, and a particularly intricate one. Of course, it is also a piece of double-exegesis. We have Luther commenting on Rom. 4.7, a quote from Psalm 32 ('Blessed are those whose lawless deeds have been forgiven / And whose sins have been covered'). And, he is thinking intertextually, bringing in a Christological reading of the Parable of the Good Samaritan. What of the analogy itself, though? There are two central points being driven home. The first is that we are both, simultaneously, wholly sinners and righteous. It is not that we have a sinful aspect and a righteous aspect. '*So then, I of myself,* that is, as one and the same person am at the same time spiritual and carnal'.[12]

> Note that one and the same man at the same time serves the law of God and the law of sin, at the same time is righteous and sins! For he does not say: 'My mind serves the law of God,' nor does he say: 'My flesh serves the law of sin,' but: 'I, the whole man, the same person, I serve a twofold servitude.'…The saints at the same time as they are righteous are also sinners.[13]

Luther does not mean to say primarily, or at least not exclusively, that we are becoming more righteous and less sinful. That would spoil what it means to be new creatures in Christ, as it would reduce 'us' to the verifiable data of our lives *hic et nunc*. No, this sick man – all of him – is both sick ('a sinner in fact')[14] and well ('he is entirely healthy in hope')[15].

11.   *LW* 25:260.
12.   *LW* 25:66. A few pages earlier, he refers to *simul iustus et peccator* explicitly: 'Therefore I am at the same time a sinner and a righteous man, for I do evil and I hate the evil which I do' (*LW* 25:63).
13.   Luther continues: 'righteous because they believe in Christ, whose righteousness covers them and is imputed to them, but sinners because they do not fulfill the Law, are not without concupiscence, and are like sick men under the care of a physician; they are sick in fact but healthy in hope and in the fact that they are beginning to be healthy, that is, they are "being healed." They are people for whom the worst possible thing is the presumption that they are healthy, because they suffer a worse relapse' (*LW* 25:336).
14.   'For if we are righteous only because God reckons us to be such, then it is not because of our mode of living or our deeds. Thus inwardly and of ourselves [i.e., "in fact"] we are always unrighteous' (*LW* 25:257).
15.   In addition to the quote above, see *LW* 25:258.

At the same time, and here is our second point, it *is* true that we are in a process of becoming well. And so, in a derivative sense, we *can* speak of becoming more righteous and less sinful.[16] While Luther wants to avoid focusing on the wrong subject (i.e., us rather than the God who promises to heal in Christ), he does affirm that we who have been sick are in the midst of a life-long healing process. Our doctor and good Samaritan, Christ, has begun to heal us and has prescribed a regimen for us as we heal ('He prohibits him from doing or omitting things'). We are getting better, which motivates us all the more toward health; and yet the very fact that we continue to be tended by the doctor reminds us that we are still and always sick. What's more, we are reminded of our sickness, as well as of our growing health, by the fierce struggle within us.

> For when the Samaritan had poured wine and oil on his wounds, he did not immediately recover, but he began to do so. Thus our sick man is both weak and getting well. Insofar as he is healthy, he desires to do good, but as a sick person he wants something else and is compelled to yield to his illness, which he himself does not actually want to do.[17]

16.   Tuomo Mannermaa notes the relative lack of attention paid to this 'partial' aspect of the *simul* in Lutheran scholarship. See Tuomo Mannermaa, *Christ Present in Faith* (ed. Kirsi Stjerna; Minneapolis: Fortress Press, 2005), p. 58. For a helpful discussion of Luther's *simul* which harmonizes the partial and total senses of the paradox, see Jüngel, *Justification*, pp. 214–24. Daphne Hampson argues that Luther's position in the lectures on Romans in regard to justification (and, by extension, the *simul*) is an 'analytic proleptic' position which still retains something of the sense of man on the way and has not reached the 'full "extrinsic" position' of the more mature 1517–18 Hebrews lectures. See Hampson, *Christian Contradictions* (Cambridge: Cambridge University Press, 2001), pp. 15, 26. This can be seen in his treatment of the *simul*, as it echoes in part Augustine's take: 'Within the Augustinian framework (which became that of Catholicism), whereby life is a *via* for our change, the term *simul iustus et peccator* could only mean that we are in part just, but in part still sinner' (p. 27). If one follows Augustine in taking both terms 'to refer to *homo viator*...the human cannot be held to be both fully just and wholly a sinner' (p. 117). It is Luther's more relational construal – speaking of one's status as just or sinner in light of one's relation to another rather than in terms of an intrinsic quality which can be spoken of apart from such a relation – which transforms the terms. David Steinmetz, while affirming Luther's relational construal of the *simul*, nevertheless denies that 'the contrast of righteousness "in hope" with sinfulness "in fact" is based entirely on an analytical proleptic judgment' which 'reckons the believer righteous in the present because he will be righteous in the future'. Rather, even as early as the first lectures on Psalms, hope is a category that corresponds to the *hidden* rather than *incomplete* or, worse, *conditional* nature of justification (David Steinmetz, *Luther and Staupitz* [Durham, NC: Duke University Press, 1980], pp. 118–19). We might want to affirm some sort of incompleteness in justification, but never in the sense that we are thrown back upon ourselves or return to an estimation of the human *in se* to determine the relative completeness of justification. Rather, we might simply say that our justification, which is now in faith and hope, will then be in sight.

17.   LW 25:340. This Christ-as-physician trope is a commonplace in Augustine's theology and must be seen to take its bearings from an Augustinian context. See the brief discussion of 'the just man a convalescent' in Eugene F. Durkin, *The Theological Distinction of Sins* (Mundelein, IL: Saint Mary of the Lake Seminary, 1952), pp. 64–7.

Romans 7 becomes the paradigm for the Christian life for Luther. The man who does what he would not is one in whom a cure has begun, in that something 'in him' fights against the cancer of original sin which had eaten him away.[18] A painful, restorative process has begun. In Luther, Romans 7 has even greater paradigmatic significance than it had for Augustine.[19] This may be in part due to the fact that, though Augustine affirmed the Christian's status as *simul iustus et peccator*, his affirmation is 'remarkable for its triviality'.[20] In McCue's analysis, this can be traced to the lack of interest in self-examination in Augustine's sermons (even if his *Confessions* would point us in another direction).[21] More to the point, however, is Augustine's sense of the Christian life as a *via* along which one gradually moves from sinner to righteous. Thus, while the Christian is always properly said to be both sinner and righteous, it is equally appropriate to speak of being 'more righteous' and 'less sinful'. It is not, as we have seen, that Luther resists a process and sanative account of justification. He does, however, strictly subordinate the *partim* sense of being righteous and sinful to the *simul*.[22]

Nevertheless, the place Luther gives to progress in righteousness will not sit well with those who have been taught that Luther's is purely a forensic doctrine of justification. Forensics involves legal judgments made at one point in time. A judge declares a person innocent; he can go free. Luther's comment above that 'we are righteous through God's imputation' of Christ's righteousness surely fits this mould, but it must be held along with his claim that this is 'through faith', a faith which is equated to our believing 'Him who promises to free us'. Or as he puts it elsewhere in the same passage, this sick man is 'well because of the sure promise of the doctor, whom he trusts and who has reckoned him as already cured, because he is sure that he will cure him'.[23] He is well because the doctor knows what he is doing and is himself sure of a cure. He trusts that the doctor knows best here, and so is healthy in hope. It is not for naught that Luther's formula of *simul iustus et peccator* has been called a paradox. And so it is, but it also must be acknowledged to be an *eschatological* paradox. George Hunsinger is helpful here:

18.   Paul speaks of himself 'as a pugilist between two contrary laws, but not as a defeated fighter for whom there is no longer a war...as is the case with the carnal man' (*LW* 25:335).

19.   Though note that it is Augustine who Henri Rondet called 'the doctor of the spiritual combat' (H. Rondet, 'L'anthropologie religieuse de saint Augustin', *Recherches de science religieuse*, XXIX [1939], p. 176; cited in Durkin, *The Theological Distinction of Sins*, pp. 64–5).

20.   James F. McCue, '*Simul iustus et peccator* in Augustine, Aquinas, and Luther', *Journal of the American Academy of Religion* 48 (1947), pp. 81–96 (83).

21.   Ibid., p. 84.

22.   The difference at this point is also reflected in the much deeper sense in which Luther saw the Christian life as itself a confession of faith in a hidden reality. 'For Luther, the believer is righteous *coram Deo*, whereas the unbeliever is righteous *coram hominibus*... For Augustine, the righteousness bestowed upon man by God in his justification was recognisable as such by man – in other words, the justified sinner was *iustus coram Deo et coram hominibus*' (McGrath, *Iustitia Dei*, p. 199).

23.   *LW* 25:260.

Justification, as Luther understood it, was an eschatological event that centered on the person of Christ. As such it was an event that had three tenses...Justification, from the first perspective, had already occurred *extra nos*...From a second perspective, however, justification in all its fullness had yet to take place...Finally, from a third, more existential perspective, justification occurred not in the past or the future but here and now...It was in this sense that justification occurred by faith.[24]

We are justified now, then, by faith in what has occurred and what is to come, that is, by remembering God's work in Christ and hoping in his promise for the future. This is a faith that is not yet sight, which is what Luther is safeguarding as he commends the healing process to the Christian. He is not falling back into mediaeval works-righteousness but is castigating those who would presume to make 'in fact' what is still 'in hope'. 'This life, then, is a life of being healed from sin, it is not a life of sinlessness, with the cure completed and perfect health attained. The Church is the inn and the infirmary for those who are sick and in need of being made well. But heaven is the palace of the healthy and the righteous.'[25] In what might seem an ironic move, given caricatures of Luther's thought, Luther attacks those who would make a heaven on earth by thinking they have been justified and do not need to be justified. These statements seem to point to an inconsistency in Luther's doctrine of justification (which *is* his theology)[26] in which he equivocates on the question of when and if one can speak of justification being completed. If, however, our justification is real precisely in faith and hope rather than in fact ('entirely healthy in hope, but in fact he is still a sinner'), these statements can be seen as an altogether appropriate way of speaking of the justification of men and women in Christ.

We pointed out at the beginning of this section that Luther uses *two* analogies when speaking of a person being *simul iustus et peccator*. We will look at the second as a way of tying together some of the major points in his treatment of this theme.

Suppose that a house which has fallen into disrepair is in the process of reconstruction, is then its construction and present condition one thing and its state of disrepair something else? It is one and the same thing. It can be said of the same house that because of its being under construction it is a house and that it is in the process of becoming a house, but because of its incompleteness it can at the same time be said that it is not yet a house and that it lacks what is proper to a house.[27]

24.   George Hunsinger, *Disruptive Grace* (Grand Rapids: Eerdmans, 2000), p. 296.
25.   *LW* 25:262–63.
26.   Ian Siggins points out that, despite 'Luther's insistence that justification is the magisterial doctrine, the chief article, the head and cornerstone of the Church...Luther often intends much more by the word "justification" than the formal or systematic content of "the doctrine of justification".' What's more, 'justification is only one aspect, however vital, of a far broader theme – the theme "by Christ alone." As a result, Luther rarely deals with justification as a separate locus' (Siggins, *Martin Luther's Doctrine of Christ* [London: Yale University Press, 1970], p. 144).
27.   *LW* 25:341.

Notice the coincidence of its state of being under construction and being in disrepair. One and the same house is said to be both. Its *becoming* a house is precisely what makes it a house, but as soon as we call it a house we must point out that it is *not yet* a house. A family that hears, 'Your house is coming along nicely', needs to hear as well, '...but you can't move in yet'. There is no denying that this house is not finished, and there is plenty about it to condemn. ('Note that every saint is a sinner and prays for his sins. Thus the righteous man is in the first place his own accuser')[28] As Luther writes, 'Sin remains and at the same time it does not remain'.[29] We certainly do lack what is proper to a Christian, really, to a person. We are still curved in on ourselves. But we are in the process of being drawn out of ourselves, of becoming who we are in Christ. And while the *simul* remains, we have faith in him and hope that, when he is revealed, we also will be revealed with him in glory.[30]

Fuel to the Fire: The Persistence of the fomes

In discussing original sin, Luther frequently describes our now inherent sinfulness as *fomes* ('tinder') or *fomes concupiscentiae*.[31] Picking up on this terminology (standard since Augustine), he affirms that prior to any willing or doing on our part, we are sinful participants in the original sin of Adam. Where Luther departs from the regnant doctrinal position is in his insistence that this tinder of concupiscence is *itself* sin. Paul is also speaking of this tinder when he laments: 'It is no longer I that do it, but sin which dwells within me' (Rom. 7.20). What's more, this sinful concupiscence 'remains, and no one is ever cleansed of it, not even the one-day-old infant'.[32] Original sin, then, is not removed at baptism (as Scotus and Ockham had taught); rather is our *guilt* removed as God refuses to impute original sin to us.[33] 'And the works of sin are the fruits of this sin' which we share with Adam.[34] The ubiquity of the tinder of concupiscence in no way mitigates the justice of God in condemning sinners. Entertaining the objection that 'God condemns no one without sin, and he who is necessarily in sin is unjustly condemned', Luther answers: 'We are all of necessity in sin and damnation, but no one is in sin by force and against his will'.[35] That is, necessity is not to be confused with and need not imply coercion. Original sin

---

28.   *LW* 25:258.
29.   *LW* 25:258.
30.   See Col. 3.4. Note Hunsinger's remark: 'The first theologian, it seems, whose christocentrism had assigned such comprehensive hermeneutical significance to this particular verse [Col. 3.3] was Luther' (Hunsinger, *Disruptive Grace*, p. 287 n. 12).
31.   For uses of *fomes*, see *LW* 25:62, 65, 259, 299–300. On concupiscence, see *LW* 25:22, 51, 62, 69, 262, 313, 357.
32.   *LW* 25:259.
33.   *LW* 25:259–61.
34.   *LW* 25:259.
35.   *LW* 25:376.

exists whether I perform it or even know about it. I am conceived in it, but I did not do it. It began to rule in me before I began to live. It is simultaneous with me...This iniquity and sin existed and they were not mine; I was conceived in them without my consent. But now they have become mine. For now I understand that I do evil and disobey the Law...The sin is now my own, that is, by my will it has been approved and accepted by my consent, because without grace I have been unable to overcome it in myself; therefore it has overcome me, and I am, because of that same tinder and evil lust [*fomite et concupiscentia*], through my work also an actual sinner and not merely under original sin.[36]

That which was, properly speaking, not mine I have made my own by embracing it and living (albeit necessarily) willfully in accordance with it.[37] I have not been able to avoid the tinder's becoming a conflagration of sin, yet I am still entirely guilty of arson.

'What, therefore, is original sin?' Luther asks in his scholium on Rom. 5.12. We have been speaking in a rather vacuous, formal manner so far; and a look at Luther's defining of his term against 'the subtle distinctions of the scholastic theologians' will help flesh out the picture.[38] The scholastics tended to define original sin in terms of *privatio* alone (it was 'the privation or lack of original righteousness') and saw the *iustitia* of which it is a privation 'under the category of a quality' as 'only something subject in the will'.[39] Luther counters:

> It is not only a lack of a certain quality in the will, nor even only a lack [*privatio*] of light in the mind or of power [*virtutis*] in the memory, but particularly it is a total lack [*privatio*] of uprightness and of the power of all the faculties both of body and soul and of the whole inner and outer man [*totius hominis interioris et exterioris*]. On top of all this, it is a propensity toward evil. It is a nausea toward the good, a loathing of light and wisdom, and a delight in error and darkness, a flight from and an abomination of all good works, a pursuit of evil.[40]

Luther's makes two points here. The first is that original sin distorts, even realigns the *totus homo*, the whole person. It is more than a deficiency in a localized 'part' of the human person.[41] We will return later to Luther's holistic anthropology, with its dismissal of talk of 'faculties' within the person in

---

36.   *LW* 25:274. *WA* 56:287. It should be noted that, though concupiscence does retain a hint of an older suspicion and even degradation of sexuality in Luther (he can equate 'the tinder of sin' with 'sinful lust' [p. 273]), lust is by no means the dominant note in his understanding of *concupiscentia*. Nor is lust to be flatly equated with illicit sexual desire.

37.   'That original sin is the actual sin of Adam himself...Therefore this one sin of the one man is the sin of all, by which all have died with him' (*LW* 25:45).

38.   *LW* 25:299. Note that Gabriel Biel is the primary target of Luther's anti-scholastic polemics in the Romans lectures (Janz, *Luther and Late Medieval Thomism*, p. 22).

39.   *LW* 25:299. This is a direct refutation of a view Luther held as late as 1509–10. See Janz, *Luther and Late Medieval Thomism*, p. 51.

40.   *LW* 25:299. *WA* 56:312.

41.   'There is, apparently, for Luther, no *terra immacula* in the life of man' (Steven Ozment, *Homo Spiritualis* [Leiden: E. J. Brill, 1969], p. 93).

favour of modes of being or 'inclinations' of the *whole* person. His second
point is that original sin is more than *privatio*. While it includes a privation
of all uprightness and power of the *totus homo*, it is in addition a positive
reality, a real 'propensity toward evil'. This language of 'propensity' evokes
Augustine's use of metaphors of directionality and 'inclination', but its
emphasis on the positive nature of such a propensity departs from Augustine's
strictly negative treatment of the *privatio boni*, though this may be due
simply to Augustine's discussion of it in reference to the first sin. Certainly,
in our postlapsarian condition, privation also carries the stronger notion of
corruption.[42] Nevertheless, the sheer weight Luther places on sin, coupled
with his radically holistic anthropology, leads him to a starker diagnosis than
Augustine. Corresponding to this divergence in diagnosis is a divergence
in treatment. Augustine speaks of healing: 'an evil is eradicated not by the
removal of some natural substance which had accrued to the original, or
by the removal of any part of it, but by the healing and restoration of the
original which had been corrupted and debased'.[43] Luther speaks of amputation: 'Because it is impossible for concupiscence to obey God, therefore we
must not strive to be cleansed of it, but we must labor to tear it out by the
roots'.[44] The danger in abandoning a privative account of sin and evil is that
sin obtains an autonomy which allows it to actually transform the person
into something other than God's good creature. As a result, salvation comes
to be seen as a certain (perverse) kind of *creatio ex nihilo*, which amounts
more to a wiping of the slate and starting over rather than the vindication of
creation. This has all too often been the case in Protestant soteriology and is
no doubt involved in the scanty doctrines of creation, environmental apathy
and disembodied spirituality endemic to much of Protestantism.

Copernicus Redux

Anders Nygren famously described Luther's insistence, '*in opposition to all
egocentric forms of religion, upon a purely theocentric relation to God*'.[45]

---

42.   Karl Barth writes: 'For Augustine privation is *corruptio* or *conversio boni*. It is not
only the absence of what really is, but the assault upon it. Evil is related to good in such a
way that it attacks and harms it' (*CD* III/3, p. 318). Tatha Wiley sees substantial agreement
between Augustine and Luther at this point, arguing that 'like Augustine, original sin for
Luther was a *something*, not an absence' (Tatha Wiley, *Original Sin* [New York: Paulist Press,
2002], p. 90).

43.   Augustine, *City of God*, XIV.xi.569. See pages 34–5 above.

44.   *LW* 25:69 n. 6. Luther does make use of healing as a metaphor for salvation as
well, though the actuality of original sin is stressed.

45.   Nygren, *Agape and Eros*, p. 681 (emphasis his). The first to refer to the 'Copernican
Revolution' seems to have been Heinrich Boehmer in the 1930 English edition of his work,
Luther and the Reformation in the Light of Modern Research (Philip Watson, *Let God Be
God!* [Philadelphia: Muhlenberg Press, 1947], p. 67 n.1).

Nygren's is a particularly fitting insight, signifying more than a theological paradigm shift. What Luther is doing in his talk of salvation coming from *extra nos* and of the *iustitia alienum* of Christ is redrawing the solar system. If we read 'humanity' for 'earth' and 'God' for 'sun', we find that Luther made a parallel 'discovery' to Copernicus. The sun does not orbit a fixed earth. It is precisely the opposite. While his metaphors are crudely spatial, they have the desired effect. We are no longer found here, but there, no longer *in se*, but *in christo*. Taking his departure from Col. 3.3 ('you have died, and your life is hidden with Christ in God'), Luther asserts a new centre. Humanity is truly re-created in Christ as it dies and is raised from the dead with him. The common charge that this is merely a 'legal fiction' which says nothing about 'the way things are' with the person herself misses the point entirely. The 'legal fiction' charge operates under the old paradigm with a geocentric cosmology. It says, 'I am looking at this person, and she looks no different, not even on the inside. She may be reckoned righteous, and that may hold sway with God; but nothing has changed.' But Luther's whole point is that we are to look no longer at her! She has died, and her life is hidden with Christ in God.

A more subtle claim – that Luther's doctrine of justification and new life in Christ is 'extrinsicist' – still only grasps half of Luther's point. Louis Bouyer sees Luther's extrinsic justification as gaining prominence and becoming more closely aligned with his positive principle of *sola gratia* as he advances in his conflict with Rome: 'That is to say, he himself unites two statements so closely that they become inseparable – one an affirmation, grace alone saves us; the second a negation, it changes nothing in us in so doing'.[46] Bouyer's comments are right as far as they go, and they avoid the disparaging dismissal of the legal-fiction charge.[47] Indeed, Luther insists that 'these good things and this peace are not exhibited to the senses but announced by the Word and can be perceived only by faith, that is, without personal experience until the future life comes'.[48] What Bouyer misses, however, is the further affirmation of our re-location (literally, our being given a new *locus*) in Christ which, of course, changes everything. While God's good things are only perceived 'by faith, that is, without personal experience' *hic et nunc*, Luther can still speak of eternal life as 'the grace which is in us in Christ personally and through faith in Him as we participate in it and receive it through imputation'.[49]

In a careful argument on Luther's approach to mysticism, Heiko Oberman notes the connection of Luther's *extra nos* (the extrinsic element) with *raptus*

---

46.   Louis Bouyer, *The Spirit and Forms of Protestantism* (trans. A. V. Littleday; London: Collins, 1963), p. 170.

47.   A few pages later the spectre of a 'legal fiction' appears though (ibid. p. 186).

48.   *LW* 25:416.

49.   *LW* 25:56. Note the commingling of extrinsic and intrinsic terminology in this short quotation. For more on the theme of Christ in us, see Mannermaa, *Christ Present in Faith*.

(a characteristically mystical category).[50] As Oberman demonstrates, Luther rejects mystical strains that tend to bypass the incarnate Word in favour of the uncreated Word as capitulations to a theology of glory which obscure Christ.[51] He stands against the speculation and escapism all too often found in mysticism. He also rejects any sense of the believer's absorption into God. At the same time, Luther does emphasize a real union with God in this life. He insists, however (as we have seen above), that it is grasped by faith rather than the senses.[52] *Raptus*, then, for Luther, 'is the reliance on the righteousness of Christ outside ourselves (*extra nos*) and can be described as a complete transformation into Christ'. Thus, '*raptus* does not mean an ontological transformation but a transformation of *affectus* and *fiducia*, of our love and trust'. Oberman himself suggests that this undercuts 'one of the major arguments for a forensic interpretation of Luther's doctrine of justification'. 'Though we have no claim to the *iustitia Christi* which is not our "property" (*proprietas*), it is granted to us as a present possession (*possessio*). *Extra nos* and *raptus* indicate that the *iustitia Christi* – and not our own powers – is the source and resource for *our* righteousness. Epithets such as "external" and "forensic" righteousness cannot do justice to Luther's doctrine of justification.'[53]

Oberman's insights notwithstanding, the one place he does not go far enough is in his description of the transformation which is *raptus*. We take his (and Luther's) point that this is not a Dionysian absorption into the divine in which we are placed in a sort of metaphysical melting pot. But a more relational ontology would provide a *via media* which allows us to speak of true ontological transformation while maintaining the appropriate distinctions

---

50.   See Heiko A. Oberman, '*Simul Gemitus et Raptus*' in *The Dawn of the Reformation* (Grand Rapids: Eerdmans, 1992), pp. 126–54. Oberman notes Erich Vogelsang's description of three strands of mysticism known to Luther and Luther's relation to each. Luther rejected 'Dionysian mysticism', was more ambivalent towards 'Latin mysticism' and embraced the 'German mysticism' he found in Tauler and the *Theologia Germanica* (p. 130). For a far more critical view of Luther's relation to mysticism which argues for a fundamental incompatibility between faith and mysticism, see Walter von Loewenich, *Luther's Theology of the Cross* (trans. Herbert J. A. Bouman; Belfast: Christian Journals Limited, 1976), pp. 147–67.

51.   'Therefore those who approach God through faith and not at the same time through Christ actually depart from Him...For the incarnate Word is first necessary for the purity of the heart, and only when one has this purity, can he through this Word be taken up spiritually into the uncreated Word' (*LW* 25:287).

52.   Here a critique of the *Schwärmer* (or 'enthusiasts') comes in. 'The amazing thing is that he does not criticize the *Schwärmer* for being too radical, but for not being radical enough. They separate faith in the heart and Christ in heaven, whereas, for Luther, these are inseparably intertwined. As regards this identification of Christ and the Christian, Luther says concisely: "Es geht nicht speculative sed realiter zu" – it is not an imagined but a real matter' (Oberman, '*Simul Gemitus et Raptus*', p. 144).

53.   Oberman, '*Simul Gemitus et Raptus*', pp. 150–1. Luther's words bring this point home: 'And in this way we are already good as long as we recognize nothing as good except God's good and our own good as evil, for he who is wise in this way with God is truly a wise and good man. For he knows that nothing is good outside of God and that in God everything is good' (*LW* 25:383).

between creator and creature. More to the point, Luther's 'transformation of *affectus* and *fiducia*' is caught up in our finding a new life in a new 'place', that is, in Christ. We have been renewed and reconciled in our relationships, first (at least logically) with God and then with one another. Thus, we are truly new people, which *must* mean ontological transformation. It seems that we often face a false dilemma in which *either* something happens that is or becomes 'one's own' in this life *or* we are merely reckoned righteous based on an alien, external righteousness, that of Christ. Neither option can support the eschatology or the relational anthropology of the New Testament, however. A relational ontology circumvents the either/or and allows for a *real transformation* that happens, yet not first and foremost in the (old) substance of the individual but *in fides* and *in spe*.[54] The person relies on God/God's promise/Christ for her substantiation.[55]

Luther makes an early exegetical move that will help explain his revolutionary re-location of the self. In his Psalm 68 scholia, Luther redefines *substantia*, such a key ontological and anthropological term in ancient and mediaeval philosophical and theological thought, with reference to its use in Scripture.[56] Substance must be understood

> not as the philosophers talk about it, but in the sense of a foothold or settled ground, on which a man can stand with his feet, so that they do not slip into the deep and are submerged...Thus 'substance' refers to everything by which anyone subsists in his life...For they will be that kind of people just as long as those things last. And so 'substance' properly is a quality or something from the outside rather than the very being of a thing. For Scripture is not interested in the quiddities of things, but only in their qualities. Thus in whatever manner a person exists and acts, according to that he has substance, and if he does not have it, he no longer subsists. Therefore the pauper, the despondent, the self-afflictor are without substance...Therefore, in short, whatever is in the world by means of which anyone can subsist and prosper in this life is called substance. But the saints do not have this kind of substance.[57]

54. Not only must our anthropology be relational, always having faith and hope in an object; it must also be eschatological. Here David Steinmetz is helpful: 'When Luther insists that the object of faith is invisible, he does so for two reasons, neither of which has very much to do with Plato or with heavenly archetypes. The object of faith is invisible either because it is future (who of us can see next Wednesday?) or because it is hidden in the present under the form of a contrary and contradictory appearance' (David C. Steinmetz, *Luther in Context* [Grand Rapids: Baker Academic, 2nd edn, 2002], p. 39).

55. Also see Steinmetz, *Luther in Context*, pp. 39–40. It would be fascinating to ask Luther about the ecclesiological implications of a similar statement he makes later in *The Freedom of a Christian*: 'A Christian lives not in himself, but in Christ and in his neighbor... By faith he is caught up beyond himself into God. By love he descends beneath himself into his neighbor. Yet he always remains in God and in his love' (*LW* 31:371). Would he affirm that there is a similarly substantiating dynamic to our living in our neighbour through love, even if it is one that always follows (logically) upon our living by faith in Christ and never departs from that *fundamentum*?

56. Luther's redefinition comes in the scholia on Ps. 69.1 (Ps. 68.2 in the Vulgate with which Luther worked). See *LW* 10:355–56. On this, see Ozment, *Homo Spiritualis*, pp. 105–11.

57. *LW* 10:355–56.

Luther appeals to the usage of substance in Heb. 10.34 and 11.1 in speaking of *substantia* as that from which we receive life, that which grounds and establishes our existence and flourishing as the people we are. As Ozment puts it, '"Where" one lives and "how" one lives constitutes his "substance" in this life'.[58] Luther's interest in speaking of people in terms of qualities which come *ad nostrum* from *extra nos* rather than quiddities which are ours *in se* means that the person who seeks to live *in se* and *ex se* rather than *in christo* and *extra se* lives an impossible life, having none of the resources needed to establish himself. The lover of money, for example, is in some sense on the right track in that he at least recognizes that he must be substantiated by something external to himself. Of course, he (like all sinners) attempts to live on that which cannot give eternal life. He may have a temporary subsistence, but as soon as his money is gone, 'he no longer subsists'.[59]

Luther is concerned with eternal subsistence, however, and particularly with the soteriological problem of substantiation. At this point, it will be useful to bring in Luther's concept of *humilitas* and its relation to the Law–Gospel distinction. Scholars are divided on the extent to which *humilitas* acts as a *praeparatio evangelica*, particularly in Luther's early lectures.[60] It clearly plays a vital role in the making of a Christian in both the lectures on Psalms and those on Romans.[61] The tearing down of pride and establishment of humility is 'the whole purpose and intention of the apostle in this epistle', which means to

> break down all righteousness and wisdom of our own, to point out again those sins and foolish practices which did not exist (that is, those whose existence we did not recognize on account of that kind of righteousness), to blow them up and to magnify them (that is, to cause them to be recognized as still in existence and as numerous and serious), and thus to show that for breaking them down Christ and His righteousness are needed for us.[62]

Our righteousness needs to be broken down and replaced by Christ's, something which can only happen as our sins are blown up and magnified. Living in our own righteousness *coram hominibus* shields from us the fact that we live in unrighteousness *coram deo*.[63] Paul magnifies sin in Romans by appealing to the law. It is the law that 'exposes and arouses' the old man[64] and causes sin to

---

58.   Ozment, *Homo Spiritualis*, p. 105.

59.   *LW* 10:355.

60.   Siggins suggests that *humilitas* plays a significant role in Luther's early career (Siggins, *Martin Luther's Doctrine of Christ*, p. 103). With his remark that humility is not itself a virtue but a renunciation of all virtues, von Loewenich would suggest otherwise (von Loewenich, *Luther's Theology of the Cross*, p. 129).

61.   For Romans, see *LW* 25:108, 137, 177, 183, 198, 200, 220, 223, 226, 232–33, 301, 393, 441, 455, 463.

62.   *LW* 25:3.

63.   See *LW* 25:151.

64.   *LW* 25:59.

be recognised.[65] 'Sins are made manifest by the Law but are not taken away'.[66] All the law can do is announce wrath.[67] In short, through the law, we become sinners[68] – that is, we come to know ourselves as the sinners we actually are, as those under the wrath of God's condemnation in the law, as those who are 'outside of Christ'.[69] Here Luther appeals to Isa. 28.21 to describe God's *duplex opus*.[70] His *opus alienum* is to expose and condemn us in his law that we might be made sinners. Such ground-clearing is the means God has chosen by which to announce peace in the gospel (his *opus proprium*).

We return, then, to *humilitas*: 'the Spirit and grace of God can arise only when the pride of the flesh has been humbled'.[71] 'None but the humble can receive the Word of God.'[72] We are humbled when we come to the knowledge of ourselves as sinners and when we justify God.[73] Justifying God (following Ps. 51.4) is agreeing with God that we are sinners, that we are *not* righteous.[74] Even in the process of being humbled, then, we find ourselves drawn out of ourselves. We justify God's wrathful word of judgment announced in the law and acknowledge our sinful (not merely creaturely) insufficiency. Returning to Luther's redefinition of *substantia*, we find him remarking that the 'self-afflictor' (we might say, 'the humble person') is 'without subsistence'.[75] Thus Ozment describes 'the soteriologically de-substantial nature of all anthropological resources'.[76] Where, then, is the sinner to look for soteriological substantiation? How is he to avoid the quicksand of his old life *incurvatus in se*? Where will he be able to place the 'feet of his soul'?[77] Luther is instructive as he chides those sceptics who cannot recognize the divine 'Yes' hidden under the 'No', who close their eyes to the *opus alienum* for which God works his *opus proprium*.

---

65. *LW* 25:302.

66. *LW* 25:302.

67. 'For the Law shows nothing but our sin, making us guilty, and thus produces an anguished conscience; but the Gospel supplies a longed for remedy to people in anguish of this kind. Therefore the Law is evil, and the Gospel good' (*LW* 25:416).

68. On the concept of 'becoming sinners', see *LW* 25:214–15, 217, 218.

69. *LW* 25:174.

70. 'What is said in Is. 28:21 takes place here: "He does a strange work in order to do His own work"' (*LW* 25:365). Luther speaks of the *opus alienum* as a work God does for the sake of his *opus proprium*. Althaus writes that for God 'this alien work is only a means through which he accomplishes something else' (Paul Althaus, *The Theology of Martin Luther* [trans. Robert C. Schultz; Philadelphia: Fortress Press, 1966], p. 168).

71. *LW* 25:385.

72. *LW* 25:226.

73. For the concept of our justifying God in his words, see *LW* 25:26, 210.

74. Our justifying God is 'not on the basis of a *weighing up between Yes and No*, but…*in obedience* to God's Word' (Jüngel, *Justification*, p. 240).

75. *LW* 10:355.

76. Ozment, *Homo Spiritualis*, p. 185.

77. Ozment again: 'By "substance," Luther means a "solid place" where one can place the "feet of his soul" (*affectus* and *intellectus*), confident that he will not sink into the abyss of sin and death' (Ozment, *Homo Spiritualis*, p. 202).

Rather they ought to rejoice because He has not put our hope in ourselves but only in Himself, in His mercy. [*Quod spem nostrum non in nobis, sed in seipso, in misericordia sua posuerit.*] All who are of this mind are secretly saying in their hearts: 'God acts in a tyrannical manner, He is not a Father, but an enemy,' which is also true. But they do not know that one must agree with this enemy and that thus, and only thus, He becomes a friend and a Father.[78]

God has put our hope 'only in Himself', wrenching it from its old home in ourselves. This makes him look like an enemy – indeed, he *is* an enemy to the old man. But such a sense of discontinuity is for the sake of the birth of the new man. He has put our hope in him, and we are called to agree with this transfer, to justify God and thus be justified *per fidem*. Ozment reminds us that, for Luther, 'what constitutes and defines man is not what he quid-ditatively is but what he looks for and expects'.[79] Thus it is just this *fides* and *spes* which are 'the "substance" of Christian life'.[80]

Two points need to be made which hold together the eschatological tension which is the Christian life. The first is that this is a real substantiation through humble dependence on another for our very life.[81] Faith and hope in Christ are truly life-giving, grounding the Christian.[82] This does not transform these virtues (which are always the Spirit's gifts) into pious works, thus catapult-ing us back into self-righteousness. They are life-giving because they are the means by which God has seen fit to relate us rightly to the one who has life in himself – Christ. The second point is that this substantiation, though *already fully real*, is *not yet fully realized*. T. F. Torrance helpfully speaks of our sal-vation in Christ (which is our substantiation in him) as *hic et tunc* ('here and then').[83] We have heard and placed our faith and hope in the promise of God,

---

78.   *LW* 25:358. *WA* 56:368. See a similar passage at *LW* 25:439.
79.   Ozment, *Homo Spiritualis*, p. 202.
80.   Ibid., p. 107.
81.   'Faith and hope are the very reverse of one's own prideful understanding. They do not presume to possess the power to create saving objects and conditions, but rather recognize and confess what we can now describe with precision as the soteriologically "de-substantial" character of self and world' (ibid., p. 119). See Ozment's cautionary note: 'we emphasize that the "de-substantial character" of which we speak is *soteriological*, and it is not to be construed as a philosophical statement in the realm of ontology. It has reference to the absence of resources, *post peccatum Adae*, requisite to a salutary standing before God and in the face of sin and death' (ibid. p. 110 n. 3). It is difficult to determine what realm of ontology Ozment intends by his statement. Certainly the universality of sin is such that his soteriological statement refers equally universally (with the exception in both cases of Christ). We may wish to qualify or transform our patterns of speech on these issues *post obsequium Christi*, but separating soteriology out from ontology seems a specious effort. It may also betray a lack of thinking the reality of our being in Christ out to its relational conclusions even in ontology.
82.   'Christians are only seemingly "idealists," in truth they espouse a "higher realism"' (von Loewenich, *Luther's Theology of the Cross*, p. 90).
83.   Torrance writes: 'That the believer is imputed righteous means that he possesses a righteousness which is *real* (*justus*), though not yet fully *realised* (*justificandus*), as real as Christ who dwells in his heart by faith, but who as yet is discerned only by faith and not by sight. *Imputatio* describes the *hic et tunc* of our salvation in Christ, and tells us not to

but we do not yet see its fulfilment. Thus, the '"place" where the faithful live is not yet present *in re*, only *in fide* and *spe*'.[84] In summary, we find that the critique of extrinsicism in Luther's doctrine of justification accurately portrays the fact that justification is an event completely *extra nos* while at the same time entirely missing the point in its persistent anthropocentrism. It is a red herring (more, it is the height of sin) to look at *me* to determine whether there is a 'real' change, in that 'I' am no longer the prime subject of my life (Gal. 2.20). Luther's christocentrism (which is always a theocentrism) is the very feature of his doctrine of justification that makes it a reality, if always (this side of the eschaton) in faith and hope.

Before we turn to consider directly *homo incurvatus in se*, two more points of relevance vis-à-vis Luther's theological anthropology are in order.

The Logic of Person and Works[85]

Only sinners sin. Only the righteous live righteously. With this simple logic, moving from person to works and never the other way around, Luther dismisses Aristotle's definition of justice.[86] 'According to [Aristotle], righteousness

judge our actual righteousness by the appearance of the flesh, for it is concealed under hope until Christ comes' (T. F. Torrance, 'The Eschatology of Faith', in George Yule [ed.], *Luther* [Edinburgh: T&T Clark, 1985], pp. 145–213 [150]).

84.   Ozment, *Homo Spiritualis*, p. 121. He notes: 'Luther's conviction that all *fideles* (and Jesus) live "by sheer hope alone" "in God's Word alone," "*res*-less" before men' (p. 108).

85.   Romans as a whole is structured according to the distinction between person (Romans 1–11) and works (Romans 12–16), according to Luther, for 'being comes before doing, and suffering comes before being. Therefore the order is: becoming, being, and then working' (*LW* 25:104 n. 2). Luther's structuring of the epistle would surely invite comment from recent Pauline interpreters whose diverse cluster of concerns falls under the umbrella of the 'New Perspective'. One common critique is that Luther's frequent caricature of Jews in his lectures on Romans as little more than exemplars of works-righteousness misses nuances of Paul's thought and threatens to distort the salvation-historical grounding of the gospel and the shape of the epistle. Romans becomes a dehistoricized handbook for individual justification by faith alone, what is perhaps a contextually appropriate reading in Luther's day, but which finally cannot do justice to Paul's far more ambiguous relation to the law as well as the central concern he has to speak both of the inclusion of the Gentiles in the people of God and the final eschatological re-incorporation of Israel. Even given the critiques of the New Perspective, it is encouraging to note the emphasis on themes surrounding participation in Christ in Pauline scholarship (earlier in Albert Schweitzer, more recently in E. P. Sanders; see N. T. Wright, *What Saint Paul Really Said* [Grand Rapids: Eerdmans, 1997], pp. 11–23), which dovetails nicely with the work of Tuomo Mannermaa and the Finnish school of Luther research since the mid-1970s. For an introduction in English to the largely untranslated work of the Finnish school, see Carl E. Braaten and Robert W. Jenson (eds.), *Union with Christ* (Grand Rapids: Eerdmans, 1998).

86.   Original sin is the locus of our entrée into sin. Our participation in the original sin follows Luther's person–works logic (*LW* 25:46), but Adam and Eve constitute a special case in their existence *posse non peccare* in which we can only say the logic from person to works holds less firmly.

follows upon actions and originates in them. But according to God, righteousness precedes works, and thus works are the result of righteousness.'[87] 'God
does not accept a person because of his works but the works because of the
person, therefore the person before the works.'[88] There is a common sense
to Luther's argument (really, it is often little more than a bald assertion) that
could cause one to rush by the radically new picture that results from such a
move. The first implication of Luther's departure from Aristotle is rather obvious: not only do only sinners sin, but also sinners only sin. 'We sin even when
we do good', Luther admits.[89] 'We of ourselves are by nature evil', and our
evil inclination means that we cannot do good apart from grace.[90] Further, we
'are in sin until the end of our life'.[91] This is what it means to be part of the
massa perditionis.[92]

87.   *LW* 25:152. On the same page, Luther rejects a key scholastic distinction between
fides informis (unformed faith) and *fides caritate formata* (faith formed by love). Luther
has in mind Nicholas of Lyra's exegesis, in which he had wanted to read 'from faith to
faith' in Rom. 1.17 as meaning from unformed faith to a more robust faith formed by love.
Luther responds that 'no righteous person lives from an "unformed faith," neither does the
righteousness of God come from it'. This is a step beyond his position in his lectures on the
Psalms, where he still held to the *fides informis*, if tentatively. See Lohse, *Martin Luther's
Theology*, pp. 202, 59.

88.   *LW* 25:256. An important research contribution could be made in looking at the
implications of Luther's distinction in light of the current vogue in virtue ethics, which looks
to Aristotle's *Nicomachean Ethics* as its fountainhead. There is a *prima facie* tension between
the two approaches, as virtue ethics operates with a more dialectical approach to the person–
works distinction (if it accepts it) and personal identity than Luther. Whereas virtue ethics
seems to argue for person and works mutually informing one another, Luther is adamant
that what a person does is entirely a function of who that person is. On this supposedly
inimical relation, Hauerwas and Pinches write: 'To put the point directly (as Luther might):
virtue is a category Catholics use, but this only demonstrates how strong and resilient is their
belief in works righteousness' (Stanley Hauerwas and Charles Pinches, *Christians among the
Virtues* [Notre Dame, IN: University of Notre Dame Press, 1997], p. 27). Luther's ethics and
his account of sanctification ring hollow to the ears of virtue ethicists, though this may be
due as much to a deficient Christology on their part as it is to a deficient account of human
transformation on Luther's. For a vigorous contemporary defence of Luther's distinction,
see Jüngel, *Justification*, and Eberhard Jüngel, 'On Becoming Truly Human', in *Theological
Essays II* (Edinburgh: T&T Clark, 1989), pp. 216–40.

89.   *LW* 25:276.

90.   *LW* 25:222. Steinmetz notes that the claim that we cannot do good apart from
justifying grace sets Luther apart from Aquinas in addition to the more optimistic Biel.
(Steinmetz, *Luther and Staupitz*, p. 113) As Janz has shown, however, the mature Aquinas of
the *Summa* is in substantial agreement with Luther on this point and in his overall theological
anthropology, which is fundamentally Augustinian. There is a striking developmental parallel
between Aquinas and Luther in their moves from an earlier, more optimistic theological
anthropology to a later, more Augustinian one emphasizing slavery to sin and the inability
of humanity to contribute to its salvation. Luther's critique of Thomism as Pelagian can
be traced to Karlstadt's misrepresentation of Aquinas' theological anthropology. It also
reflected 'a shift in the Thomas-interpretation of the late medieval Thomist school in a non-
Augustinian direction on vital questions of theological anthropology'. See Janz, *Luther and
Late Medieval Thomism*, pp. 154–7.

91.   *LW* 25:308.

92.   See *LW* 25:156, 348, 394.

Such a dire analysis could lead one to despair.[93] Indeed, this would be entirely fitting, even salutary, in Luther's view. For even as it casts the darkest shadow over humanity, despair gives place to the brilliance of the fact that God loves *sinners*. 'God saves no one but sinners, He instructs no one but the foolish and stupid, He enriches none but paupers, and He makes alive only the dead; not those who merely imagine themselves to be such but those who really are this kind of people and admit it.'[94] Daphne Hampson makes much of this as a defining feature of Luther's theology, as well as being a locus of continual misinterpretation on the part of Catholic Luther scholars who almost universally seek to read Luther according to Catholic structures of thought. The misunderstanding is itself understandable, as Hampson argues that

> it would appear almost impossible for Catholicism to accept the basic Lutheran proposition, that God accepts sinners. It is fundamental to the Catholic structure of thought, embedded in the philosophical context of the ancient world within which Catholicism grew, that our relationship to God is founded on our likeness to God.[95]

Another correlate of Luther's distinction between person and works is his doctrine of election. While helpfully and appropriately circumspect about election (he notes that what comes first in Lombard's *Sentences* – discussion of God's foreknowledge, predestination and will – should come last),[96] he speaks of the firmness of God's election and is clear that 'nothing except election distinguished' Isaac from Ishmael and Jacob from Esau.[97] We note the absolute exclusion of any human cooperation in salvation, seen most dramatically in Luther's well-known use of phrases like *aliena* and *extra nos/se* to describe the coming to us of what is not properly ours. 'Salvation comes in no way from something working in itself but only from outside itself, namely, from God, who elects.'[98] 'His imputation is not ours by reason of anything in us or in our own power…within yourself there is nothing but destruction, and your deliverance is from outside of you [*Sed salus tua extra te est*]'.[99]

93.   On the significant place of despair and anxiety in Luther's understanding of the Christian life in this period, in particular in their connection to the doctrine of election see Richard Marius, *Martin Luther* (London: Belknap Press, 199), pp. 105–27.

94.   *LW* 25:418–19.

95.   Hampson, *Christian Contradictions*, p. 99. Steinmetz argues that the 'entire medieval tradition, and not simply one theological school within it, defined justifying grace or *gratia gratum faciens* as the grace which makes the sinner pleasing to God' (Steinmetz, *Luther and Staupitz*, p. 133). Ozment's conclusion is that, for Luther, '"unlikeness" was the unitive principle in religion' (Steven Ozment, 'The Mental World of Martin Luther', in *The Age of Reform (1250–1550)* [London: Yale University Press, 1980], pp. 223–44 [243]).

96.   *LW* 25:390.

97.   *LW* 25:374. On election and predestination in the early Luther in general, see Steinmetz, *Luther and Staupitz*, pp. 109–22, esp. 109–10. Luther argues that Christ did not, 'in an absolute sense', die for all, but that verses like 1 Tim. 2.4 refer to the elect (*LW* 25:375-76).

98.   *LW* 25:377.

99.   *LW* 25:257. WA 56:269. Luther writes only a few months after concluding the Romans lectures that 'to come to Christ and go out from oneself is the great cross' (*LW* 51:30, quoted in von Loewenich, *Martin Luther*, p. 102).

Totus homo: *The Postures of Flesh and Spirit*

Luther rejects a faculty anthropology in favour of a holistic focus on the whole person (*totus homo*). Two central reasons assert themselves for Luther's radical divergence from scholastic anthropology on this point. The first is a concern to return to scriptural ways of speaking.[100] Here Luther makes a similar point to Augustine regarding the Bible's use of 'flesh' as a synecdoche for humanity in general or individual humans in particular, either neutrally or in reference to sinful rebellion against God. That Luther does not read 'physical body' for 'flesh' is clear implicitly at a number of places,[101] and that he does not intend a denigration of the body is explicitly the case in a comment on Rom. 6.6: '"So there might be destroyed," not "the body" but "the body of sin," that is, to the degree to which it is a sinful body and the extent to which sin rules in it, not the nature of the body'.[102]

More to the point, Luther (again, following Augustine and Paul) usually confines his usage of 'flesh' to humanity living for its own sake and sets it in opposition to those who are 'spiritual' and live for God's sake.[103] Immediately, then, we see that Luther's anthropology is *relational* and *directional*.[104] 'Fleshly' man is man as he attempts to live in a pure self-relation, with all other potential relationships being instrumentally collapsed into the self-relation. Carnal man, we might say, asserts a gravitational pull on all around him and lives centripetally.[105] 'Spiritual' man is man living for God's sake, referring himself and all creation to its *telos* in the Father, through the Son, by the Spirit. This God–self relation relativizes the spiritual man and continually draws him out of himself ecstatically,[106] as he finds his life in Christ and then in his neighbour. Thus, *homo spiritualis* lives centrifugally and eccentrically.[107]

100. Wilfried Joest argues that Luther's rejection of the 'inseity' of the human person flowed from his exegetical work rather than a new philosophical anthropology (Joest, *Ontologie der Person bei Luther* [Göttingen: Vandenhoek and Ruprecht, 1967], p. 251).

101. E.g., *LW* 25:484.

102. *LW* 25:112.

103. Augustine and Luther both point to the same Pauline passage (Gal. 5.19ff.) in setting up the opposition of flesh and spirit.

104. He says this explicitly in a discussion of Romans 7 in his treatise *Against Latomus* (1521): 'There is the one man Paul, who recognizes himself to be in two different relationships: under grace, he is spiritual, but under the law, carnal. It is one and the same Paul who is under both' (*LW* 32:246).

105. In the words of Luther's beloved *Theologia Germanica*, 'assumption and his "I" and his "Me" and his "Mine" – that was his apostasy and his fall. And this is still the case.' 'All those in whom the true Light is not are turned upon themselves [*auff sich selber gekert*] and consider their selves as the best' (*The Theologia Germanica of Martin Luther* [trans. Bengt Hoffman; London: SPCK, 1980], pp. 62, 118–119).

106. On the 'ecstasy of faith' (rather than love) in Luther and its relation to the mystical tradition, see Steinmetz, *Luther and Staupitz*, pp. 135–140.

107. Luther's is 'an absolutely unnarcissistic I' (Bayer, 'The Modern Narcissus', p. 306). In relation to God, Joest describes Luther's anthropology in terms of a being 'carried and carried forward' in which humanity lives not from its own 'immanent quality, but only from the being-with of God' (Joest, *Ontologie der Person bei Luther*, pp. 269, 273; on the eccentric character of personal being, see pp. 233–74).

'Flesh', then, is not the physical body (which would betray a discomfort and even a denunciation of materiality), but the 'old' or 'external' man *in toto* who is turned away in hostility to God. In turn, 'spirit' is not the non-substantial part of a person, but the 'new' or 'internal' man *in toto* who is friends with God.[108] The difference between the old and new men is, quite simply, the indwelling of the Spirit of God. It is this Spirit which makes men new, leads them into friendship with God and makes their very mode of existence a 'spiritual' one. Here Luther brings out the Spirit's role in justification.[109] When Rom. 8.10 speaks of the spirit of a person being 'alive because of righteousness', Luther comments that

> the 'spirit,' that is, the inner man [*homo interior*], does not exist unless the man has the Holy Spirit; hence we can correctly permit the expression 'fruits of the spirit' to be understood as the fruits of the Holy Spirit. However, it is better to interpret 'spirit' [*Spiritus*] of the inner man, like a good tree which brings forth good fruit, and 'the flesh' [*Caro*] is the evil tree which produces evil fruit. But it is better to say that the Holy Spirit makes the tree good rather than to say that the tree is itself good.[110]

Luther's recommendation that we not even speak of a Spiritless person as 'spiritual'[111] is surely a salutary one given the current vogue in 'spirituality' defined over against 'religion' as one's (usually individualistic, often piecemeal and nearly always vague) approach to the numinous. Of course, his claim is far too particular to sit comfortably in the flux of contemporary Western speech. His treble emphasis on the divine source of 'spirit' in the statement above underscores the complete insufficiency of humanity in attempting to become spiritual, not to mention humanity's unspiritual state as flesh. The corresponding truth is that the references Luther makes to the 'spiritual' are

108. *LW* 25:69.

109. Paul Metzger argues that the Finnish school fails to highlight the role of the Spirit in union with Christ which is the beginning of justification, particularly in light of Rom. 5.5. See Paul Louis Metzger, 'Mystical Union with Christ', *Westminster Theological Journal* 65 (2003), pp. 201–13 (210–11) (though note that his comments are chiefly in reference to Tuomo Mannermaa's contributions in *Union with Christ*).

110. *LW* 25:68. *WA* 56:76. The connection of spirituality with justification is made even more explicit in Luther's description of those who are 'outside of Christ [*extra Christum*] and not yet spiritual' (*LW* 25:15; *WA* 56:17).

111. See *LW* 25:513, where Luther speaks of 'man as spirit'. While Luther's holistic anthropology would seem to give more weight to speaking of these *postures* of the whole man rather than faculties, we take note of Luther's speaking of spirit as an 'element' of man at another place in the lectures, following a generally Pauline tripartite structure (*LW* 25:473). Paul himself is evidence of how an anthropology that emphasizes postures or orientations (*coram deo/coram hominibus*) can also refer to a personal structure which, while obtaining, is nevertheless theologically less *significant* than the question of the posture of a person. In addition, while he points out that Luther draws a 'picture of a man who is operationally united (*totus homo velut unum membrum*)' and rejects any interpretation of Luther's anthropology as a faculty-based one, Ozment is careful to note that *spiritus* is 'a distinctively anthropological reality' which has a very 'down-to-earth' meaning and which ought not be elided by a premature identification with theological categories of Spirit (Ozment, *Homo Spiritualis*, pp. 100, 94–5).

pneumatological. They are references to the indwelling presence of the Spirit of God who is God himself, making the whole person new, not references to a 'part' of humanity *per se*.

This brings us to the second reason for Luther's abandonment of the faculty anthropology of the scholastics. Luther insisted that the corruption which is original sin extends to the whole person. It is not the case that our wills are curved in on themselves, while our intellects remain largely unstained by concupiscence.[112] Talk of aspects of the soul or person too often serves an agenda of locating some still-Edenic part of humanity that will serve as a suitable place for God to make his home. Consistently opposing this strategy, Luther rejects any need to look for such an unaffected region of the person as if God could only relate to that which is like him. We are sinners – all of us.

Particularly of note here is Luther's rejection around the time of his lectures on Romans of any soteriological component to the much-vaunted mediaeval concept of *synteresis*. As central as it was to much mediaeval discussion, a consensus on the definition of *synteresis* is difficult to find. It seems to have its roots in Augustinianism and Neoplatonism[113] and can refer to a natural knowledge of the moral law, an inclination or desire for the good or a spark of divine intellect.[114] In any case, what the tradition of *synteresis* sought to define is the 'inner dignity' of the person.[115] Ozment argues persuasively that, in the lectures on Romans, 'the *synteresis* becomes delimited in its significance to the sphere "before men" and has no role to play in man's achievement of a saving relation with God. It has potential ethical, but not soteriological significance'.[116] The problem is that Luther's opponents (Gabriel Biel, Pierre d'Ailly and Duns Scotus come in here), in insisting that 'man of his own powers can love God above all things and can perform the works of the Law according to the substance of the act',[117] overestimate the 'powers of the *synteresis* to underlie

---

112. Here, of course, we are again aware that the flesh's *incurvatus in se* encompasses the will, the body, the intellect, any non-Spiritual 'spirit' we may have and any other 'part' of us that might come to mind. We note, too, Tatha Wiley's observation that Luther followed Augustine and Lombard in identifying original sin with concupiscence (Wiley, *Original Sin*, p. 96).

113. Ozment, *Homo Spiritualis*, pp. 20–2.

114. See Ozment, *Homo Spiritualis*, pp. 20–1, and the editorial remark at *LW* 25:157 n. 41.

115. Ozment, *Homo Spiritualis*, p. 20.

116. Ozment, *Homo Spiritualis*, p. 197. See pp. 186–97 for his discussion of *synteresis* in the Romans lectures. On the 'disappearance of the *synteresis*', see Michael G. Baylor, *Action and Person* [Leiden: E. J. Brill, 1977], pp. 173–208. Baylor questions even the ethical significance *coram hominibus* of the *synteresis* (pp. 184–89).

117. *LW* 25:261. Luther explicitly rejects the soteriological implications of the *facere quod in se est* as Pelagian here and at *LW* 25:496–97. On Luther's rejection of the distinction between fulfilling the law according to the substance of the act and according to the intention of the lawgiver and his corresponding rejection of the nominalist doctrine of grace, see Steinmetz, *Luther and Staupitz*, pp. 115–16. On Luther's rejection of the *facere quod in se est* see Heiko A. Oberman, '*Facientibus quod in se est deus non denegat gratiam*', in *The Dawn of the Reformation*, pp. 84–103, especially p. 103; Oberman, 'Wir sein pettler. Hoc est verum', in *The Reformation* (Grand Rapids: Eerdmans, 1994), pp. 91–115 (105–8, 111–13).

the claim that man can love God above all things. For Luther's opponents, man's natural *ability* grounds salutary *activity* before God.'[118] Baylor, though agreeing with Ozment's judgment regarding the tendency to over-estimate the *synteresis*' efficacy, argues that Luther's rejection of it is in the context of a larger rejection of the scholastics' locating of conscience within an Aristotelian framework in which it judges actions but not the whole person who acts.[119]

Thus, for Luther, a holistic anthropology emphasizing modes of being – we might even say existential *postures* – wins out over a faculty anthropology and its languages of 'parts' of the person for biblical and polemical reasons.[120] Of course, there is an autobiographical component here as well. Luther knew the battle of flesh and spirit, and in reading Romans 7 as the angst-ridden cry of the Christian he found himself. The coarse, conniving carnality Luther read of in Paul's epistle was his own – was himself, *in toto*. The victory of the Spirit of which Paul spoke really did make Luther an entirely new man, if one who battled against this 'old man' who lingered on even after his death.

It might be natural to assume that, when Luther rejects any sense that 'part' of us is pristine while 'part' of us is sinful, he is left with one option – the claim that we are *either* wholly holy *or* wholly sinful. But it is just here, where Luther's *totus homo* meets his *simul iustus et peccator*, that he is at his most innovative.[121]

> The man who by faith in Christ is Spirit, is simultaneously flesh by virtue of his self. And that is as *totus homo*. The old man, the flesh, is not merely the 'lower' part of man (the real self minus the empirical piety); but it is man in his totality. The struggle in man is therefore not a struggle between a higher and lower part of man's nature, but between man's real self and the Spirit of God. Therefore, that which the struggle is against is our total real self, and that which fights it is the Spirit.[122]

The bleakness of the picture for 'man's real self' is seen in that nothing remains unstained by sin. No 'empirical piety' is left which counts for anything, as it is precisely the *totus homo* – even the *totus homo religiosus* – who is

---

118. Ozment, *Homo Spiritualis*, p. 193. Steinmetz concludes that there is little difference between Luther's early account of *synteresis* and Calvin's mature understanding of the *sensus divinitatis* (Steinmetz, *Luther and Staupitz*, p. 114).

119. Baylor, *Action and Person*, p. 201.

120. This is not to say that Luther never had recourse to talk of faculties but, rather, that he deemed them theologically insignificant in comparison to the far more fundamental sense in which we are *coram hominibus* and *coram deo*, *simul iustus et peccator* or flesh and spirit. Furthermore, despite Luther's emphasis on holism in his anthropology, Cavanaugh suggests that Luther's doctrine of the two kingdoms underwrote a stark bifurcation of the person, in which soul and body are handed over, respectively, to the administration of church and state: 'What is left to the Church is increasingly the purely interior government of the souls of its members; their bodies are handed over to the secular authorities' (William T. Cavanaugh, *Theopolitical Imagination* [Edinburgh: T&T Clark, 2002], pp. 24–5).

121. When considering how the *totus homo* can be simultaneously spirit and flesh, righteous and sinful, Luther draws on the *communicatio idiomatum* (LW 25:332).

122. Regin Prenter, *Spiritus Creator* (trans. John M. Jensen; Philadelphia: Muhlenberg Press, 1953), p. 225.

homo incurvatus in se. Scripture 'describes man as so turned in on himself [*incurvatum in se*] that he uses not only physical but even spiritual goods for his own purposes and in all things seeks only himself'.[123] It is precisely in Luther's holistic anthropology where we see the seriousness of his view on sin.

And yet, it is also precisely in Luther's holistic anthropology, and in virtue of the totality of depravity, that we find the necessity for a salvation that is *extra nos*. So we find that this one who *is* flesh also *is* Spirit.[124] That one is self-induced ('by virtue of his self') and another by faith in Christ in no way militates against this being truly said of one and the same man. This must be kept in mind when Prenter at the end of the passage above calls this a struggle between 'man's real self and the Spirit of God', as this can just as truly be called a struggle between man's self *in re* and his self *in fides*, to use categories from earlier in our discussion. That is to say, for Luther, this whole man really is spiritual. The new life of the new man is circumscribed by the presence and power of the Spirit in such a way that we can truly say he is spiritual.

A further illuminating passage in which the *totus homo* dovetails with the *simul* comes from Luther's scholia on Rom. 7.17:

> The idea of the metaphysical theologians is silly and ridiculous...when they invent the fiction that the spirit, namely, our reason, is something all by itself and absolute and in its own kind and integral and perfectly whole, and similarly that our sensuality, or our flesh, on the opposite end likewise constitutes a complete and absolute whole. Because of these stupid fantasies they are driven to forget that the flesh is itself an infirmity or a wound of the whole man [*totius hominis*] who by grace is beginning to be healed in both mind and spirit. For who imagines that in a sick man there are these two opposing entities? For it is the same body which seeks health and yet is compelled to do things which belong to its weakness.[125]

Here, again, we find Luther resisting those theologians who speak of different, autonomous parts of a person. Rather, the flesh is itself a 'wound of the whole man'. We are reminded of Augustine's discussion of the sinful *privatio* that has followed on our being *inclinatus ad se*. God has begun to heal this wound, and so all of the person is being healed. Still, for all Luther's emphasis on a holistic anthropology, in his own existential interaction with Romans 7, rather than one *totus homo*, there seem to be two men fighting within. We might best describe the *totus homo* as a Janus who as flesh faces the past of the old man and as spirit faces the future of the new man. Luther's concern is to preserve the gospel that crucifies that it might resurrect.

---

123. *LW* 25:345. *WA* 56:356.
124. See *LW* 25:332-33, 336. Luther summarizes nicely, and then adds a pragmatic qualification: 'The same person is both spirit and flesh, therefore what he does in the flesh the whole man is said to do. And yet because he resists, it is rightly said that the whole man is not doing it, but only a part of him' (*LW* 25:331).
125. *LW* 25:340–41; also see 330. *WA* 56:351–52.

But human righteousness tries first of all to take away sins and change them and also to preserve man as he is; thus it is not righteousness but hypocrisy...But when a man has not died to sin and has not been taken from it, in vain does one try to take away sin and die to it. Thus it is obvious that the apostle means that sin is taken away by a spiritual means (that is, the will to commit sin is put to death), but these people want the works of sin and our evil lusts to be taken away by metaphysical means, as when white paint is taken from a wall and heat from water. Hence Samuel says in 1 Sam. 10:6: 'And you shall be turned into another man,' that is, another person. He does not say: 'Your sins will be turned,' but: 'you will be changed first and when you have been changed, then also your works will be changed'.[126]

Luther's emphasis on sin being taken away by spiritual, not metaphysical means, is akin to his insistence on the logical move from person to works. Because sin is not localized somewhere within us, but rather *we* are sinners, it cannot be removed. Rather, we must die. Any attempts at preserving continuity of selfhood ('man as he is') by pruning are vanity, as the sinful root remains and can yield only poisonous fruit. Here Luther makes a similar observation to what we have seen in Augustine, though Augustine places the emphasis on the healing of the sinner, while Luther speaks of healing in the context of being crucified with Christ. So, the discontinuity for Luther is clearly evident. True, this is a healing of the person God created; but it is a resurrection healing that comes through death.

Incurvatus in se *as Ignorance: The Critique of Natural Understanding*

In his scholia on Rom. 11.9, Luther speaks of Scripture as honey and a feast unto life to one man and poison and a feast unto death to another. To these latter, the Word of God 'is a "snare" because they do not know it, a "trap" because they want to accept as true only that which seems true to them, a "pitfall" because they turn away from the truth when it is thrown up to them and when it runs counter to their own thinking'.[127] Not knowing the true nature of the Word is involved with not accepting it as true and instead only embracing what seems true to us.[128] We set ourselves up as judge[129] and 'exchange the truth for a lie'.[130] The consequence of this is a spiral into the

---

126. *LW* 25:323.

127. *LW* 25:425.

128. Here, again, we find *homo incurvatus in se*. Luther condemns reason with such force because it is self-seeking: 'It is certainly true that the law of nature is known to all men and that our reason does speak for the best things, but what best things? It speaks for the best not according to God but according to us...For it seeks itself and its own in all things, but not God' (*LW* 25:344). Augustine could say the same thing, but he would also want to say that there is a *right* kind of seeking one's own, which is a seeking one's own in God. For Luther, on the other hand, self-seeking is *by definition* sinful.

129. Luther is adamant that only God can judge. He is the 'only true judge' who 'can be judged by no one, since He Himself is eternal law and judgment and truthfulness' (*LW* 25:16, 197–98).

130. Rom. 1.25.

darkness of ignorance and confusion. Paul continues in Romans 11 by quoting David:

> Let their eyes be darkened to see not,
> And bend their backs forever.[131]

We are to read 'their minds' for 'their backs', Luther notes in his interlinear gloss, such that 'they do not look to grace, which is from above'.[132] Rather, 'their eyes [have] become blurred, so that even though all others are seeing, they themselves are in no way moved to see anything, and while all others stand straight they remain curved in on their own understanding [*curvi in sensum suum*]'.[133] These spiritually blind and hunched are clear parodies of the godly man of Proverbs 3 who trusts in the Lord with all his heart and refuses to lean on his own understanding. This is an active rebellion in which they '"have spurned the counsel" (Ps. 107:11) of God, because they act according to their own preconceived notion and want things done that way, nor are they willing to set aside their own ideas or to be transformed'.[134] Clinging to our 'own ideas' *is* our refusal to be transformed, and it is this insistence on self-continuity that, ironically, has the rattle of death to it. Precisely in our desire to avoid death, we find our feet running towards it. 'For whenever God gives us a new degree of grace, He gives in such a way that it conflicts with all our thinking and understanding...And the preservation of one's own mind is the most harmful resistance to the Holy Spirit.'[135] It is for this reason that Luther writes against those who 'rely only on their own feelings and experience'.[136]

---

131. Rom. 11.10. The severity with which Luther views spiritual blindness, coupled with the central place he gives to a faith which comes through hearing, has led some to conclude that he (along with the Reformation as a whole) marked a shift from the mediaeval privileging of the eye to a modern privileging of the ear. Steinmetz makes a cautionary note: 'One should be careful not to mistake the contrast between ear and eye as a general preference for auditory over visual learning' (Steinmetz, *Luther and Staupitz*, p. 57 n. 136). The distinction is not so much one in which one sense is approved and another rejected as much as it is the recognition that *all* senses, indeed, human rationality *per se* is incapable of perceiving God apart from his *opening* of the eyes and ears.

132. *LW* 25:98.

133. *LW* 25:426. *WA* 56:433.

134. *LW* 25:437–38.

135. *LW* 25:438.

136. *LW* 25:438. Experience was an ambiguous category for Luther. On the one hand (we might call this 'experience *as* reason'), following his commitment to a *theologia crucis* which looked at things *sub contrario* (not to mention being influenced by a sharp distinction between reason and revelation among the Nominalists), experience was seen to be just another manifestation of humanity's carnal attempt to draw creator and creation into its orbit. On the other hand (we might call this 'experience *rather than* reason'), the clearly experiential quality of Luther's own greatest theological insights along with his conviction that knowledge of God is not true, *useful* knowledge unless it is knowledge of the *Deus pro nobis*, made experience a vital category for the Christian (see Siggins, *Martin Luther's Doctrine of Christ*, p. 80). So Luther (and here experience serves as a foil for the philosophers and, in the process, a potential foil for reason itself) writes that 'a person will never grasp this unless

The physical and spatial metaphor of curvature in this instance (its application to fleshly understanding) betrays a person withdrawn into a fixed, intense self-regard, oblivious to her surroundings.[137] The narrowness of such a gaze, caused by its attention to only one object, causes us to miss the world (not to mention God) for what it is. All else sits in the fuzziness of peripheral vision and is only seen in reference to the primary object, ourselves. The irony in the midst of our fixed focus on ourselves, however, is that our inattention to all that is not ourselves is part of the reason that we mis-read ourselves as well, not least in that we are 'lumpishly insensitive to the intensity of [our] predicament before God'.[138] This is a key point at which Luther's relational anthropology comes to the fore.[139] Who we are, bound up as it is with our relation to God (and our relation to our neighbour, though this point is not as explicit in Luther),[140] makes no sense without reference to God and our relation to him. Thus, in being curved in on our own understanding, we become *homo absconditus* and do not know ourselves. It goes without saying that we also find God to be the *deus absconditus* and know only an idol.[141]

---

he learns to know it by experience. For if practical experience is necessary in law, which is a shadowy teaching of righteousness, how much more is it necessary in the case of theology!' (*LW* 25:439) Experience and reason are again set at odds in Luther's interlinear gloss of the same passage: '*that you may prove*, that you may discover by your own experience, *what is the will of God*, because it lies hidden under things which are displeasing to us, *and perfect*, because it lies hidden under the imperfect' (*LW* 25:105).

137. Luther's far more radical solution (compared to Augustine) to the problem of sinful *incurvatus in se* needs to be seen in a pastoral context in which scruples, an anguished conscience, had as of the beginning of the fourteenth century become a 'mass phenomenon in the Latin world'. Coupled with this was a piety of relentless introspection and self-examination, exhibited most clearly in the realm of monastic perfectionism (McCue, '*Simul iustus et peccator* in Augustine, Aquinas, and Luther', p. 90).

138. Steinmetz, *Luther and Staupitz*, p. 106. As Steinmetz writes, in reference to our knowledge of ourselves as sinners as an article of faith, 'If one attempts to determine one's status in the presence of God by an empirical sifting of the evidence, by an honest examination of conscience and rigorous self-scrutiny, one enters a labyrinth from which one cannot always escape, a maze in which the evidence is ambiguous and the possibilities of self-deception are endless' (Steinmetz, *Luther and Staupitz*, p. 118). Also see Alan Torrance's devastating genealogy and critique of modernity's obsession with and elusive quest for immediate self-knowledge in Alan Torrance, 'The Self-Relation, Narcissism and the Gospel of Grace', *Scottish Journal of Theology* 40 (1987), pp. 481–510.

139. 'Luther treats "nature" not as a substance, but rather as a relational concept. Thus human nature is corrupt only insofar as it refuses to ground its existence in God' (Janz, *Luther and Late Medieval Thomism*, p. 20; also see p. 30).

140. In practice, though, relationships with others played a significant role in the transformation of people curved in on themselves. 'Time and again he said that those tempted to melancholy should shun solitude' (Marius, *Martin Luther*, p. 121).

141. Brian Gerrish accounts for two types of God's hiddenness in Luther's works. 'Hiddenness I' refers to God hidden *in* his revelation, while 'Hiddenness II' is God hidden *behind* or *outside* his revelation (B. A. Gerrish, '"To the Unknown God"', *Journal of Religion* 53 (1973), pp. 263–92). What is surprising is how infrequently scholars have spoken of another type of hiddenness – that which is a function of humanity's sinfulness and refers to God hidden from those who are curved in on their own understanding.

But they want to be like God, and they want their thoughts to be not beneath God but beside Him, absolutely conformed to His, that is, perfect, which is as possible, or rather as little possible, as that clay which by nature is suitable for a pitcher or some kind of vase can in its present form be like the form or the model which the potter has in mind, into which he intends to shape the clay. They are foolish and proud over this and know neither God nor themselves...Therefore these people who do not have the Spirit flee and do not want the works of God to be done but want to form themselves.[142]

Curved in on our own understanding, we seek to set ourselves up as judge beside and with God. We want to be 'like God, knowing good and evil' (Gen. 3.5) and in seeking to be his peer we simultaneously play the role of usurper. This is a folly and pride which keeps the *duplex cognitio* of God and ourselves at arm's length. Rather than gladly being formed in the Word by the Spirit, we flee from God's works in an attempt at self-formation. In insisting that we *do* know ourselves, that we *do* know God, we betray and exacerbate our ignorance of both. Not surprisingly, then, Luther follows his mentor Staupitz in rejecting 'self-scrutiny as a source of consolation' in favour of looking to the wounds of Christ – particularly appropriate pastoral counsel for men and women *incurvatus in se*.[143]

There is a second reason besides sin for our lack of knowledge regarding God, ourselves and the world – eschatology. Luther speaks of understanding from the end of things. Indeed, such a mode of rationality is characteristic of God's work in distinction from our own (and here we understand all of creation to be God's work). 'We understand our own work before it is done, but we do not understand the work of God until it has been done.'[144] Luther criticizes the philosophers who 'so direct their gaze at the present state of things that they speculate only about what things are and what quality they have' and contrasts them with 'the apostle [who] calls our attention away from a consideration of the present and from the essence and accidents of things and directs us to their future state'.[145] Eschatology, that is to say, is the best philosophy.[146] Luther's eschatological language is also teleological. True knowledge of creation is with a view to its eschatological *telos*. Foolish philosophers are like a builder's assistant 'marveling at the cutting and hewing

---

142. *LW* 25:366.

143. Steinmetz, *Luther and Staupitz*, p. 110. See *LW* 25:389–90.

144. *LW* 25:356.

145. *LW* 25:360. These remarks bear on our earlier discussion of Luther's abandonment of a faculty anthropology for a more holistic one. He continues that Paul 'no longer directs his attention to or inquires about the creation itself, but rather to what it is awaiting' (*LW* 25:361). Indeed, in its present state, nature has become 'totally unrecognizable', thus making it futile to look to 'the way things are' to come to a proper knowledge of the creation (*LW* 25:351).

146. 'Therefore you will be the best philosophers and the best explorers of the nature of things if you will learn from the apostle to consider the creation as it waits, groans, and travails, that is, as it turns away in disgust from what now is and desires that which is still in the future' (*LW* 25:361).

and measuring of the wood and the beams' who is 'content and quiet among these things, without concern as to what the builder finally intends to make by all of these exertions'.[147] They think only of the mechanics of creation without any appreciation of its *telos*. Not only does this give only half the picture; it distorts the whole, mistakenly treating the 'not-yet' as an 'already'. Luther laments how far afield philosophy has taken us:

> Look how we esteem the study of the essences and actions and inactions of thing, and the things themselves reject and groan over their own essences and actions and inactions! We praise and glorify the knowledge of that very thing which is sad about itself and is displeased with itself! And, I ask you, is he not a mad man who laughs at someone who is crying and lamenting and then boasts that he sees him as happy and laughing?[148]

Luther carries this opposition between reason and revelation further, however, and with it magnifies the perversion of an understanding curved in upon itself. He speaks of all that is good, all that is of God being hidden *sub contrario*. Truth and righteousness 'always really appear' ugly, a principle exemplified 'in the case of Christ, for whom "there is no form or comeliness" (Is. 53:2)'.[149] Christ – God himself – is hidden *sub contrario*. 'For He is near us and in us, but always in a form which is strange to us, not in the appearance of glory but in humility and gentleness, so that He is not thought to be who He really is.'[150] While not equivalent terms, Luther's sense of things hidden *sub contrario* is closely related to his *theologia crucis*.[151] The *theologia crucis* stands directly opposed to a *theologia gloriae* which refuses the offer of a suffering saviour, preferring a glorious king. Never denying that Christ is King of Glory, Luther insists, however, that we can only know the glorious one in his suffering and that to presume to peek at his glory this side of the eschaton is to leave the triune God for an idol. Suffering may seem – indeed, always will seem – a strange form to us, but this is the only way 'He is near us and in us'.

> But those who have the Spirit are helped by Him. Thus they do not lose hope but have confidence, even though they are aware of what goes contrary to what they have so sincerely prayed for. For the work of God must be hidden and never understood,

147. *LW* 25:361–62.

148. *LW* 25:362. Related to this is Oberman's note that in his first Psalms lectures, 'Luther repeatedly slights the fourth sense of Scripture, the anagogical interpretation. It is certainly not completely absent; but when it occurs it stands increasingly for the horizontal perspective of the faithful and not for the vertical ascent of the aristocrats of the Spirit'. He goes on to note the parallel between *fides* and *gemitus* [groaning]. *Gemitus* is not the *synteresis* or any sort of pre-condition for faith. Rather, it 'presupposes faith' and at the same time 'characterizes the life of the *sancti*, whose righteousness is hidden. It describes the state of complete identification with Christ' (Oberman, '*Simul Gemitus et Raptus*', pp. 149, 151–3).

149. *LW* 25:230.

150. *LW* 25:243.

151. Though Luther did not use the phrase *theologia crucis* until his lectures on Hebrews in 1517–18, the concept is clearly found in the Romans lectures (see von Loewenich, *Martin Luther*, p. 99).

even when it happens. But it is never hidden in any other way than under that which appears contrary to [*sub contraria specie*] our conceptions and ideas.[152]

This hiddenness *sub contrario* is in no way an arbitrary, fickle thing, though. It is designed for redemption.

> God does not want to redeem us through our own [*domesticum*], but through external [*extraneam*], righteousness and wisdom; not through one that comes from us and grows in us, but through one that comes to us from the outside; not through one that originates here on earth, but through one that comes from heaven. Therefore, we must be taught a righteousness that comes completely from the outside and is foreign [*aliena*]. And therefore our own righteousness that is born in us must first be plucked up.[153]

Here we recall 'the chief purpose' of Romans, which is 'to break down, to pluck up, and to destroy all wisdom and righteousness of the flesh'.[154] Luther finds the same thrust in Jeremiah 1, a vision of Daniel and Psalm 45. It is the theme of his dialectical hermeneutic of law and gospel. God hides himself and his works in just such a form that the revelation of him and them will destroy our self-satisfaction.[155] Thus, we learn to rely in faith and hope on God who has come to us in Christ by his Spirit. And in so doing, we are drawn out of ourselves (from *incurvatus in se* to *excurvatus ex se*), the crooked is made straight, and we are substantiated outside ourselves (*extra nos*) in Christ, who is our life (Colossians 3).[156] It is in this sense that Jüngel can call faith 'self-discovery'.[157]

---

152. *LW* 25:366. *WA* 56:376–77.

153. *LW* 25:136. *WA* 56:158.

154. *LW* 25:135.

155. This is necessary even for the saints, who are *simul iustus et peccator* and daily beginning anew. Bernard's influence is evident when Luther writes that 'they would not be Christians if they had not already arisen; but to stand still on the way to God is to retrogress, and to advance is always a matter of beginning anew. Hence the Preacher does not say: "When a man has made progress" but "when a man has finished, then shall he begin" (Ecclus. 18:7)' (*LW* 25:478; see Steinmetz, *Luther and Staupitz*, p. 92). What is striking in Luther's portrayal is the wedding of progress with daily beginning anew. The believer can grow, but never in such a way that she is no longer fully dependent on God's grace and gifts. Indeed, progress is, more than anything, a continual returning to the Giver.

156. As Luther writes later in his career: 'And this is the reason why our theology is certain: it snatches us away from ourselves and places us outside ourselves, so that we... depend on that which is outside ourselves, that is, on the promise and truth of God, which cannot deceive' (*LW* 26:387).

157. Jüngel, *Justification*, p. 241. This needs to be balanced with Moltmann's insight that our being *homo absconditus* is a function of eschatology (as well as being a consequence of sin, as we have seen). He writes that the Christian 'comes "to himself" – but in hope... Thus the believer becomes essentially one who hopes. He is still future to "himself" and is promised to himself...Thus he comes into harmony with himself *in spe*, but into disharmony with himself *in re*. The man who trusts himself to the promise is of all people one who finds himself a riddle and an open question, one who becomes in his own eyes a *homo absconditus*...

Reason *versus* revelation. Things hidden under their opposite. A third corollary of these dialectics is the opposition of nature and grace. 'Nature', at least in its anthropological reference, is not a category of creation for Luther. Instead, it refers to existence under the Fall. Thus, when he speaks of 'nature', it is as if to say humanity according to the flesh. And it is this nature which is at odds with grace. 'In vain do some people magnify the light of nature and compare it with the light of grace, since it is actually more a shadow and something contrary to grace...This light [of nature] came into being right after sin did, as the Scripture says, "Their eyes were opened" (Gen. 3:7).'[158] Nature 'came into being' *not* at the point of creation, but 'right after sin did'; and its existence is directly tied to the curved-in understanding of Adam and Eve, whose 'eyes were opened'. Like Adam and Eve in their greed for autonomous judgment, nature is self-seeking and self-glorifying, characterized by 'a terrible curving in on itself'.[159] It is this nature, not humanity as God created it, which

> rejoices and is peaceful when these things are flowing in upon it but...becomes disturbed and disquieted when they go the other way. Not so grace, which remains at rest, in all things loving only to do the will of God and seeking to perform it, so that whatever things befall it, it is content both with itself and with all other things.[160]

Luther is rooting out all human self-maintenance which would attempt to ensure a broad continuity of selfhood. Where nature grows anxious at the sight of things flowing away from it – that is, where it is intent on preserving itself – grace is content to obey, freed from the strictures of self-preservation.

The hiddenness of God and the Christian life *sub contrario* is such that adversity becomes a mark of God's good will. There is a real sense that the worse things appear, the better they are. It is this theme that later led Luther to add suffering to the traditional marks of the Church,[161] and we see it throughout the Romans lectures. We hear that 'every Christian ought to rejoice most heartily when something is done which is diametrically contrary to his own

Hence the man who hopes is of all people the one who does not stand harmoniously and concentrically in himself, but stands ex-centrically to himself in the *facultas standi extra se coram Deo*' (Moltmann, *Theology of Hope* [trans. James W. Leitch; Minneapolis: Fortress Press, 1993], p. 91).

158. *LW* 25:345–46.

159. Nature 'sets itself in the place of all other things, even in the place of God, and seeks only those things which are its own and not the things of God. Therefore it is its own first and greatest idol. Second, it makes God into an idol and the truth of God into a lie, and finally it makes idols of all created things and of all gifts of God...This is spiritual fornication, iniquity, and a terrible curving in on itself...as it turns all knowledge in upon itself, it is the most complete darkness. Nor can it by its nature do anything else than turn in upon itself' (*LW* 25:346).

160. *LW* 25:347.

161. In his *On the Councils and the Churches* (*LW* 41:164–65). So Oberman writes: 'The Reformation symbol of Christ's presence is not the halo of the saint, but the hatred of the Devil' (Oberman, *Luther*, p. 155).

thinking, and he ought to be in the greatest fear when it goes according to his own thinking'.[162] Indeed, so nervous is Luther of founding justification *in nobis* that he speaks of a willingness to be damned as the one assurance of salvation.[163] There can be no moral proof that gives us assurance, for that would amount to a *theologia gloriae* that presumes to pull back the veil that can only be pierced by faith and hope, not sight. That being said, a problem arises here that is also reflected in Luther's distinction between use and enjoyment (as we will see below). In his caution to cast a theocentric cosmology, he wants to hold to a kind of disinterested love for God. That is, I love God because he is God, rather than because he, for instance, saves me. Thus, my willingness to be consigned to hell because it is the will of God, while an appropriately penitential stance on the part of *homo incurvatus in se*, seems to lay too heavily into the mystery of election in its emphasis on the inscrutability of the divine will which calls for a willingness to be resigned to hell and thereby misses the fact that God was in Christ reconciling the world to himself.

At the same time, we must hold this in tension with Luther's insistence that all signs of divine displeasure are for the sake of our coming to know his good will. It may be that a willingness to be damned is in part an assurance of salvation, in that the very extremity of our agreement with the judgment of God points to his already working for our salvation. Thus we are to

> be most pleased at the time when the most unpleasant things happen, for then it is certain that the acceptable will of God is at work ...For in this way we prove the will of God, when we do not judge according to our experience and our feelings, but rather walk in darkness.[164]

> If the Word of God comes, it comes contrary to our thinking and our will. It does not allow our thinking to stand, even in those matters which are most sacred, but it destroys and eradicates and scatters everything, as Jer. 23:29 (cf. also 1:10) says: 'Is not My Word like fire, says the Lord, and like a hammer which breaks the rock in pieces?' Hence it is an infallible sign that one really has the Word and carries it in himself, if he finds nothing in himself which pleases him, but only what is displeasing, that he is sad at all he knows, says, does, and feels, and finds pleasure only in others or in God. On the other hand, the clearest sign that the Word of God is not in a certain person is if he finds pleasure in himself, and rejoices in what he says, knows, does, and feels...in order that it thereby may teach us to have pleasure, joy, and confidence only in God, and outside ourselves happiness and pleasure in our neighbor.[165]

---

162. *LW* 25:439.
163. See *LW* 25:381–82. For Luther, Paul's statement about willing to be damned for the sake of the Jews becomes a willingness to be damned for God's sake, that is, a perfect denial of self.
164. *LW* 25:443.
165. *LW* 25:415.

Using, Enjoying: Incurvatus in *se* as Egoism

While Luther probably had some familiarity with Augustine's works from the *studium generale* at the Erfurt monastery, his keen personal interest in Augustine[166] seems to have begun around 1509, when he made marginal notes on *The Trinity* and *City of God*.[167] Coupled with these in the German edition of Luther's works are his 1510/11 marginal notes on Peter Lombard's *The Four Books of the Sentences*.[168] As a *Baccalaureus Sententiarius*, Luther was required to lecture on the *Sentences* at the Erfurt cloister,[169] as it was the standard textbook of mediaeval theology. Every bachelor at a university was required to write a commentary on it as part of his theological education.[170] Lombard mediated Augustine to a great extent, beginning the *Sentences* with a detailed discussion of Augustine's sign theory in *De doctrina christiana*.[171] He opened up this question by attempting to sort out Augustine's inconsistent use of a distinction between *usus* and *fruitio*, use and enjoyment. Significantly, however, Lombard restricted himself to Augustine's use of the distinction in *De doctrina christiana* and *The Trinity* and neglected to mention any of the references in *City of God*. While the semiotic context of Lombard's concerns need not have necessitated an exhaustive treatment of Augustine's distinction, Lombard's canonical status, coupled with his careful treatment of the distinction (as far as it went) might lead one to believe that Book I of the *Sentences* gives us the final formulation of Augustine's thinking. What one is left with at the end of Lombard's first distinction is the impression that only God is to

---

166. 'Hitherto he had not been drawn to St. Augustine, but now he really devoured him with the rapture of a younger theologian for his first theological love' (Rupp, *Luther's Progress*, p. 21). Also see Lohse, *Martin Luther's Theology*, p. 46. On Luther's later pitting of his theology as biblical and Augustinian over against the teachings of Aristotle and Lombard, see his letter to John Lang, Prior of the Augustinian Eremites at Erfurt on 18 May 1517 (*LW* 48:42).

167. See the editor's notes in *LW* 48:24 n. 6 and, on the *studium generale*, *LW* 48:28 n. 3. The marginal notes on Augustine are in *WA* 9:15–27. Luther comments on all of the books of *The Trinity* except Book XI. His notes on *City of God* are on Books 1, 3, 4, 7–19.

168. *WA* 9:28–94. Luther discusses the first three books of the *Sentences* in detail, but only gives half a page to Book IV in reference to Distinction 44. Above is the *Weimar Ausgabe* dating of the marginal notes.

169. See Lohse, *Martin Luther's Theology*, p. 45. For the theology of the marginal notes on Augustine and Lombard, particularly as it bears upon the growth in Luther's understanding of justification, see Uuras Saarnivaara, 'The Growth of Luther's Teaching of Justification' (doctoral dissertation, University of Chicago, 1945), pp. 106–15. Luther's familiarity with Lombard extended at least back to 1507 (and probably much earlier, given his prominence), when Johannes Nathin pointed Luther to Biel's dogmatics, which Biel structured as a commentary on the *Sentences*. See Oberman, *Luther*, p. 138.

170. Janz, *Luther and Late Medieval Thomism*, p. 34. Janz notes that this provided significant common ground even in the rich diversity of late mediaeval scholastic theology, as 'Lombard was the property of all the schools'.

171. Book I, dist. 1.

be enjoyed. Augustine's later emphasis on enjoying one another in God finds little place. When the early Augustine as mediated by Lombard entertains the objection of Philemon 20, which speaks of enjoying someone 'in the Lord', he places the accent heavily on this latter phrase and concludes that Paul is really enjoying God *rather than* Philemon.

Such an either/or misses the nuance of Augustine in his later usage of the *usus/fruitio* distinction, in which he moves to speaking of people truly enjoying one another, if only in God. In Book XIX of *City of God*, Augustine speaks of the 'heavenly peace', which is 'the perfectly ordered and completely harmonious fellowship in the enjoyment of God, and of each other in God'.[172] This harmonizes well with his concern for an *ordo amoris* which both refers all loves to love of God and also allows for a love of relative goods appropriate to their ontological arrangement.[173] Indeed, such harmony produces peace in the heavenly city. This patterned peace is a 'tranquility of order'[174] which issues in and from joyful fellowship. We become a community as we enjoy God together and as we enjoy one another in God. While Augustine does continue to hold to a view that *usus* and *fruitio* are mutually exclusive *per se* in *City of God*, he sets up the distinction in this late work as one between using the world and enjoying God (or the reverse, if speaking of perverse attempts at using God and enjoying the world). Augustine makes no reference to persons in this, and while he does not make the connection with his earlier distinction (where only God is said to be enjoyed) explicit in his later references to enjoying one another in God, the force of such language is such to signal a shift from his earlier work. Furthermore, after *De doctrina christiana*, Augustine never again referred to neighbour-love under the banner of use but transferred love of neighbour to enjoyment, 'although he continued to speak with comfort of loving the neighbour "for God's sake".'[175]

But what is the significance of such minutiae for understanding Luther's treatment of sinful *incurvatus in se* and his relational anthropology? What is odd is that Luther seems to take Augustine's earlier understanding of *usus/fruitio* without evincing any knowledge of its later formulation in Book XIX of *City of God*. He had clearly read at least through this book by 1509 (his marginal notes stop there, with nothing on Books XX–XXII), but when he distinguishes use from enjoyment it is in the strict sense allowing for the

---

172. Augustine, *City of God*, XIX.xvii.878. Also see also XIX.xiii.872. We should note, too, that Augustine does allow for the enjoyment of another in God as early as *De doctrina christiana*, though, as we have seen, this is a *fausse joie* or, rather, a joy whose proper object is God rather than another person. The evocative eschatology of Augustine at the close of *City of God* shows how far he had come since his earlier work on this point.

173. 'Enjoyment is an absolute love, use a relative one' (Nygren, *Agape and Eros*, p. 505).

174. Augustine, *City of God*, XIX.xiii.870.

175. Oliver O'Donovan, '*Usus* and *Fruitio*', *Journal of Theological Studies*, N.S. 33 (1982), pp. 361–97 (395).

enjoyment of nothing but God, who alone is to be enjoyed *propter se*. It is likely, given this as well as the proximity of the Romans lectures to his lectures on the *Sentences*, that Luther adopted Lombard's rendering of the distinction without adapting it in light of Augustine's mature formulation in *City of God*. What this would have led him to, however, as we noted above with reference to Philemon 20, is the conclusion that even if we *can* speak of enjoying one another in God (Augustine's later emphasis), this enjoyment is really one of God rather than of one another. One danger implicit in this is that Luther will find it difficult to recognize and valorize relative goods. That is, he might highlight the instrumentality implicit in Augustine's earlier conception of *usus/ fruitio* in such a way that he mitigates the very neighbour-love he is intent on retaining.[176]

Luther made much of the *usus/fruitio* distinction in reference to *incurvatus in se*.[177] In two passages in which he explicitly makes reference to being curved in upon oneself, Luther paints the sinner as one who uses God to enjoy the world.

> Our nature has been so deeply curved in upon itself [*in seipsam incurva*] because of the viciousness of original sin that it not only turns the finest gifts of God in upon itself and enjoys them (as is evident in the case of legalists and hypocrites), indeed, it even uses God Himself to achieve these aims, but it also seems to be ignorant of this very fact, that in acting so iniquitously, so perversely, and in such a depraved way, it is even seeking God for its own sake. Thus the prophet Jeremiah says in Jer. 17:9: 'The heart is perverse above all things, and desperately corrupt; who can understand it?' that is, it is so curved in on itself [*curvum in se*] that no man, no matter how holy (if a testing is kept from him) can understand it.[178]

> In all these things he 'enjoys' the gifts of God and 'uses' God [*fruitur donis Dei et utitur Deo*]. Nor can he be freed of his perversity (which in the Scriptures is called curvedness, iniquity, and crookedness [*curvitas, iniquitas et perversitas*]) except by the grace of God.[179]

As both passages point out, Luther's use of the language of curvature to describe our sinfulness is part of his privileging of biblical ways of speaking. While he still retains some of the scholastic terminology in which he was schooled (in

---

176. While this is a danger in the systematic implications of Luther's theocentrism, we note these words: 'Hence it also enjoys all things in and with God' (*LW* 25:352). Also see *LW* 25:415, where Luther writes that we are to 'have pleasure, joy, and confidence only in God, and outside ourselves happiness and pleasure in our neighbor'. Clearly Luther rejoiced in other people as well as in God. When he speaks against enjoying the gifts of God, he is criticizing a joy in them without reference to God, as *ultimate* ends.

177. Nygren reads Luther as finding in the *usus/fruitio* distinction an attempt by Augustine 'to overcome the selfish idea of love' (Nygren, *Agape and Eros*, p. 715).

178. *LW* 25:291. *WA* 56:304–305. Note that a few lines later Luther explicitly references Lombard (p. 292).

179. *LW* 25:313. *WA* 56:325.

spite of often filling it with strikingly new content), Luther is re-casting his vocabulary according to the mould of scriptural usage.[180]

The Scriptures tell us not only that our sinfulness is a crooked and curved perversity, but also that we are ignorant of this fact and could not understand it even if we were aware of it. The first passage above (in Luther's scholia on Rom. 5.4) is set in the context of a discussion of testing, which (seen as functioning within or analogously to law – never mind that Romans 5 speaks of those who *have* been justified by faith) is for the sake of self-knowledge. For 'God accepts no one as righteous whom He has not first tested…And this testing takes place in order that each person may see his own state of mind, that is, that each may know himself, namely, whether he really loves God for the sake of God'.[181] Here we see the law at work in its second use (what Luther calls the 'theological' or 'proper' use), in which it reveals sin and humbles hearts, even leading us to despair before God's judgment and wrath.[182] As Gerhard Ebeling describes it, 'Law is therefore not an idea or an aggregate of principles, but the reality of fallen man'.[183]

Of course, our blithe ignorance of our own perversity is at the same time an ignorance of the grace of God. As such, it is an ignorance of God himself, the *Deus pro nobis*. Knowledge of man and God are inseparable for Luther, as they would be for that second-generation reformer, John Calvin. Not that we are to localize the problem of being curved in on ourselves to a problem of knowledge. No, ignorance follows on the prior corruption of our nature – a corruption so deep that it seems (and in a certain sense can be said to be) *natural*. Strictly speaking, it is not natural (if by that we mean to refer to human nature as created by God), but is a result of the 'viciousness of original sin'.

Returning to Luther's handling of the *usus/fruitio* distinction, we can see the strength of original sin's gravity in that we do not stop at turning the 'finest gifts of God' in upon ourselves in an effort to enjoy them. We go further, using

180.	See the chapter on 'A Crisis of Vocabulary' in Rupp, *The Righteousness of God*, pp. 81–101, which points to the beginnings of Luther's linguistic transformation. According to Joest, Luther's critique of the 'theological adequacy of the philosophical idea of being' was motivated by 'a new encounter with the theological "*Sache*"' (Joest, *Ontologie der Person bei Luther*, p. 114). Steinmetz notes Luther's adoption and transformation of Biel's language of 'doing what is in one': 'When one asks what Luther means by "doing what is in one," Luther responds with a string of verbs: "ask," "seek," "knock," "cry out." The sinner does what is in him when he cries out for a virtue which he does not have and which he is all too painfully conscious that he lacks' (Steinmetz, *Luther and Staupitz*, p. 88). This, in effect, turns Biel's meaning on its head.

181.	*LW* 25:291.

182.	On the uses of the law, see Wayne G. Johnson, *Theological Method in Luther and Tillich* (Washington, DC: University Press of America, 1981), pp. 5–7. Also see Thomas M. McDonough, *The Law and the Gospel in Luther* (Oxford: Oxford University Press, 1963), pp. 87–8, 143–5. It may be that Luther's frequent talk of proper use of not just the law but also the sacraments, Scripture and the work of Christ may be an extension of Augustine's distinction. On proper use, see Gerhard Ebeling, '*On the Doctrine of the Triplex Usus Legis*', in *Word and Faith* (London: SCM Press, 1963), pp. 62–78 (72–3).

183.	Ebeling, '*Triplex Usus Legis*', p. 75.

even God for our own sake. We bring him into our orbit to suit our purposes. The crux of the matter for Luther seems to be this: 'it would be the enjoyment [*fruition*] of the creature instead of the Creator'.[184] This is largely due to his following Augustine and Lombard in speaking of *fruitio* in tandem with the phrase *propter se*. We enjoy and love things for their own sake, whereas we use things with reference to the enjoyment of another.[185] Thus, enjoyment of the creature *rather than* the creator (and the either/or is as stark as it looks) amounts to idolatry, immediately evoking Rom. 1.25: 'they exchanged the truth of God for a lie, and worshiped and served the creature rather than the Creator'. Not only is this enjoyment idolatrous, but it is also futile. That is, in enjoying creatures we treat them as final ends in themselves, expecting them to provide all the good which is only God's to give. So, we have reduced God to an instrumental role in the fulfilling of our desires. Rather than the only one who is to be loved, enjoyed and worshipped for his own sake, we have used him with reference to ourselves. And, ironically, in our inordinate enjoyment of God's gifts, we have frustrated them. Our enjoyment of these gifts in themselves and the consequent divorcing of them from the context of meaning found in being gifts of God, forces them to play a role as final ends in themselves which they can never fulfill. 'All these [gifts of God], I say, man turns in [*inflectit*] upon himself, in them he seeks his highest good, and of them he makes for himself horrible idols in place of the true God insofar as he does not refer them to God.'[186] Such is the perversity of our turning God's gifts and himself in on ourselves.[187]

Homo religiosus *as* homo incurvatus in se

But we are not crass. We are not the heirs of Johannes Tetzel, Luther's early nemesis who helped make indulgences big business, complete with marketing campaign.[188] We do not pretend to buy God's favour. As Luther points out above, though, even our *seeking* God is using him, insofar as it is a seeking him for our sake (his words spoke of our nature 'even seeking God for its own sake'). Here he clearly moves beyond Augustine, for whom humanity is defined by desire.

184. *LW* 25:292.
185. Though again, recall our earlier discussion of enjoying one another in God. In this case, our love for one another is a love *propter Deum*, our enjoyment a *fruitio propter Deum*. Rist notes the connection: '"Because of God" [the *propter Deum* language] is enriched by "in God" – to emphasize that one really does enjoy one's neighbour, but that the only way to do so without reducing his status to that of a material object is to enjoy him "in the Lord"' (Rist, *Augustine*, p. 165).
186. *LW* 25:351. *WA* 56:362.
187. See *LW* 25:363, where Luther talks about vain/perverted enjoyment of creation which subjects it to futility.
188. Tetzel even used a catchy jingle: 'As soon as the coin in the coffer rings, / The soul from purgatory springs' (Roland H. Bainton, *Here I Stand* [London: Hodder & Stoughton, 1951], p. 78).

> It is easy, I say to understand how in these things [i.e., sensual evils] we seek our fulfillment and love ourselves, how we are turned in upon ourselves and become ingrown at least in our heart [*in nos ipsos inflexi et incurvi affectu saltem*], even when we cannot sense it in our actions.
>
>   In spiritual matters, however (that is, in our understanding, our righteousness, our chastity, our piety), it is most difficult to see whether we are seeking only ourselves in them. For the love of these things, since it is honorable and good, often becomes an end in itself for us and does not permit us to regulate them in accord with God and refer them to Him, so that as a result we do them not because they are pleasing to God but because they delight us and quiet the fears of our heart, because we are praised by men, and thus we do them not for the sake of God but for ourselves [*non propter Deum, Sed propter nos*].[189]

There is a sort of common sense that recognizes the ingrown sinfulness of sensuality. Even if we do not sense it in each of our actions, Luther thinks it is enough to point out this selfishness for it to be acknowledged for what it is. Spiritual matters are more subtle, however, and therefore more dangerous. It is precisely because the love of such things (and notice the list – understanding, righteousness, chastity, piety!) is a very good thing that we can slip into treating them as ends in themselves 'for us' (and this is the key phrase for Luther). But even doing such self-evidently good things as thinking well, repenting, remaining celibate and praying can become a corkscrewed perversion when they are done for the sake of some advantage accruing to us (our own delight, avoidance of fear or praise from others) rather than for the sake of God. Nygren notes that Luther expanded here on Augustine's notion of *incurvatus in se* in his application of it to *homo religiosus*. Augustine saw the remedy to our being ingrown in the soul's directing

> its desire upwards towards God and the heavenly world. Luther has discovered that even the soul that is turned towards heaven can be bent upon itself – that is, if it is governed by desire and longing. 'Even in heaven they only seek their own,' he can therefore say. It is from this point of view that he criticises Catholic piety.[190]

In this one phrase – 'if it is governed by desire and longing' – a chasm has opened between Augustine and Luther. As Nygren accounts for Luther (and he would seem to be right on this point), desire and longing are the very categories of a life lived for one's own sake. Augustine, as we have seen, is one for whom 'the whole life of the good Christian is a holy longing'. Consequently, he structures the Christian life around desire and accounts for sin as a corruption of and misdirection of desire. Certainly, Luther levelled his critique at the crass manipulation (on all sides) of the indulgence controversy (though Luther would not enter the fray on this issue for a few years). But his attack on religious anthropocentrism goes much further and, in the process, reveals how endemic

189. *LW* 25:245. *WA* 56:258-59.
190. Nygren, *Agape and Eros*, p. 486 n. 3.

such egoism is.[191] He refuses to entertain on any level seeking God out of fear or out of desire for reward. Indeed, these two motivations are condemned throughout the lectures on Romans in connection with ethical action of any sort. We are not to love God out of fear or desire; nor are we to love others for these reasons. We might say, playing on O'Donovan's words, that whereas for Augustine self-love is *problematic*, for Luther it is simply a *problem*.[192]

Love of God

We begin with the first part of the twofold love commandment – loving God. God's love, by which we love God, 'loves nothing but God alone, not even His gifts, as the hypocritical self-righteous people do. Therefore, when physical and spiritual blessings flow in, it does not get excited.'[193] Indeed, 'to love Him for the sake of His gifts or for some advantage is the lowest kind of love, that is, to love Him with a selfish desire [*concupiscentia*]. This is using God but not enjoying Him [*Quod est uti Deo et non frui*].'[194]

There is a danger here of splitting person and works in God. When Luther speaks of loving God not for what he does for us but for who he is in himself, this seems to sit uneasily with his later ever stronger emphasis that God is none other than the God we meet in Christ,[195] that the God we meet in Christ is always the one who is *pro me/nobis*.[196] Furthermore (and more to the point, in terms of Luther's concerns), such a split between who God is and what he does cannot do justice to the Scriptures. The psalmist gives voice to the whole of Scripture when he sings:

I love the Lord, because He hears
My voice and my supplications.[197]

We love God for who he is, that is, for being the one who hears our voice and our supplications.

191. 'To be sure, there are many who for God's sake consider the goods of the left hand, that is, temporal goods, of no value and gladly give them up, as the Jews and the heretics are doing. But there are few who for the sake of obtaining the righteousness of Christ consider the goods of the right hand, the spiritual goods and righteous works, worth nothing. This is something the Jews and heretics cannot do. And yet, nobody will be saved unless this takes place' (*LW* 25:137–38).

192. The book is O'Donovan, *The Problem of Self-Love in St. Augustine*.

193. *LW* 25:293.

194. *LW* 25:294–95. *WA* 56:307.

195. See Siggins, *Martin Luther's Doctrine of Christ*, p. 8.

196. It may be that this is something drawn from Staupitz which Luther later abandons, though the centrality of this love for God for who he is rather than for the benefits we derive from him to Luther's critique of *incurvatus in se* would suggest that it is retained throughout his career. On Staupitz's treatment of this theme in his 1497–98 sermons on Job, see Steinmetz, *Luther and Staupitz*, p. 40.

197. Ps. 116.1.

This objection notwithstanding, it is instructive to keep in mind the axe Luther is grinding and to remember his urgent sense of the need of a sharp blade to hew the gnarled trees of a mediaeval philosophy, theology and spirituality that had been planted in the coarse ground of works-righteousness. What Nygren terms the 'egocentric tendency' means more than that man has become the centre of the story. Not only has salvation become 'more or less' man's work. 'At the same time, everything also centres upon man's own *interest*.'[198] So Luther's diatribe against loving God for his benefits is set against the background of late mediaeval concern for, to put it simply, results without relationship. It is not that Luther wanted to diminish the significance of soteriology. It is rather that he wanted to *maintain* the indissoluble connection between the doctrine of God and soteriology. In fact, he is attacking the split between person and works which occurs when people love God for his gifts without due reference to who he is.[199] Luther rejects any form of instrumentalism in pious approaches to God as flatly egocentric. In the same scholia on Rom. 5.5 in which Luther has been attacking love for salvation without reference to the Saviour, he remarks that 'it is not enough to have the gift unless the giver also be present'.[200]

Fear as an illicit motivation is merely the flip side of self-love. Both wallow in self-consumption and self-absorption. Both bespeak what Luther calls 'covetous love' (whether this desiring for oneself is for the sake of acquisition or avoidance). He describes

> those who think that they are righteous and love God with a covetous love, that is, because of their salvation and eternal rest or because of their escape from hell, and not for the sake of God Himself, but for their own sakes, men who babble that ordered love begins with itself and that each person must first desire salvation for himself and then his neighbor's salvation as his own.[201]

We do not love God aright if we love him for what he does for us, because that is making us the *telos* of our love. We are then doing things *propter nos* rather

---

198. Nygren, *Agape and Eros*, p. 681. Mannermaa critiques Nygren for dismissing union with Christ as irreducibly bound up with *eros*. Rather than the result of an ascent of desire (which Nygren rightly criticizes), union is the fruit of the descent of God to humanity which is known in faith – a faith whose form is Christ (Tuomo Mannermaa, 'Why Is Luther So Fascinating?', in Braaten and Jenson [eds.], *Union with Christ*, pp. 1–20 [17]). The significantly overlapping semantic fields of desire and love as well as Nygren's banishment of union as an improper category for Christian theology may explain in part why he speaks of Christian love almost exclusively in terms of love for neighbour rather than love for God. Our relation to God is one of faith. Veli-Matti Kärkkäinen, on the other hand, draws faith in and love for God together (see Kärkkäinen, '"The Christian as Christ to the Neighbour"', *International Journal of Systematic Theology* 6 [2004], pp. 101–17 [109]).

199. In many ways, this anticipates the reduction of the *Deus pro nobis* to an action ('*pro nobis*') in search of an actor ('*Deus*'), as seen in later liberal Protestant theology. That many of these theologians (e.g., Schleiermacher, Ritschl, Herrmann) were Lutherans or deeply indebted to Luther shows the razor's edge Luther walked in attempting to articulate a theology that was at once theocentrically grounded and experientially directed.

200. *LW* 25:296.

201. *LW* 25:380–81.

than *propter deum*. But such a move on our part denies the soteriological sufficiency of God's prior move towards us in Christ. It amounts to a practical atheism, or at least an idolatry that denies that what God has done for us is in itself enough – for salvation, for life itself. Instead, 'we should approach all of these things as people about to serve God freely and happily and not out of fear of conscience or punishment, nor in the hope of reward or honor'.[202] If our salvation had not been accomplished in the first advent of Christ *in carnem* and his second (spiritual) advent *per gratiae* and eagerly anticipated in his future advent *per gloriam*,[203] we would have every reason to anxiously work to accomplish it. Now that it has been accomplished, though, our self-concern is needless and merely evidences the persistence of our original incurvature in Adam. Galatians rebukes such a posture: 'It was for freedom that Christ set us free'.[204] It is freedom that undercuts the validity of and the need for lives of desire or fear. We have been freed from sin, death, the world, the flesh and the devil. Now we can love God with a pure love precisely in that we are not required to love him above all things in order to be saved. There is a near parallelism between love and faith at this point for Luther. We can approach God only 'by faith', 'through Christ', Luther insists,[205] the inseparability of the two being seen in that 'He is our life, and through faith He flows into us and remains in us by the rays of His grace'.[206] Luther similarly regards God's love and the presence of the Holy Spirit as inseparable. At first glance a comment like this can look like a mere reiteration of Gabriel Biel's insistence that we can and must love God above all things in order to be saved. So Luther begins by commenting that God's love 'is the purest feeling toward God, and alone makes us right at heart, alone takes away iniquity'. The first hint that this is not a reversion to works-righteousness (besides the fact that this verse comes only four verses after Paul's statement that we are justified by faith) is that this love 'alone extinguishes the enjoyment of our own righteousness'.[207] Moreover, this is a love 'where nothing is visible, nothing experiential, either inwardly or outwardly, in which we can trust or which is to be loved or feared' but which 'is carried away beyond all things into the invisible God'. This is a type of desire for God, but it is one marked by its trust in him alone in

---

202. *LW* 25:493. Also see p. 495: 'If we are pleasing to God, all of these things must be done not by the compulsion of necessity or by the drive of fear but in happiness and a completely free will.'

203. 'Thus the whole root and origin of our salvation lies in God who sends' (*LW* 25:413). For a discussion of Christ's threefold advent, with reference to Luther's earlier lectures on the Psalms, see Ozment, *Homo Spiritualis*, pp. 127–30, 163, 173, 176. Also see Steinmetz, *Luther and Staupitz*, pp. 63–4, who notes Luther's 'hermeneutical rule for his students that whenever any verse is explained or can be explained with reference to Christ in the flesh, it ought at the same time (*simul*) to be interpreted with reference to his coming in grace and his last advent in glory' (p. 64).

204. Gal. 5.1.

205. *LW* 25:286–87.

206. *LW* 25:315.

207. *LW* 25:293.

the face of contrary experiences. And it is a love which is 'not born in us or originated in us' but which '*is poured* into us...*through the Holy Spirit*'.[208] Luther admonishes his students to remember that 'the apostle unites the spring with the river...For it is not enough to have the gift unless the giver also be present.'[209] The love for God of which Luther speaks is one which *presupposes* God's presence as Spirit in the believer. Only on such terms can he continue to speak of loving God above all things,[210] and in so doing he flatly contradicts Biel's assertion that this is within our natural powers.[211] On the contrary, it is our 'curvedness [which] is now natural for us, a natural wickedness and a natural sinfulness [*Curvitas est nunc naturalis, naturale vitium et naturale malum*]. Thus man has no help from his natural powers, but he needs the aid of some power outside of himself [*ab extrinseco*]. This is love.'[212]

But in addition to being freed to love God with a pure love, we can give our lives to others. Our participation in Christ, in whom we now live, provides the resources for an effective *imitatio Christi* (always *in Christi*) in a life of self-giving love for others.[213] As Luther would later write, 'We should devote all our works to the welfare of others, since each has such abundant riches in his faith that all his other works and his whole life are a surplus with which he can by voluntary benevolence serve and do good to his neighbor'.[214]

Love of neighbour[215]

Turning to the second part of the twofold love commandment – loving one's neighbour as oneself – Luther again rejects any ethical motivations of fear or desire. His reason is simple: both betray a primary self-concern that is incompatible with love, which 'seeks not its own'.[216] Fearful people act to avoid evil or the loss of good. Those motivated by desire act for the sake of their own gain. Both use people in the wrong sense. That is, they manipulate people for

208. *LW* 25:294.

209. *LW* 25:295–96.

210. *LW* 25:294–95.

211. On Biel on loving God, see Heiko A. Oberman, 'Gabriel Biel and Late Medieval Mysticism', *Church History* 30 (1961), pp. 259–87 (272). On Luther's rejection of this, see Steinmetz, *Luther and Staupitz*, p. 110.

212. *LW* 25:345. *WA* 56:356.

213. George Hunsinger writes that Barth learned from Luther that Christ 'is not the source of our righteousness without also being its reality and ground, that the righteousness we receive from him by faith does not come by portions and pieces but is already ours whole and entire, that *it is participatory before it is intrinsic*' (Hunsinger, *Disruptive Grace*, p. 286 [emphasis mine]).

214. *LW* 31:365–66.

215. A helpful summary of Luther's theology of love is Kärkkäinen, '"The Christian as Christ to the Neighbour"', which offers a digest of the Finnish school's work in this area. His reading of Luther on human love is, I think, too optimistic.

216. 1 Cor. 13.4 is a constant refrain in the Romans lectures. His other theme in speaking of Christian ethical action is Philippians 2.

their own ends (themselves being their own final ends). Luther is particularly perceptive in his description of the subtle ways in which this occurs. It can often be under the guise of kindness. There is a 'human, or worldly, type [of *benignitas*], that is, the imperfect type, which endures only as long as it finds an echo and ceases over against evil and ungrateful people'.[217] A subterranean conditionality obtains with this worldly kindness, which is a kindness in search of kindness for itself. It calls out, eagerly awaiting (and expecting) its reciprocation. Luther further speaks of 'the manner of the mercenary to give honor with the hope of being honored in return'[218] and commends 'those who are hospitable out of free love and not of mercenary desire'.[219]

Contrasted with the manner of the mercenary is that of the one who is free. Paul 'understands the term "hospitality" [in Rom. 12.13] in terms of something freely given and not the mercenary or commercial kind'.[220] Indeed, 'if we are pleasing to God, all of these things must be done not by the compulsion of necessity or by the drive of fear but in happiness and a completely free will'.[221] The fundamental ethical shape of the Christian life for Luther is that of free, self-giving love which is not hampered by fear or desire. To say that love is self-giving is an analytic judgment, as is saying that love is free. Thus, Luther speaks often of the ease and joy of this freedom in which nothing – not the flesh, the world or the devil – constrains a person.[222] In fact, it is the freedom of the Christian which enables her self-giving. Luther's is truly a kenotic theological anthropology, though only by virtue of its prior status as a christocentric one.[223]

On the necessary impossibility of self-love

Such a definition of love immediately rules out reflexive love. Luther remarks that 'love keeps nothing for itself and seeks only those things which are in the interest of others'.[224] Self-love, then, is *not* love.

> Charity is love not for oneself but for another. Likewise as soon as the apostle rejected self-complacency, he immediately went on to teach that we should please our neighbor. Therefore to please our neighbor means not to please oneself...For as long as we first use each good for ourselves, we are not concerned about our neighbor.[225]

217. *LW* 25:169.
218. *LW* 25:455.
219. *LW* 25:463.
220. *LW* 25:463.
221. *LW* 25:495.
222. See *LW* 25:330.
223. We will have occasion to return to this theme in the next chapter, when we look at Daphne Hampson's critique of Luther's anthropology, particularly its motifs of self-emptying, discontinuity and a certain form of heteronomy.
224. *LW* 25:455.
225. *LW* 25:512.

Charity is, *by definition*, love for another. It means *not* pleasing ourselves as much as it means pleasing another. It means *not* using goods (including our neighbour) for ourselves, but always with reference to our neighbour's edification and, ultimately, God's glorification.

Of course, that people *do* love themselves in some sense is self-evident. Luther acknowledges this in reflection on the twofold love commandment:

> Therefore I believe that with this commandment 'as yourself' man is not commanded to love himself but rather is shown the sinful love with which he does in fact love himself, as if to say: 'You are completely curved in upon yourself [*Curvus es totus in te*] and pointed toward love of yourself, a condition from which you will not be delivered unless you altogether cease loving yourself and, forgetting yourself, love your neighbor.'[226]

Luther has earlier tried two readings of Mt. 19.19, rejecting the first way of understanding the commandment 'in the sense that both the neighbor and one's own self are to be loved'. The 'better interpretation' is the sense in which 'we are commanded to love only our neighbor, using our love for ourselves as the example'. But why is this better? 'Because man with his natural sinfulness does love himself above all others, seeks his own in all matters, loves everything else for his own sake, even when he loves his neighbor or his friend, for he seeks his own in him.'[227] In the same way that one cannot serve both God and Mammon, Luther argues that one cannot love both one's neighbour and oneself. Either one seeks one's own in everything, even in one's neighbour, forgetting all others but oneself, or one forgets oneself and seeks the good of one's neighbour in everything.[228] There is no allowance for degrees. And here Luther stands again in stark contrast to Augustine, for whom self-love was a much more knotty problem. In fact, of the two readings Luther considers for the command to love one's neighbour as oneself, Luther rejects the Augustinian interpretation that argues that 'ordered love...begins with itself'. Really, he accepts this statement at face value, but so redefines it that it is unrecognizable in the Augustinian matrix. Indeed, saying that the *ordo amoris* begins with self-love will actually serve to lead us 'away from love as long as we do not understand it'. How, then, are we to understand it? Simply put, 'true love for yourself is hatred of yourself...Therefore he who hates himself and loves his neighbor, this person truly loves himself. For he loves himself outside of himself [*Quia iam extra se seipsum diligit*], thus he loves himself purely as long as he loves himself in his neighbor.'[229] Luther is consistent in locating all our good *extra nos*, here arguing that a right self-relation is one in

---

226. *LW* 25:513. *WA* 56:518.

227. *LW* 25:475.

228. 'Moreover, a man cannot be diligent in the case of other people unless he is negligent of his own interests' (*LW* 25:451). It is comments like this, which seem to encourage self-denigration, that will provoke the critique of feminists like Daphne Hampson, as we will see in the next chapter.

229. *LW* 25:512. *WA* 56:517.

which, strangely, we are related to ourselves outside ourselves. But we must be careful even at this point not to have love for ourselves as the goal of our loving our neighbour or, again, we have curved our neighbour in upon ourselves. Luther is razor sharp in his suspicion of even psychological egoism, and his critique here echoes his critique of loving the gifts and not the giver. In all this, direct self-love is flatly rejected.

One small postscript is necessary, and it is a small one. Luther does seem to allow that we can truly love ourselves, but only indirectly, as a happy consequence (never a motivation) of our loving others kenotically. Recall that 'by this very fact [i.e., by your loving your neighbour as yourself] you most truly love yourself, and all in turn love you'.[230] Even here, of course, we remember Luther's early and frequent insistence that the sense of desperation that inevitably accompanies self-love is simply out of place in light of our dying and rising with and in Christ. And so, while this indirect self-love is salutary, it can only be a cause for a slight smile rather than a great shout of joy or sigh of relief. It matters little.

The horizontalizing of good works

A last word about love of neighbour in terms of its relation to the problem of good works is in order. It would be easy, and many have fallen prey to the temptation, to dismiss Luther in his insistence on our inability to read off someone's standing before God from her moral character and his re-location of our life in faith and hope in Christ as being at best an irrelevancy (at worst a corrosive) in Christian ethics. As we have seen, though, it is precisely our having been relativized and re-established in a new *locus* that enables ethical human action. We have been set free from the bondage of an ethics that seeks to tips the scales of salvation in our favour. There is no one left to please who matters, because those in the Son know the good pleasure of the Father. Oberman's colourful comment brings the point out vividly: 'Good works are not repudiated, but their aim and direction have been radically "horizontalized": they have moved from Heaven to earth; they are no longer done to please God but to serve the world'.[231] This is the freedom of the sons and daughters of God which is, nevertheless, a kind of servitude. At the same time, 'this kind of servitude is the highest freedom, for it lacks nothing and receives nothing, but rather gives and bestows. Thus it is truly the best freedom and one which is the peculiar property of Christians.' In the same passage Luther writes: 'To be sure, the apostle and spiritual men also performed these works and still do so, but not because they have to but because they want to; not because the works are necessary but because they are permitted'.[232] This freedom can give without thought to what it receives (without listening for

230. *LW* 25:514.
231. Oberman, *Luther*, p. 192.
232. *LW* 25:474.

an echo, as Luther remarked) because it already has everything in Christ.[233] Nothing else is necessary.

The Violation of Vocation: Transgressing the Limits of Calling

A final feature of living *incurvatus in se* is a violation of the limits of one's calling. In his re-valorization of the laity, Luther extended the notion of *vocatio* to the everyday life of the believer. The Church's unity and health depends on each believer living in joyful, self-giving freedom in the station (which would include particular gifts the Spirit gives) in which God has placed her. *Vocatio* actually discovers, or confers grace.[234] Unity is threatened, though, by transgressions of the salutary limits of one's vocation.[235] Yet such transgressions, or at least the desire for them, seem an inescapable feature of human existence.

> Therefore those who have this ability and have been called [*vocati*] ought not to take time for other matters, although in our day this has become common practice, as also the heathen Horace knew: 'The lazy ox longs for the saddle, and the nag longs to plow,' for no one is content with his own lot in life, but he praises those who follow other paths. And Terence says: 'Most of us are of a mind that makes us dissatisfied with our own lot.' Those who are suited for a job dislike it, and the incompetent pant for it.[236]

There is a faint echo here of Augustine's emphasis on sinful *inordinatio*. A disorder is manifested in and results from the desire to do something other or more than what God has given and gifted us to do. It is an absurd disorder, too, with oxen longing for saddles and those who are unfit longing to do just what they cannot and should not do. Vocation lends dignity to particularity.

> Therefore the works of the saints are not to be preached in an absolute sense, that is, they are not to be commended to men in the sense that they should do exactly the same things, but the added advice should be given: 'See here, he lived in his own station in such and such a way as an example for you, so that you in your station may do

---

233. Even the Christian's goodness is only a goodness in and from Christ. 'The "goodness" of human action is thus received *ab extra*; like justification and sanctification, it is "alien". And one consequence of this idea of the "alien" character of the goodness of good works is that the prime agent in good works is God himself: once again, "God alone works in us"' (John Webster, *Barth's Moral Theology* [Grand Rapids: Eerdmans, 1998], p. 164; quoting Luther's 1520 *Treatise on Good Works*). The recognition and rejoicing in the fact that there is a new primary subject of our life, namely Christ, is itself a sign of God's salvation. As Luther writes: 'Note how the voice of the flesh is always saying "my," "my"; get rid of this "my" and rather say: "Glory to Thee, O Lord!" And then you will be saved' (*LW* 25:376).
234. *LW* 25:447.
235. *LW* 25:105.
236. *LW* 25:448. *WA* 56:455.

likewise, but not in such a way that you must do the same things to the neglect of your own station and by jumping over into his.'[237]

Luther transforms the tradition of *imitatio* in two ways. First, he radically subordinates it to the doctrine of justification. He gives no place to imitation of Christ or the saints as a form of self-establishing or self-forming piety.[238] Such a form of piety would fall foul of the person/works distinction that grounds Luther's understanding of justification. In a fascinating essay, Robert Jenson remarks that 'the Reformation began as an attack on medieval counseling practice, which in those days they called the rite of penance'. He speaks against the 'Socratic' tendency to speak of potential and continuity. Rejecting the developmental metaphor of an acorn, Jenson writes: 'The doctrine of justification says that righteousness is not potentially in the acorn, that it has to be given to the acorn from outside it, that the acorn is not what it is to be but must receive what it is to be...God *crucifies* human personality in order thereby and only thereby to bring it to fruition.'[239] One can only truly imitate Christ and the saints (Luther continues to speak of the value of *imitatio Christi* and, to a lesser extent, *imitatio sancti*) from the secure ground of having been given oneself by God, in Christ. Thus *imitatio* with its tendency to emphasize self-perfection gives way to *Nachfolge Christi*, a decidedly derivative activity (in its subordination to justification) that emphasizes conformity to the one in whom we live.[240] In other words, discipleship does not establish holiness but is the life that follows from being sanctified in Christ.

Second, Luther emphasizes the particularity of an individual's 'station' with reference to the freedom of the Christian.[241] The joyful freedom experienced

---

237. *LW* 25:410.

238. Hampson writes that 'for Luther there can be no saints', quoting his remark that 'God has nothing to do with holy men. A holy man is a fiction' (Hampson, *Christian Contradictions*, p. 51). Such a one-sided statement captures Luther's Christocentric orientation as well as the fundamental *hiddenness* of Christian holiness which refuses empirical tests of holiness. But it misses the true sanctification of the believer *in Christ*. Joest is closer to the mark: 'What differentiates this sinner from an unholy sinner is this alone, that *the* holy one is *with* her' (Joest, *Ontologie der Person bei Luther*, p. 261).

239. Robert W. Jenson, 'The Doctrine of Justification and the Practice of Counseling', in *Essays in Theology of Culture* (Grand Rapids: Eerdmans, 1995), pp. 105–16 (109).

240. See Hampson, *Christian Contradictions*, p. 51. She continues: 'It is not for the Christian to become in himself like Christ, but rather to look to another [i.e., Christ]. (Indeed one could contend that what Catholicism has often understood by sanctification is very close to what Luther thinks *par excellence* sin)' (p. 52). See her later discussion of Kierkegaard's continuing in this Lutheran tradition of discipleship which nevertheless finds more room for *imitatio* (pp. 266–7). Also see Siggins, *Martin Luther's Doctrine of Christ*, pp. 159–60.

241. Vocation has a 'local' character which contrasts it with imitation of a pattern. 'The only saint who could in any sense be the proper object of my imitation would be one who had precisely the same neighbor as I and stood in the same relation to him as I do...The saints are patterns for us only in that we should resemble them in their faithfulness to their tasks, not that we should make their tasks ours. We must show our faithfulness in our own tasks' (Gustaf Wingren, *Luther on Vocation* [trans. Carl. C. Rasmussen; Philadelphia: Muhlenberg Press, 1957], pp. 172, 182).

here is the freedom I have been given to love others without concern for myself, right where I am. Luther's strong emphasis on ethical spontaneity, which many commentators have noted,[242] trades in any wooden, thinly literalistic forms of *imitatio* for a Spirit-led obedience that is peculiar to one's vocation in life. Implicit here is an affirmation of the basic goodness of secular stations – the life and work of a mother, a prince, a baker. We cannot overstate the significance of Luther's growing sense of what Regin Prenter calls 'the gospel of the *vocation*, the good news that Gracious God may be served in an ordinary, everyday job in the world, with no less dedication and holiness than in a monastery'.[243] Luther is still a monk as he gives these lectures with, as far as we know, no plans of leaving his own religious vocation. But even at this point, we see him moving towards his later position (and maybe in some sense having already arrived) in which the range of holy options is dramatically broadened. And there are two impulses at work here. The first is 'a gradual movement from an objective piety [in which acts themselves are the locus of piety] toward a subjective one', which begins before but finds unique expression in Luther, not least in his rejecting of sacramental efficacy *ex opere operato* in favour of a focus on the sacramental benefits being present to faith.[244] The second is Luther's unwavering insistence on the derivative nature of this subjective piety, in which imitation or discipleship always follows on justification. It is a piety of faith, hope and love, all of which are in response to the promise of God heard in the gospel.[245]

242. See Regin Prenter, 'Holiness in the Lutheran Tradition', in Marina Chavchavadze (ed.), *Man's Concern with Holiness* (London: Hodder & Stoughton, 1970), pp. 121–44 (136–37); Nygren, *Agape and Eros*, pp. 726–33.

243. Prenter, 'Holiness in the Lutheran Tradition', p. 133. Also see Philip Watson, 'Luther and Sanctification', *Concordia Theological Monthly* 30 (195), pp. 243–59. Watson makes the interesting suggestion that part of the reason there is often 'little outward difference' between the works of a Christian and those of a 'decent heathen' is because 'the works that God appoints for the Christian are simply those given in the daily round and common task of life. From this point of view Luther can say that good works are a quite inadequate index of a person's faith and his standing with God. Yet there is a great difference in the spirit in which true Christians do their works: namely, the Holy Spirit, who is the Spirit of willing love' (p. 253).

244. William A. Dyrness, *Reformed Theology and Visual Culture* (Cambridge: Cambridge University Press, 2004), p. 36. This movement, whose origins pre-date the Reformation, is seen in the Devotio Moderna and the Brethren of the Common Life, as well as in Thomas à Kempis, whose *Of the Imitation of Christ* is 'the best-known product of this school' (pp. 32–3).

245. By way of anticipation, Nigel Biggar notes that Barth's notion of our 'correspondence to God's action in Jesus Christ differs from classic notions of the *imitatio Christi* and Christian discipleship in its indirect method of moving from Scripture to ethics. It also differs in the very low level of specificity that characterizes its moral conclusions' (Nigel Biggar, *The Hastening that Waits* [Oxford: Clarendon Press, 1993], p. 114). In fairness, a similar criticism could be levelled against Luther, though Barth would resist even Luther's commitment to the *via crucis* as a principalization unbecoming of one whose Lord is the One who loves in freedom. So Biggar: 'As Barth explicitly rejects principial monasticism, so he implicitly rejects principial suffering. Self-sacrifice is not *the* principle of Christian life. There is no such thing' (pp. 108–19).

Hampson argues the symbolic force of two moves: 'Augustine left the world for the monastery, whereas Luther left the monastery to live a "secular" life in the world'. In applying these moves to the larger traditions which stemmed from these two men, Hampson finds a self-preoccupation in the former, 'as though a little too much of Plotinus' dictum "never cease to chisel your statue" has rubbed off on Catholic faith'.[246] That Augustine's move, historically, was far from the inward retreat Hampson suggests is seen in his sorrow at being pressed into the priesthood – something which, if anything, signalled the *end* of his hopes for unharried contemplation.[247] This was a being thrust *into* the world. Where Hampson is right, however, is in locating Luther within a world that has become holy again. Gone is a privileged sense of vocation which sees monastic orders as uniquely 'spiritual'. As we have seen, the presence of the Spirit in the believer sanctifies all of life such that 'getting married was, for Luther, nothing if not a theological statement!'[248]

Conclusion: *Augustine* versus *Luther?*

Anders Nygren concludes that Luther means 'something quite different' from Augustine in his use of *incurvatus in se*.[249]

> In Augustine, the sinful soul is '*bent down to earth*'; in Luther, it is '*bent upon itself.*' The difference is clearest of all if we notice how this situation is thought to be changed. For Augustine it happens when the soul directs its desire upwards towards God and the heavenly world. Luther has discovered that even the soul that is turned towards heaven can be bent upon itself – that is, if it is governed by desire and longing. 'Even in heaven they only seek their own,' he can therefore say. It is from this point of view that he criticises Catholic piety.[250]

Nygren is right to point out, as we have seen, the extension of *incurvatus in se* in Luther to its application to the whole person as *homo religiosus*. This may have been a matter of context, but Luther's development is no less significant for that reason. In calling even the most glorious of human activity into question, Luther revealed the totality of humanity's incurvature. In this, Luther's solution to the problem of sin – salvation coming to us from outside

246. Hampson, *Christian Contradictions* (London: Faber & Faber, 2000), p. 286.

247. Peter Brown, *Augustine of Hippo* (London: Faber & Faber, 2000), p. 395.

248. Hampson, *Christian Contradictions*, p. 286.

249. Robert Crouse suggests that the abiding appeal of Nygren's rather simplistic thesis is due to its being 'so neatly consistent with the anti-Hellenic temper of twentieth-century Christian thought' (Robert Crouse, '*Paucis Mutatis Verbis*' in Dodaro and Lawless (eds.) *Augustine and His Critics*, pp. 37–50 [39]).

250. Nygren, *Agape and Eros*, pp. 485–86. Nygren is followed, nearly word for word, in this by A. Skevington Wood, 'The Theology of Luther's Lectures on Romans', *Scottish Journal of Theology* 3 (1950), pp. 1–18 (7); Rupp, *The Righteousness of God*, p. 165; Hampson, *Christian Contradictions*, p. 37.

of us – is as radical as his diagnosis of that problem.[251] But Nygren's critique of Augustine, via Luther, goes much further. He rejects the category of desire which structures human life in Augustine's thinking. He acknowledges that, for Augustine, this is simply a way of saying that 'we, unlike God, have not life in ourselves and of ourselves, but from Him. *Desire is the mark of the creature.*' Human life 'has not its "bonum" in itself; its existence depends entirely on something which is outside it'.[252] From here, Nygren criticizes Augustine's claim that all human love is intrinsically acquisitive, which is coupled with an explicit endorsement of self-love. That is, if *all* love seeks its own, the question is not *whether* we seek our own good but *in what* we seek that good. Augustine's *ordo amoris*, with its concern for right self-love[253] (rather than none at all) is still held captive to the egoism which is central to Luther's radical conception of *agape*, in which self-love is banished.[254] Augustine's scheme, according to Nygren, is one in which '*the descent of Christ has as its aim our ascent…*Augustine thus teaches a *theologia humilitatis*, but merely as a means for rising to a *theologia gloriae*.'[255]

Unquestionably, Luther's complete rejection of self-love represents a radicalizing and even at points a rejection of Augustine's *ordo amoris* and corresponding understanding of *incurvatus in se*.[256] Luther's view of the *total* depravity of humanity shows up Augustine's claim that we all seek our good. Rather, according to Luther, do we inescapably look in the wrong places for our good and, when any good is found, do we mis-use and thereby abuse it. That Luther continues to think of Augustine as his one friend (along with the Bible) amidst a sea of theological foes, though it should give us pause in attributing to Luther the project of uprooting Augustinianism, does not diminish this point. Indeed, in criticizing Augustine's reading of the command to love one's neighbour, Luther clearly draws a line between the two. Further, there is a clear divergence between Augustine's picture of God as the *summum*

---

251. It is in keeping with Luther's sense of sin and his corresponding doctrine of salvation that Oswald Bayer writes, 'Self-reflection will cease in the consummation of creation. The one praying Psalm 17:15 says, "As for me, I shall behold your face in righteousness; when I awake I shall be satisfied, beholding *your* likeness"' (Bayer, 'The Modern Narcissus', p. 313).

252. Nygren, *Agape and Eros*, p. 479.

253. See Nygren, *Agape and Eros*, pp. 547–8, for a helpful division of Augustine's notions of self-love into three kinds.

254. Not, of course, that Augustine had no place for egoism, as we have seen. Sin began with pride. What's more, even if we were to focus on sin as *inordinatio* in Augustine, we would have to acknowledge that Adam and Eve's love for the temporal simply *is* a sinful egoism. Conversely, for Luther, man's egoism is an inordinate love for a creature in that it is not giving God his due. Thus, while not wanting to flatten out the distinction between these two, we see that there is an extensive overlap in their judgements and even in the concepts they use to explain these judgements, if not always in the structures of their larger thought.

255. Nygren, *Agape and Eros*, pp. 529, 532.

256. Though Nygren overstates his case, as in the statement that 'it is immediately obvious that [Luther] uses this term ["bent" or "curvatus"] in an entirely different sense from Augustine' (Nygren, *Agape and Eros*, p. 713).

bonum, the satisfaction of all our desires, and Luther's insistence that we love God for who he is and not simply for his gifts. Surely God is more and often other than merely the answer to the achings of our hearts (*contra* Augustine). At the same time, surely he is none other than the God who has in Christ saved and loved sinners, restoring them to the most joyous (and desirous) of communions with him and one another.

It is in his rejection of ascent that Nygren misses the point. Luther, too, could speak of ascent.[257] In fact, he and Augustine make strikingly similar statements on this point.

> God himself, the blessed God who is the giver of blessedness, became partaker of our human nature and thus offered us a short cut to participation in his own divine nature.[258]

> He placed this ladder on earth so that we might ascend to God on it.[259]

For both Augustine and Luther, Christ's descent *does* have as its aim our ascent. An ascent need not signal a collapse back into egoism.[260] Indeed, Luther's ascent of faith resembles Augustine's ascent of desire in that both are caught up in the descent and ascent of the Word made flesh.[261] That is, both are, in this movement of Christ, drawn out of themselves into another. This is an ascent which is also a reconciliation, an ascent on Christ, our Jacob's ladder. This is salvation.

257. Applying the label of 'Neoplatonist' (which is frequently paired with the motif of ascent) to Augustine to clearly draw a line between him and Luther similarly misses the point. Though Augustine's Neoplatonism and Luther's biblical personalism certainly lead to their drawing different conclusions about the nature of humanity and its sin, we should be cautious about making too much of this. Luther's lavish praise for the *Theologia Germanica* would at least seem to imply that *he* saw little to condemn in the Neoplatonism in which the mystical text was soaked. See *The Theologia Germanica of Martin Luther*, p. 54.

258. Augustine, *City of God*, IX.xv.361.

259. WA 40/III:656.25 (cited in Siggins, *Martin Luther's Doctrine of Christ*, p. 33).

260. Though it may very well do so. Nygren describes a '*threefold mode of ascent*' in Augustine: 'by the ladder of Virtue, of Speculation and of Mysticism' (Nygren, *Agape and Eros*, p. 513 [emphasis his]). We would critique any places in which Augustine attributes ascent to human action (via any of these three modes), but we would further point out that, for Augustine, participation in Christ is the primary mode of ascent.

261. And so Lutheran faith and Augustinian desire come to resemble one another as well. Gerard Loughlin offers a helpful term in 'dispossessive desire' which hints at how the dispossession of Luther's categories and the (salutary) acquisition of Augustine's might be brought together. See Loughlin, *Alien Sex* (Oxford: Blackwell, 2004), pp. 17–19.

Chapter 3

(How) Do Women Sin?
Daphne Hampson and the Feminist Critique of Luther

Introduction

We turn now to what may be the most forceful critique levelled against seeing sin paradigmatically as humanity curved in upon itself. This is the feminist critique of sin as pride.[1] In particular, we will examine the post-Christian feminist critique of Daphne Hampson.[2] Besides having written extensively on Luther's understanding of the self, Hampson is an apt conversation partner in that she advocates a relational understanding of personhood and of sin (and reads Luther as doing the same) while herself rejecting the way this is conceived in Luther and the broader Christian tradition. Following Joest's depiction of Luther's abandonment of Aristotelian categories, Hampson succinctly summarizes Luther's position:

> Luther understands the human *relationally*, whether in relationship to God, or as attempting to be independent of God...Just as faith is relational in nature (it has to do with the relationship to another), so equally is sin (the non-relationship of attempting

---

1.   That being *incurvatus in se* and being prideful are not identical conditions we have seen in both Augustine and Luther, and we will have occasion to revisit this later in this chapter. Furthermore, while assuming Augustine's definition of original sin as pride at the outset of her work (advancing an argument along 'Wesleyan-holiness–feminist' lines), Diane Leclerc acknowledges that the definition comes from Augustine's later, anti-Pelagian writings and suggests that other alternatives *within* Augustine's corpus might dovetail nicely with her own project. That she later rejects incurvature is an unfortunate consequence of her equation of it with pride (Leclerc, *Singleness of Heart*, pp. 13 n. 2, 158). In calling attention to Augustine's privileging of pride after considering various options (pride, sensuality – note the parallels with Kierkegaard and Niebuhr – and the threefold formula of 1 Jn. 2.16 are considered), O'Connell points to his reading of Ecclesiasticus 10 as convincing, or at least confirming him in this conviction. See O'Connell, 'Augustine's Exegetical Use of Ecclesiasticus 10:9-14', pp. 247–8.

2.   Hopefully, this will prove to be an exercise in 'generous orthodoxy' characterized by 'the willingness to give another voice airtime, the willingness and openness to test without immediate charge of wrongdoing, wrong doctrine, or incipient schism' (Katherine Greene-McCreight, 'Feminist Theology and a Generous Orthodoxy', *Scottish Journal of Theology* 57 [2004], pp. 95–108 [97]).

to establish oneself in the face of God). Neither is understood 'substantially' in terms of the inward attributes of a person.[3]

Thus, while we will have occasion at times to nuance Hampson's reading of Luther, we acknowledge from the outset that it is a profound analysis of the structure and radical implications of his thought. Accordingly, I do not intend in this chapter to continue to re-argue for the reading of Luther set out in the previous chapter. What is at issue here are questions of reality and morality – whether Luther's particular relational understanding of sin and the relational anthropology which accompanies it are true and good.[4] Whereas Hampson is advocating a relational theory of selfhood while rejecting a paradigmatic portrait of sin as *incurvatus in se* (conceived of as prideful egoism), I am advocating a relational theory of selfhood and seeing it complemented in the relational account of sin as *incurvatus in se*. What's more, as I will argue below (following Hampson), one's understanding of sin informs and is informed by one's theological anthropology. As a consequence, though Hampson and I both argue for the fundamental relationality of personhood, relationality in a Lutheran versus a post-Christian context will look strikingly different.

Hampson's Critique of Luther on Sin, incurvatus in *se and the Self*

In Hampson's account of Luther, sin is fundamentally a refusal of dependence. The state of sin correlates with Luther's understanding of salvation as 'the consent in faith to dependence on God'[5] in that sin involves one attempting 'to establish oneself in the face of God', thus making a 'bid for independence from God'.[6] Such an independence can take a number of forms,[7] but 'within the Lutheran tradition sin is basically conceived of as *hubris*; as that pride in

---

3.   Hampson, *Christian Contradictions*, pp. 13, 36. Furthermore, for Luther, '*iustus* and *peccator* are relational terms and we are involved in a relational understanding of what it is to be justified' (p. 25).

4.   Hampson confesses to having reached the conclusion that 'Christianity...is neither true nor moral' in Hampson, *Theology and Feminism* (Oxford: Basil Blackwell, 1990), p. 1.

5.   Salvation thus represents a 'reinstantiation of creation', in that prelapsarian existence was characterized by this dependence on God (Hampson, *Christian Contradictions*, pp. 35–6). It is worth noting that, for Luther, the primal sin was the idolatrous unbelief of Eve, which is a turning from God. In his gloss on Gen. 3.4-5, he writes: 'Although she has not yet eaten the fruit, she has already sinned against the Word and faith; for she has turned away from the Word to a lie, from faith to unbelief, from God to Satan, and from the worship of God to idolatry' (*LW* 1:159).

6.   Hampson, *Christian Contradictions*, p. 36. Elsewhere, she writes: 'There is thus a dichotomy running through the center of Lutheran thought, the dichotomy between trying to exist by myself (sin) in which I shall fail to be a self, and living from God (faith) whereupon I come to live as God intended that I should live' (Hampson, 'Luther on the Self', *Word & World* 8 [1998], pp. 334–42 [336]).

7.   Hampson treats pride, idolatry, egoism, isolation, insecurity and despair.

which the creature attempts in and of himself or herself to be "God", thereby denying the true God'.[8] This idolatrous self-deification lands one in despair[9] and the insecurity of attempting to go it alone in the universe. It is also characterized by an egoistic referencing of all of reality to oneself. So, by virtue of his expulsion or denial of God as the ground of his life, 'the human is insecure and will misuse others in the bid, which must always be in vain, to secure himself'.[10] Not surprisingly, the usurping of God and (ab)use of others lands one in a place of isolation.[11] This description as a whole serves to describe *homo incurvatus in se* in Hampson's treatment of Luther.[12]

Adopting the methodology of the Scandinavian school of motif research, Anders Nygren in particular, Hampson continually draws the reader's attention to the structural context of theological words and ideas.[13] Claims about

8.   Hampson, *Christian Contradictions*, p. 36. For her analysis and critique of sin seen paradigmatically as pride in Niebuhr, see Hampson, 'Reinhold Niebuhr on Sin', in Richard Harries (ed.), *Reinhold Niebuhr and the Issues of Our Time* (Grand Rapids: Eerdmans, 1986), pp. 46–60; *Theology and Feminism*, pp. 121–26; and *After Christianity* (London: SCM Press, 1996), p. 140. Also see *Christian Contradictions* for her discussion of sin as pride in the context of the overall structure of Luther's thought (pp. 36–7).

9.   A technical term taken from Kierkegaard. There are two kinds of despair, the will to be oneself by oneself and the lack of the will to be oneself at all. The former is a distinctly 'manly' form of despair which Hampson matches up with her discussion of pride. See her discussion of Kierkegaard's *Sickness Unto Death* in *Christian Contradictions*, pp. 271–7. See also 'Reinhold Niebuhr on Sin', pp. 48–9.

10.   Hampson, *Christian Contradictions*, p. 37.

11.   See 'Luther on the Self', p. 337: 'For Luther such a person is caught up in himself, bent into himself: the human in sin is *incurvatus in se*. Thus the move from sin to faith is a move from an essential isolation to a connectedness to another who is God'. We note that Hampson sees in Christianity as a whole a tendency towards isolation, even in its understanding of salvation. This is a predictable outcome, according to Hampson, given what she sees to be its rootedness in an oppressive, male-dominated system of symbols and meaning.

12.   It is their description of *homo incurvatus in se* that allows us to 'contrast rather neatly Luther's understanding of sin with that of Augustine' (*Christian Contradictions*, p. 37). Following A. Skevington Wood (who follows Nygren), the contrast is as follows: 'Augustine speaks of sin as being bent (or curved) down to the ground', but means this ('Neo-Platonist that he is') to refer to man's inordinate desire for the temporal and earthly. Luther uses the same term but 'speaks of the human as being curved in upon himself (which is egoism)' (*Christian Contradictions*, p. 37). Even here, Hampson would argue, the different structures of thought are seen. Where Augustine thinks in terms of man in a hierarchy of being, Luther thinks in terms of man *coram Deo* and *coram hominibus*. See our discussion of Nygren's comparison of Augustine and Luther on *incurvatus in se* at the conclusion of Chapter 2.

13.   Though where motif research claims to be historical and neutral ('though in fact Luther is always its hero', as is clear from even a cursory perusal of Nygren's *Agape and Eros*), Hampson wants to ask theoretical questions which involve critique (*Christian Contradictions*, p. 143). In a chapter on 'Motif Contexts' in his *Meaning and Method*, Nygren neatly summarizes the problem which launches Hampson's book: 'Two judgments which are verbally similar can have totally different meanings if they are governed by different fundamental motifs'. We note that, according to Nygren, 'the fundamental Christian motif is *the Agape motif* (pp. 366, 374). Of course, the opposite is also true, a point which seems at times lost on Hampson (and, presumably, Nygren). Two judgements which are verbally

how sinful man is (in both senses of that phrase) affect the rest of one's approach to both theology and spirituality. And of course, the reverse is true. Thus, Hampson points out that it is not surprising that when sin is described in terms of the *hubris* of man there is a corresponding view of self and salvation that majors on the humbling of the proud. This is certainly a common biblical theme, and it is Luther's lens for reading Romans.[14] Thus, Luther speaks in terms of discontinuities, of a breaking of the self, of heteronomy. What this means is that salvation involves the crucifixion of the old man and the recreation of the self as a new man who lives entirely in dependence on God. Luther's de-centring of the self and speaking of our living *extra nos* is a prime example of this for Hampson. Such heteronomy places value on authority ('God's will') obedience, and worship, all of which Hampson categorically rejects.[15] Coupled with this soteriology is an ethic of self-giving love. That is, where the *eros* of egoism is the problem, the *agape* of kenotic, self-abandoning love is the solution.[16]

different can have very similar meanings if they are governed by the same fundamental motif. In the previous footnote, we argued for greater continuity between Augustine and Luther in regard to sin by appealing to verbal similarity and implied that, though their concepts (notwithstanding their overlapping understanding of sinful curvature) may be rather different, their judgements are strikingly similar. So on the other side of this argument, we take David Yeago's distinction between concepts and judgements, whereby the important thing to pay attention to is the judgements (while still acknowledging that concepts are a material part of the judgements). Due to the fact that 'the same judgement can be rendered in variety of conceptual terms', the unity of the Church's teaching should be sought 'at the level of judgements and not at the level of concepts' (David S. Yeago, 'The New Testament and the Nicene Dogma', in Stephen E. Fowl (ed.), *The Theological Interpretation of Scripture* [London: Blackwell Publishers, 1997], pp. 87–100 [93–94]).

14.　See page 61 above.

15.　Daphne Hampson, 'On Autonomy and Heteronomy', in Daphne Hampson (ed.), *Swallowing a Fishbone?* (London: SPCK, 1996), pp. 1–16 (9). Also see *After Christianity*, pp. 78, 251 (they are 'hierarchical modes of being'). Later in *After Christianity*, the three Christian values she rejects as harmful to women are self-sacrifice, humility and obedience, though we note that she does not reject all acts of self-sacrifice (p. 270).

16.　This is a rather simplistic distinction (though one with significant theological warrant in Luther's writings) made popular by Nygren. There seem, *prima facie*, to be at least two forms of *eros*. The first is the rather straightforward egoism which Hampson identifies. A second would be the erotic mode of much mediaeval spirituality, which at times seems to issue in the self's being lost in the divine. This is also seen in many treatments of (human) romantic love, where the self is lost in the lover. Indeed, mediaeval mysticism often uses the language of romantic love to speak of the union of the soul and the bridegroom. St John of the Cross sings: 'Oh night that joined the lover / To the beloved bride / Transfiguring them each into the other. / ... / Lost to myself I stayed / My face upon my lover having laid / From all endeavour ceasing: / And all my cares releasing / Threw them amongst the lilies there to fade' (St John of the Cross, *Poems of St. John of the Cross* [trans. Roy Campbell; London: Pantheon Books, 1951], p. 13). C. S. Lewis writes of this second form of *eros* when he says that 'Eros...wonderfully transforms what is *par excellence* a Need-pleasure into the most Appreciative of all pleasures' (C. S. Lewis, *The Four Loves* [London: Fount Paperbacks, 1960], p. 88). Loughlin calls into question the equation of egoistic acquisition and possession with the desire for another by challenging Nygren's 'sharp distinction between a possessive

While the above outline could be nuanced, Hampson is remarkably lucid and straightforward in her analysis. Certain theological commitments imply a larger, Christian worldview, and this worldview is simply no longer tenable – for both feminists and post-Enlightenment Westerners in general.[17] What interests us at this point is the unacceptability of these claims (focusing on casting sin in the mould of pride) for feminists and, indeed, for women in general. Hampson's critique is twofold. First, sin conceived of as pride is not true to women's experience. Worse, the (male) theologians who have shaped the doctrine of sin in this way (she most frequently refers to Augustine, Luther and Reinhold Niebuhr) do not realize this, assuming it to characterize sin *per se* rather than sin in the lives of men.[18] This is not surprising, given the tendency of dominant groups to read their experience as *normal* and to move from that to holding it to be *normative*.[19]

Hampson rebuts the *hubris* model, as described above, point by point. First of all, it is not that women refuse to be dependent. If anything, they can be said to lose themselves in their various dependencies. Rather than egoistic pride in which one refers all others to oneself ('Women are not typically self-enclosed'),[20] it is self-hatred or a losing of oneself in relationships (a kind of

eros and a dispossessive agape' with his own category of 'dispossessive desire' (Loughlin, *Alien Sex*, pp. xvii, 17–19). Where the two forms of *eros* correspond, however, is in a fundamentally anthropological concern. God and creation are both seen as objects of desire, which for Luther amounts to a sinful confusion of Augustine's *usus/fruitio* distinction.

17.   Hampson has challenged repeated criticism that she is simply a child of the Enlightenment (see, for example, Daphne Hampson, 'A Reply to Angela West', *Scottish Journal of Theology* 51 [1998], pp. 116–21 [116–17]), but her commitment to certain (largely Troeltschian) principles about the way history and the universe work is striking for its resolute faith and unwillingness to entertain other possibilities, at least Christian ones. One repeatedly gets the sense that we have simply moved beyond Christianity as an intellectually viable option, not least because it seems to be conventional wisdom that (1) historical particularity and uniqueness (in the strong sense that Christian claims require) are impossible and unethical (Hampson's claim is that Christianity is 'particular, hence partial' [the words are West's in her *Deadly Innocence* (London: Mowbray, 1995), p. 64]) and (2) the causal nexus cannot be broken (such that an event like the resurrection can have any significant meaning or such that we could speak of a God who transcends the universe, who is above or before creation, or who is an 'other' in apposition to the creation).

18.   Hampson does say more than once that the analysis of sin in terms of egoism and pride is profound and true when applied to men. So she writes of Reinhold Niebuhr in this case: 'The argument is not that Niebuhr's analysis is false, but that it is inapplicable to the situation of all of humanity, while failing to recognize that this is the case' (*Theology and Feminism*, p. 121; see also 'Reinhold Niebuhr on Sin', pp. 46–7).

19.   For a concise survey of the opposition of male and female (in which the woman becomes defined as 'not man') and its relation to canons of rationality, see Elizabeth Morelli, 'The Question of Woman's Experience of God', in Alvin F. Kimel Jr (ed.), *Speaking of the Christian God* (Leominster: Gracewing, 1992), pp. 222–36 (224–25). The origins of this, notes Morelli, were in the role of opposition in pre-Socratic cosmology; and the incorporation of gender into the scheme occurred in Aristotle's table which included ten pairs of opposites (something he dates to the Pythagoreans).

20.   Hampson, 'Luther on the Self', p. 339.

sensuality)[21] that has characterized women. Not isolation,[22] but a lack of cen-tredness due to self-diffusion is the norm. A woman may experience despair, but it is Kierkegaard's second type of despair, the lack of the will to be oneself at all in which she 'wishes to be rid of herself by losing herself in another'.[23] As a consequence, women do not typically know the anxiety and insecurity of isolation. Instead, they tend to be much more at home in the world. Women are naturally more relational, thinking in terms of webs of relationship rather than the hierarchies in which men live and which are reflected in the worlds they construct. What's more, women have simply never been in the position of power which would give one the opportunity and the imaginative resources to conceive of a prideful setting oneself in the place of God.[24] Pride is a winner's sin, and women have consistently been (painted) the losers.

The second part of Hampson's critique follows on the first and demon-strates her concern for the integration of systematic theology and spirituality. As conceiving of sin as pride is not true to women's experience, it follows that it is not a helpful (indeed, it is a harmful) paradigm from which to understand women's spiritual lives. Women, who already incline towards self-hatred and self-diffusion, who despair of themselves, are only encouraged to remain in that condition when they hear sermons preached against their prideful self-assertion. What's more, men continue to take advantage of such a theological justification for their belittlement of women. So, the focus on pride actually serves to entrench women in the sins to which they *do* incline – sensual-ity, self-diffusion, this second type of despair. And, because of such a gross mis-diagnosis, the wrong medicine is prescribed.[25] Rather than a restorative

21.   Here Hampson notes Niebuhr's remark that sin can be seen as pride or sensuality, only to ignore the latter ('he hardly analyses this') and put his emphasis on the former. ('Reinhold Niebuhr on Sin', p. 47). Hampson is right to note that Niebuhr sees pride as 'more basic than sensuality', with sensuality being derived from pride. (The quote is from Reinhold Niebuhr, *The Nature and Destiny of Man* [New York: Charles Scribner's Sons, 1964], vol. 1, p. 186.) He hardly ignores sensuality, however, giving a sensitive, extensive treatment of it (thirteen pages, compared with eighteen for pride) which clearly recognizes the potential problems of subsuming sensuality under pride, even admitting finally that sensuality involves both self-love and 'an effort to escape from the self' (pp. 233–4). It is not our contention that Niebuhr is right in these points, but rather to point out that he is not blind to the issues at stake. Nevertheless, Plaskow notes that Niebuhr's subordination of sensuality to pride leads him to look for only those aspects of sensuality which 'follow from pride, entirely neglecting important dimensions of the human flight from freedom' (Judith Plaskow, *Sex, Sin and Grace* [London: University Press of America, 1980], p. 63).

22.   Hampson, *Theology and Feminism*, p. 145.

23.   Hampson, 'Reinhold Niebuhr on Sin', p. 49. Contrast this with the man who wants to be 'another greater than himself'. Hampson does note that Kierkegaard 'says that each sex can experience the other form', though there are few, if any instances in her writing which provide examples of this (p. 47).

24.   Hampson, *Theology and Feminism*, p. 121.

25.   Alistair McFadyen captures the implications of such a move: 'Ironically, naming pride as sin may nonetheless work to preserve male dominance. For, ironically, the possibilities of women's liberation are undercut in the very basis of the recognition of the male sin of pride...And so theological feminism finds the declaration of female innocence works to keep women passive in the face of their own oppression' (McFadyen, *Bound to Sin*, p. 138).

process of healing, women are encouraged to do as men do – be crucified with Christ, be broken, live lives of dependence on another, being found entirely in others (Christ and neighbour).[26] The themes of discontinuity and decentring are clear, and it is not surprising that each of these remedies has a poisonous effect in the lives of women.[27] Her reasons for rejecting an ethic of kenotic *agape* are similar.[28] It is precisely because *agape* is 'that love which does not count the cost' that it presents a problem for women.[29] She expresses a hesitancy about the usefulness of Eastern spirituality for this generation of Western women who 'at this moment in their history are seeking not to lose the self but to come into their own as articulate agents'.[30] And so the gospel's call to self-sacrifice is misplaced: 'He speaks of the need for sacrificial love on the part of the powerful. But he fails to speak of the need for those who are powerless to stake a claim for power'.[31]

It is important to keep in mind that Hampson's critique of Luther is a critique of Christianity. She is, of course, careful to note that there are points in the Christian tradition which offer refreshingly other conceptions of sin,

26.   Hampson, 'Luther on the Self', p. 335.
27.   Derrida's discussion of the ambiguity of the Greek word *pharmakon*, which can mean both remedy and poison, comes to mind here. See Jacques Derrida, 'Plato's Pharmacy', in *Dissemination* (Chicago: University of Chicago Press, 1983), pp. 61–172.
28.   Sarah Coakley roundly critiques Hampson, offering an account of spiritual *kenosis* grounded in contemplative prayer and characterized by '"power-in-vulnerability", the willed effacement to a gentle omnipotence which, far from "complementing" masculinism, acts as its undoing'. In contemplative prayer, there is a 'unique intersection of vulnerable, "non-grasping" humanity and authentic divine power, itself "made perfect in weakness"' (Sarah Coakley, *Powers and Submissions* [Oxford: Blackwell, 2002], pp. 37, 38).
29.   Daphne Hampson, 'On Power and Gender', *Modern Theology* 4 (1988), pp. 234–50 (238).
30.   *After Christianity*, p. 250. Also see p. 282. Hampson surprisingly enlists Luther at this point, rightly pointing out that, for Luther, one must be secure in God's loving acceptance before one can effectively love others. But she speaks of this coming as a result of self-acceptance rather than the crucifixion of faith, seriously misapplying Luther's insight (p. 276). Contrast Hampson's earlier remark that 'to come into one's own is to reject the male God' (*Theology and Feminism*, p. 109). Though in a still earlier comment, while rejecting an anthropomorphized God, Hampson wants to speak of God 'as personal, though not as a person' and 'as being one who will enable us to come into our own' (Daphne Hampson, 'The Challenge of Feminism to Christianity', *Theology* 88 [1985], pp. 341–50 [349]). And with this, contrast Eberhard Jüngel's remark that righteousness 'signifies a well-ordered relation' in which 'all the persons (or dimensions) included in these relations come into their own (right), without needing to *seize* it for themselves – or for the other.' (Eberhard Jüngel, 'Living Out of Righteousness', in *Theological Essays II*, pp. 241–63 [247]).
31.   Hampson, *Theology and Feminism*, p. 125. Also see p. 123. McFadyen describes the potential problems with an ethic of *agape* as it relates to persons in relation: 'The power to be genuinely oneself in relations is easily dissipated where such self-giving is systematically not reciprocated' (McFadyen, *Bound to Sin*, p. 152). Hampson's critique is full-throttled, extending to the discipleship commended in Phil. 2.5-11, a following after the kenotic Christ, as similarly misguided: 'The theme of self-emptying and self-abnegation is far from helpful as a paradigm' (*Theology and Feminism*, p. 155).

self and salvation. Nor does she take 'pot shots' at a rigidly defined, carefully caricatured Christianity. Her definition is simple[32] (as is her definition of feminism),[33] and Luther comes out simply as a classic example (albeit with his own particular contextual concerns) of Christian thinking. But one thing is certain – Christianity and feminism are incompatible. This has been her stance since at least 1985 (in her essay 'The Challenge of Feminism to Christianity')[34] and is the thesis of her first book, *Theology and Feminism*, published in 1990. Moreover, her argument has changed little since then, with the exception of her introduction to French feminist theory (chiefly Luce Irigaray's work) and her recognition (which does little to alter her argument, but does clarify her position) that 'the basic incompatibility between feminism and Christianity lies in the fact that Christianity is necessarily heteronomous, in that it understands God as other than the self and known through revelation. Feminists must stand for human autonomy (though not isolation).'[35] So, as we examine her alternative understanding of selfhood, it is to be remembered that she believes this understanding is simply incompatible with Christianity.

Hampson's Alternative

The feminist anthropology that Hampson commends is one that conceives of 'persons centred in relation'. She continues: 'In using such a phrase I wish to capture the sense that the self is both "centred" and "relational"; moreover that it is not that there is conflict between the two. Thus we are able to acquire centredness because we are in relation.'[36] 'Again, to be in relation is to be a centred self who reaches out to another.'[37] We see with these two comments that neither personal centredness nor relationality is to be given primacy in Hampson's account, though given her concern to rehabilitate women's self-understanding, she tends to emphasize a 'coming to oneself'. Of course, as a

---

32. 'Christians are those who, in whatever way they may speak of uniqueness (and they have done so in various ways), find themselves compelled to speak of the Christ event as having had such a uniqueness...What cannot...be held to be a Christian position, if one is not to muddle terms, is the belief (simply) that Jesus was a very fine person who was deeply in tune with God' (Hampson, *After Christianity*, p. 21). Or an even more concise, but substantially identical definition: 'Christians are those who proclaim Jesus to have been unique' (Hampson, *Theology and Feminism*, p. 50).

33. 'The proclaimed equality of women and men' (Hampson, *Theology and Feminism*, p. 50). Elsewhere, feminism is defined as 'the coming into our own of women' (Daphne Hampson, 'Feminism', *The Month* 19 [2nd series] [1986], pp. 96–9 [96]).

34. In the essay Hampson argues that Christianity presents an insoluble theodicy problem for women (p. 348).

35. Hampson, *After Christianity*, p. vii. On this issue, see Hampson, 'On Autonomy and Heteronomy'.

36. Hampson, *After Christianity*, p. 106.

37. Hampson, *Theology and Feminism*, p. 165.

post-Christian[38] feminist, Hampson categorically rejects any notion of God as an 'other' set in apposition to humanity. God is not an 'other' with whom we relate, which is both absurd in a post-Enlightenment context and ethically unacceptable due to its heteronomous implications. Consequently, the coming to oneself she advocates is not something one does in relation to or dependence on a personal God.

> Far from wishing to deny the self, or to say that an individual should be broken open and based on someone or something other than herself, feminists have wished to affirm the self. Feminists will that women should come into their own. In theological terms, feminism might well be said to be aligned with a 'high' doctrine of creation. Feminists believe, not in the undoing of the self, castigating a person for her pride, but rather in building up what is already given. Feminists will therefore look askance at a doctrine which advocates turning away from the self to God. They will be skeptical about the contention that the self is only itself when it is based on that which is not the self, namely God.[39]

The relationality Hampson speaks of, then, is strictly horizontal. Even here, there is a difference between speaking of coming to oneself in relationships and being based on another. Thus, Hampson's critique of what she reads as a patriarchal conception of God that requires heteronomy and the breaking of the self is at the same time a critique not only of patriarchy on the human scale, but of any anthropology that speaks primarily in terms of one being based on another. Her alternative anthropology, in turn, uses metaphors of growth, maturity, construction and affirmation.[40] She urges her reader to see the self and say that it is good.

Sin is described in similarly relational terms. 'Feminists, then, would wish to name as "sin" unjust relations which prevent community, whether found in the personal or the political sphere'.[41] Men and women prevent community differently, as we have seen above, and this is a fundamental part of

---

38.   For her understanding of herself as 'post-Christian', see Hampson, *Theology and Feminism*, p. 42; *After Christianity*, p. 57. For a brief, early account of what God and prayer might look like in post-Christian theism, see Hampson, 'On Power and Gender', pp. 248, 250.

39.   Hampson, *After Christianity*, p. 282.

40.   Paul Sponheim, in a critically sympathetic response to Hampson, suggests that the 'category of "growth" may materially have been so usurped by a given culture that it is simply next to impossible to pry it loose and fill it with new content'. He goes on to quote a comment Luther makes on Zech. 3.8-9:

> Christ is being preached in the gospel and *is growing and increasing in the world*. But this is a *strange growing*, one that looks to the world like something withering and perishing. For we find the cross of Christ in it and all kinds of persecution. But we also find pure growth in it; for in the midst of death there is life, in poverty riches, in disgrace honor, and so forth.

(Sponheim, 'On Being and Becoming before God', *Word and World* 15 [1995], pp. 332–41 [340]; quoting *LW* 20:217 with Sponheim's emphasis).

41.   Hampson, *Theology and Feminism*, p. 126.

Hampson's argument. 'What men then need to learn is to be a self in *relation*; while women, to be a *self* in relation.'[42] Relations require at least personal centres by definition,[43] just as persons are only persons in relation. Without reasonably healthy individuals, the relations which constitute those very individuals will suffer. In short, person and relation are mutually edifying categories which constitute one another. So, we name as 'sin' any unjust relation which is really no relation, in the strong sense which we reserve for those relations which provide and foster community.

These comments on sin relate directly to Hampson's understanding of salvation. As the sins of men and women are different, their salvations will be different. We will focus, as Hampson does, on the salvation of women. 'Rather than breaking the self, women, it may be suggested, need to come to themselves.' Salvation, instead of involving a discontinuous crucifixion and resurrection in which we are based on and live in another, is a healing in which the self comes to itself.[44] But note that it is not a being healed as much as it is a self-healing: 'If women's ills have been the result of an undervaluation of the self, then their healing must consist in self-actualization'.[45] This is a process of basic continuity, such that women are better described as 'once-born' than 'twice-born', using William James' categories.[46] In all this, Hampson seeks a difference that enriches rather than one that dichotomizes and divides.[47] To this understanding of sin and salvation she (following Elizabeth Johnson) adds an ethic of loving mutuality based on *philia*.[48] In place of the discarded values of authority, obedience and worship, Hampson offers attention, honesty and ordering.[49]

One more comment is in order. For all her commitment to a model of persons in loving relation, Hampson is adamant about retaining a proper sense of autonomy. This is not an autonomy of independence and isolation,[50]

---

42. Ibid., p. 118.

43. A point Jürgen Moltmann has made in reference to the doctrine of the Trinity. It is not that the Trinitarian persons *are* relations, but that persons are only persons as they are in relation with other persons. They are irreducibly and essentially relational. See Moltmann, *The Trinity and the Kingdom of God*, p. 172.

44. The problem with Reinhold Niebuhr's call for faith in response to pride, then, is that it 'precisely does not tolerate the self coming to itself' (Hampson, 'Reinhold Niebuhr on Sin', p. 53).

45. Hampson, *Theology and Feminism*, p. 127; see also Hampson, 'Reinhold Niebuhr on Sin', p. 51.

46. Hampson, *Theology and Feminism*, p. 129. In suggesting that women may better be described as 'once-born', Hampson means to say both that women really *are* once-born and also that they *should be* and *should consider themselves to be* once-born. Schleiermacher, whom Hampson finds so conducive to her own constructive proposal, makes a nearly identical point to James (and suggests that 'conversion' may be an inappropriate model for women) in Friedrich Schleiermacher, *Christmas Eve* (trans. Terrence N. Tice; San Francisco: The Edwin Mellen Press, 1990), pp. 54–5.

47. Hampson, *Theology and Feminism*, p. 130.

48. Hampson, *After Christianity*, pp. 157, 163.

49. Ibid., pp. 260ff.

50. Ibid., p. vii.

which is what she is so critical of in monotheism.[51] This is an important point, as Hampson wants to affirm that autonomy 'need not imply conceiving of oneself as an isolated atom in competition with others...as though the only way to be oneself, to take responsibility for oneself, were to set oneself up over against others'.[52] Hampson explicitly conceives of autonomy along Kantian lines, however, in which one is self-legislating.[53] She begins *After Christianity* with a discussion of Kant's bold challenge to abandon one's self-incurred immaturity and *Sapere aude!* ('Dare to know').[54] But while 'to be "autonomous" is to let one's own law rule one',[55] Hampson is careful here: 'Women are saying, "I want to be at the centre of 'my' world", not "at the centre of 'the' world" – as men have not infrequently thought themselves to be'.[56] Nevertheless, 'my world' is still one in which I make the rules. Self-legislation is possible because 'in a sense people bring the truth with them'. Hampson rejects revelation here and opts for something much closer to the Socratic theory of recollection.[57] It is not that people need to be told what is true; instead, they simply need to be drawn out. It is not a (preached) word (or Word) spoken to them, but them speaking themselves and *being listened to* that establishes people. Hampson picks up Nelly Morton's phrase: 'hearing one another into being'.[58] Consequently, she opposes a model of passivity (such as found in the adoration and imitation of Mary of which Hampson

51.   Ibid., p. 123. Hampson takes issue here with a God who 'represents self-enclosure, autonomy (in the sense of independence) and power, understood as power over that which is not itself'. What she does not articulate is that this power over-and-against is first and foremost in the Christian tradition a power *for*. That is, it is a power that *creates something out of nothing* and hence God's power is not defined in opposition to his creation but rather as the very thing which allows his creation to *be*.

52.   Hampson, 'On Autonomy and Heteronomy', p. 1.

53.   'The God whom Kant disallows is ruled out not simply because there is no evidence of him, and therefore no knowledge possible, but because it would be immoral that there should be an authority other than a person's inner authority' (Hampson, 'The Challenge of Feminism to Christianity', p. 346).

54.   Kant is a hero who gave us 'the first full "demythologizing" of Western religion' (Hampson, *After Christianity*, p. 1). Hampson later speaks of the manner in which feminism transforms later, more individualistic understandings of Kant's concept (p. 104).

55.   Hampson, 'On Autonomy and Heteronomy', p. 1.

56.   Hampson, *After Christianity*, p. 77. For the concept of heteronomy and how it relates to Hampson's critique of Christianity's historical particularity, see 'On Autonomy and Heteronomy' and *After Christianity*, p. 83.

57.   See Kierkegaard's account and stinging critique of Socratic recollection in his *Philosophical Fragments*.

58.   Hampson, 'On Autonomy and Heteronomy', p. 14. 'There is no authority, such as might deny that what she thinks may be thought; nor yardstick by which she should measure what she thinks. Ideally feminists listen to one another in such a way as to draw one another out, that they may allow people to think what it is they need to think, even that they may surprise themselves in its articulation.' Of course, violence can be done and selves severely distorted in listening as well, which is not an entirely passive activity (as Hampson seems to recognize).

is so critical),[59] a model which she finds to be built into the structure of Christianity.[60] Such a rejection of Christianity as heteronomous goes hand-in-hand with her rejection of seeing sin paradigmatically as pride, for both would seem to militate against women's self-actualization. In this, her concerns line up with Kant's, for whom it is not self-assertion but 'laziness and cowardice'[61] which 'are the causes of people remaining unenlightened'. That is, 'they remain unenlightened because they want to'.[62]

A more relationally conceived autonomy, however, in no way leads Hampson to countenance a theological anthropology in which the self is located *extra se*.[63] Her account of eccentric personhood diminishes, both in the sense that it excludes Luther's primary sense of our eccentricity in relation to God in Christ through faith and also in the sense that she is more cautious

59.   Hampson reflects on the possibility that Mary could have said no to Gabriel: 'That would spoil the whole story! But it would represent women's autonomy' ('On Autonomy and Heteronomy', p. 10).

60.   'It is built into the structure of Christianity that a revelation, or God, or that institution which is the church, must take precedence over what one would oneself think... Christians are not centred in themselves. They are centred on God (such is their conception of God), or on Christ, on the Bible, or bound up with the institution of the church; such that authority lies outside themselves' (Hampson, 'On Autonomy and Heteronomy', p. 2). We will turn shortly to a critique of Hampson's falsely dichotomizing autonomy and heteronomy, but it is worth noting a similarity between Kant and Luther at one point. As John Macken argues: 'Kant's emphasis in the use of "heteronomy" is placed on countering the philosophy of eudaemonism or that of utilitarianism, which made happiness the basis of morality' (Macken, *The Autonomy Theme* [Cambridge: Cambridge University Press, 1990], p. 4). Robert Paul Wolff agrees: 'The argument for the formula of autonomy turns on the notion of legislating disinterestedly, that is to say, legislating independently of or in abstraction from the particular interests of the agent'. And it is this 'quality of disinterestedness which characterizes true morality' (Wolff, *The Autonomy of Reason* [Gloucester, MA: Peter Smith, 1986], pp. 178–80). In Kant's words, we must 'abstract from all objects to this extent: that they have no *influence* at all on the will' (Kant, *Groundwork of the Metaphysics of Morals* [trans. Mary Gregor; Cambridge: Cambridge University Press, 1997], p. 48). It is precisely this emphatic rejection of an external good to be had, *particularly* some personal benefit, that Luther rejects in his ethics.

61.   Immanuel Kant, 'An Answer to the Question: What is Enlightenment?', in *Practical Philosophy* (ed. Mary J. Gregor; Cambridge: Cambridge University Press, 1996), pp. 15–22 (17). We will have occasion to revisit these concerns in our discussion of Barth's location of *incurvatus in se* in his description of sin as sloth.

62.   Macken, *The Autonomy Theme*, p. 8. This is true of 'so great a part of humankind' who 'gladly remains minors for life', the consequence of whose laziness being that 'it becomes so easy for others to set themselves up as their guardians. It is so comfortable to be a minor!' This great part of humankind includes 'the entire fair sex' (Kant, 'What is Enlightenment?', p. 17).

63.   Hampson draws chiefly on *The Freedom of a Christian* to make this point, where Luther writes: 'We conclude, therefore, that a Christian lives not in himself, but in Christ and in his neighbor. Otherwise he is not a Christian. He lives in Christ through faith, in his neighbor through love. But faith he is caught up beyond himself into God. By love he descends beneath himself into his neighbor. Yet he always remains in God and in his love' (*LW* 31:371; see Hampson, *Christian Contradictions*, pp. 10–11).

about the claims Luther makes (which he can only make in light of the prior, primary sense) about our living eccentrically in others in love. This is related to her rejection of an ethic of *agape*, to which we will return below.

As we have seen, Hampson criticizes conceiving of autonomy as if it necessarily entailed independence and, therefore, competition with others. That is, she wants to hold that one's autonomy need not represent an assault on the others with whom one relates. This is vital to uphold the twin poles of *persons* in *relation*. What is striking is that Hampson assumes that just such a competitive relation must obtain, by definition, any time one bases oneself on another. Of course, this is the heart of the Christian conception of the God–human relation which therefore can only be a competitive relation according to her rendering of the situation, such that *either* God's rule *or* the rule of the human person has primacy. She writes:

> I do not wish to conform to a mind-set which only allows of a choice between allegiance to one Lord or to another, to God or to the devil. I have more faith in humanity's ability to stand on its own feet than such a stance represents. I am a feminist. I wish an ethical position in which I do not give over my being to any person or to any God who lies outside myself.[64]

Thus, we hear her affirm Kant, for whom 'human ethics must always take precedence over some supposed will of God. Were this not to be so, human beings would cease to be autonomous.'[65]

It would be naïve to suppose that this kind of competitive relation has never been espoused in the Christian tradition, but to argue that it inheres within the structure of Christian thought is another thing entirely. Hampson's concern to avoid an ethic of passivity relies on the assumption that any passive relation to another must be harmfully heteronomous. That is, passivity discourages one from being oneself. This is just the sort of self-diffusion which has characterized women, and so passivity is hardly an appropriate posture in which to locate the healing of women. Kathryn Tanner is helpful in response at this point:

> Our passivity before Christ does not translate into passivity on any ordinary construal of that. Passivity before Christ hardly means our lives are taken out of our hands; it hardly forms an easy contrast with a modern emphasis on human responsibility for the character of our lives...Assumption by Christ cannot be identified with discrete moment of our lives in which we are merely passive; it does not divide our lives into a metaphysically or empirically passive component (say, the passive constitution of our

---

64.   Hampson, *After Christianity*, p. 38.

65.   Hampson, 'On Autonomy and Heteronomy', p. 10. Though clearly in debt to voluntarism at points, Kant's antivoluntarism comes across in his 'astonishing claim...that God and we can share membership in a single moral community only if we all equally legislate the law we are to obey'. Thus, for both God and humanity, being good is a matter of being 'willed by a will governed by the moral law' (Schneewind, *The Invention of Autonomy* [Cambridge: Cambridge University Press, 1998], p. 512).

very persons or characters); and an active one (say, the expression of such a character in our deeds).[66]

Tanner argues for a fundamental *structural* passivity[67] in which everything is a gift but which does not simply correspond to non-activity.[68] Rather, it is precisely God's boundless giving which establishes the creature *qua* creature, that (in the only real sense) allows the creature a creaturely appropriate autonomy. Tanner's notion of transcendence as *enabling* God's immanence comes in here, as does her account of a non-competitive God–creation relation: 'A non-competitive relation between creatures and God means that the creature does not decrease so that God may increase. The glorification of God does not come at the expense of creatures.'[69] The only time this relation *looks* competitive is when humans sinfully insist on their own autonomy in clear opposition to God. When this is the case, the negative aspect (that real human action is always a gift of God and is in no way something produced *in se*) must be highlighted. Such was the case in Luther's day, which may go a long way in accounting for his iconoclastic reading of Romans.[70] Tanner has given a compelling picture of the non-competitiveness of God and creation which coherently accounts for both the transcendence and freedom of God and the

66. Kathryn Tanner, *Jesus, Humanity and the Trinity* (Edinburgh: T&T Clark, 2001), pp. 71–2. Regin Prenter agrees. Commenting on Luther's comment that '*Christiana sanctitas est passiva*', Prenter writes: 'This passivity, however, does not mean inaction but receptiveness...Receiving is in itself a specific sort of labour. The scholastic terms *passive* and *active* used by Luther must not be interpreted in a psychological sense, as if a man in receiving passive sanctity were psychologically inactive' (Prenter, 'Holiness in the Lutheran Tradition', p. 126).

67. Tanner, *Jesus, Humanity and the Trinity*, pp. 71–7.

68. Tanner quotes Barth to great effect here: 'When the Reformers described faith as "a strictly passive matter" (*res mere passiva*), they did not mean that faith included only one aspect...receptivity but not spontaneity. There is no receptivity without spontaneity as well, and faith cannot of course be reduced to some sort of trance-like condition. No, reason's normal activity is not interrupted; but it is directed, guided and ordered by something superior to itself, something that has no part in its antithesis. Taken as a whole (as activity spontaneous and receptive) reason is passively related to that superior reality. It is related to it, in other words, obediently' (Tanner, *Jesus, Humanity and the Trinity*, p. 73, from Karl Barth, 'Fate and Idea in Theology', p. 54).

69. Tanner, *Jesus, Humanity and the Trinity*, p. 2. Tanner's reference to Jn. 3.30 must be held in tandem (if not finally in tension) with the gospel's proclamation that humanity's glorification is one given on the other side of crucifixion. That is, while Hampson is wrong to assume that Christianity offers an inverse relation between God's flourishing and ours, it would be a mistake to opt for a simple correlation of the two that does not take seriously the form which our flourishing takes – a dying and rising with Christ.

70. Tanner makes this point in reference to the Reformers. See page 28 above; Kathryn Tanner, *God and Creation* (Oxford: Basil Blackwell, 1988), pp. 111–12. See Hampson's discussion of Joest's work for an explication of this negative emphasis which loudly echoes Gal. 2.20 (*Christian Contradictions*, pp. 11–12).

meaningfulness of human action. Still, her basic theological premises will be rejected by Hampson.[71]

We turn now to a musicological example which counters the claim that basing oneself on another is inherently harmfully heteronomous. This will also serve as a response to Hampson's critique of an ethic of *agape* centred on kenotic, self-giving love. In an article which asks why it is that so many people have described John Coltrane's saxophone playing as 'spiritual', Steve Guthrie finds Coltrane's distinctive voice emerging directly from his submission to the tradition in which he stood.[72]

> Coltrane developed his own voice by surrendering it to another. Before he could speak on his own, he first gave himself to repeating again and again the things Monk had said. 'He'd play it over and over and over.' The paradox of artistry is that discipline is the pre-requisite for self-expression. And, conversely, the object of mastering another's voice is finding one's own. Tradition and creativity stand in a complementary relationship to one another – the former establishing the conditions for the latter, the latter providing the *telos* of the former.[73]

Hampson, of course, rejects any subjection to another – whether a God, another person, institution, tradition, history or point in history – as unacceptably heteronomous.[74] Thus, in *her* musicological example, we hear that

> Beethoven picked up what he wished to from the tradition, yet he created something essentially new. He was free both to draw on the past and to express reality as it seemed to him to be. But he did not have to measure what he wanted to write against some benchmark of truth placed in the past.[75]

In response to Hampson and the discipleship context of Christ's kenosis in Philippians 2, Guthrie draws two conclusions. The first is that there is 'no necessary connection between laying aside oneself to follow another and an oppressive and destructive self-abasement'. Furthermore, at least in relation to art, 'self-denial is the ground and the necessary condition for self-realization and self-expression'. Not that this proves 'any particular vision

71.   As McFadyen notes: 'Despite the reconception of power, autonomy and the voluntary in relational terms, feminist theologies are often wary of allowing that transcendent divine power might be reconceived as non-competitive, co-operating and empowering' (McFadyen, *Bound to Sin*, p. 164).

72.   I am grateful to Steve Guthrie for permission to cite his as yet unpublished paper, 'A Love Supreme'.

73.   Guthrie, 'A Love Supreme', p. 9.

74.   'We do not need to live in a heteronomous relationship to the past, to men, or to a God conceived in men's image' (Hampson, 'On Autonomy and Heteronomy', p. 16). Though she does admit that 'this does not mean that we shall not draw on human history', she seems committed to selecting from history as it suits women's needs. Angela West has charged Hampson with being arbitrary on this point, noting that she critiques certain elements of Western tradition while uncritically embracing others (West, *Deadly Innocence*, p. 83).

75.   Daphne Hampson, 'Sources and the Relationship to Tradition', *Feminist Theology* 3 (May 1993), pp. 23–37.

of human self-realization. But it does lend plausibility to the Christian claim that self-surrender may be ultimately creative.'[76] Simply put, basing one-self on another need not be destructive but may actually be the key to the flourishing about which Hampson is concerned. The second conclusion, one which recognizes Hampson's call for healed, whole selves, is that disciple-ship is as much about living new lives in Christ and the Spirit as it as about dying to the old. It is a call to respond creatively to our life in Christ *in our own voices.*[77]

We might characterize Luther's account, then, as moving from heteronomy to autonomy, in that it is precisely the gift and grace of Christ and the Spirit which sets one free to live in an obedience which is life indeed. It is in being found in another (Colossians 3) that we find *ourselves*, and it is precisely from this life *extra se* that we live our own, true lives. Thus, without ignoring the significant divergences between Luther and Kant,[78] we can acknowledge a significant over-lap. Criticizing post-Fichtian conflations of autarchy and autonomy, Macken writes: 'Kant's idea of autonomy is not absolute self-determination, but self-determination according to the rational and moral being which is given to man and which contains in itself the rational and moral law'.[79] Kant is not speaking of the Spirit of love poured abroad in our hearts. He has little time here for a doctrine of sin which might complicate matters of self-determination. That being said, Macken's description of Kantian self-determination might serve well as a description of the delight in obeying which defines Pauline obedience. And even for Kant, such self-determination is according to the being 'which is given to man'. There is a givenness which must be accounted for,[80] a givenness which

76.   Guthrie, 'A Love Supreme', p. 11.

77.   Here a robust pneumatology is called for, which Tom Smail articulates in arguing that the Holy Spirit enables to respond *for* ourselves if never *by* ourselves. See his *The Giving Gift* (London: Hodder & Stoughton, 1988).

78.   It is worth noting at this point that 'religion' is one of the greatest hindrances to autonomy for Kant, as is seen in his celebrated 1784 essay, 'What is Enlightenment?': 'I have put the main point of enlightenment, of people's emergence from their self-incurred minority, chiefly in *matters of religion*' (p. 21). On the first page of *After Christianity*, Hampson mentions his 'Strife of the Faculties' in this regard.

79.   Macken, *The Autonomy Theme*, p. 10. This conflation of concepts involves an 'atheist definition of autonomy as autarchy' and its adoption by theologians amounts to a 'conceding much of the ground at issue' (p. 21). Compare J. B. Schneewind's comment that autonomy 'involves two components. The first is that no authority external to ourselves is needed to constitute or inform us of the demands of morality...The second is that in self-government we can effectively control ourselves' (Schneewind, 'Autonomy, Obligation, and Virtue', in Paul Guyer [ed.], *The Cambridge Companion to Kant* [Cambridge: Cambridge University Press, 1992], pp. 309–41 [309]).

80.   Though we note, for his part, Kant's rejection of voluntarism and commitment to the notion that God and humanity, as Schneewind writes, 'share membership in a single moral community'. (See footnote 65.) If Kant were right, we might ask whether there is a givenness even in God's morality for which we must account. At this point, however, we would be in danger of positing a principle in some sense prior to God. It is in Kant's edging away from voluntarism, not in general but on this one specific point, that he arguably moves further from a Christian account.

the Christian tradition understands with reference to a triune God who creates, sustains, saves and gives new life *that we might live*. For all the profundity of her analysis of Christianity, Hampson falters right here, in her misconstrual of it in relation to autonomy and heteronomy.[81]

This excursis on the question of heteronomy might seem an unwarranted one. It is, however, central to Hampson's claim that a relational theological anthropology must be non-relational with regard to God, who is not to be understood as an 'other' and certainly not as an other on whom we base ourselves. It is also intrinsically related to questions of the appropriateness of speaking of sin as a curving in on oneself (with the implied sense of a turn away from God and others) in which God is denied or even usurped. We turn now to answer this critique.

Transition: Key Questions

Hampson's critique of pride as a paradigm for sin presents certain problems for a similarly paradigmatic account of sinful humanity as *homo incurvatus in se*. Hampson's equation of the two and her argument that pride is neither true to the experience of women nor helpful in articulating a soteriology that centres on the healing and wholeness of women would seem to cast doubt on the ability of *incurvatus in se* to meaningfully articulate how sinful humanity is. If Hampson is correct, it could at best serve to elucidate (and maybe serve as a paradigm for) what it means for men to be sinners. It could not, however, do so in relation to women. The second section of this chapter will seek to examine whether there is sufficient merit in such a gendered account of sin, to ask about the adequacy of Hampson's account of sin *per se*, and finally to re-examine the conceptual scope of *incurvatus in se* in light of Hampson's equation of it with pride.

Problems with a Gendered Approach to Sin

The category of experience is fundamental for Hampson, which is why she finds Schleiermacher such an attractive figure in the Christian tradition.[82] A

---

81.   Not that she fails to notice that Christians claim this freedom for real human action (Hampson, *Christian Contradictions*, p. 244). Rather she rejects it as a heteronomy which is no freedom. She seems, incidentally, committed to an incompatibilist model in which divine and human freedom and agency are irreducibly competitive.

82.   See, in relation to her constructive theistic proposal, her treatment of Schleiermacher in *After Christianity*, pp. 212–23. His terms for God ('the Universe', 'the One', 'the All') in *On Religion: Speeches to Its Cultured Despisers* are commended as a helpful move ('The Challenge of Feminism to Christianity', p. 346). In addition, Hampson shares with Schleiermacher a sense of God as in some sense immanent to human experience as well as a particular relational understanding of the self that follows from this. (See Keith Clements, 'Introduction', in Keith Clements [ed.], *Friedrich Schleiermacher* [Minneapolis: Fortress Press, 1987], pp. 7–65 [37]).

proper feminist methodology, she argues, makes humanity 'the primary focus of our attention'[83] and is concerned with perceptivity rather than revelation.[84] Accordingly, theology (and theological anthropology) arises from and is checked by human experience. Hampson's rejection of pride as the fount of sin is based on the assumption that women by and large are not proud. That is, Hampson argues that experience shows women to be other than egoists. It is not part of the structure of womanhood. Hampson here follows Valerie Saiving's work in 1960 in which Saiving wrote:

> The temptations of woman *as woman* are not the same as the temptations of man *as man*, and the specifically feminine forms of sin – 'feminine' not because they are confined to women or because women are incapable of sinning in other ways but because they are outgrowths of the basic feminine character structure – have a quality which can never be encompassed by such terms as 'pride' and 'will-to-power'. They are better suggested by such items as triviality, distractability, and diffuseness; lack of an organizing center or focus; dependence on others for one's own self-definition…in short, underdevelopment or negation of the self…The specifically feminine dilemma is, in fact, precisely the opposite of the masculine.[85]

This quotation from Saiving beautifully captures the concerns of more recent feminism in which feminists moved from an earlier focus on a woman's ability to do just what a man does – and better[86] – to an acknowledgment and commendation of the dignity of separate spheres. It is natural, if men and women have different strengths, that they have different weaknesses, different areas in which they are prone to sin. And surely there is something to this. What's more, we note Saiving's insistence that we are not to read this so rigidly as to say that women cannot sin in 'manly' ways, nor vice versa. But there is a 'basic feminine character structure' from which self-abasing sins issue. In her appropriation of Saiving's work, Hampson is clear that she wants to avoid an essentialist stance.[87] She inclines instead towards a social-constructivist account, though

83. Hampson, *Theology and Feminism*, p. 154.

84. Though note Hampson's frustration with the secular nature of theology. While experience is her starting point, it is experience *of God* (noting, though, that God is not a 'thou'). She is critical of feminist theology being reduced to women's experience *per se* rather than real God-talk: 'In all this, what I miss is "theology": talk of God' (*Theology and Feminism*, p. 170; also see 'Reply to Angela West', p. 118). Of course, it is difficult to say how her God-talk would finally be something other than talk of the world. Indeed, it could not be. She nuances this a bit in a recent article, calling God 'that onto which we open out; that to which we are immediately present' (Daphne Hampson, 'Reply to Laurence Hemming', *New Blackfriars* 86 [2005], pp. 24–47 [43]).

85. Hampson, 'Reinhold Niebuhr on Sin', p. 50; also see *Theology and Feminism*, p. 123. West dates the origins of modern feminist theology to this article (Goldstein, 'The Human Situation', *Journal of Religion* 40 [1960], pp. 100–12; West, *Deadly Innocence*, p. 1).

86. I am reminded of the recent American television advert in which a male and a female athlete compete against one another in a variety of events to the tune of 'Anything You Can Do I Can Do Better' from the musical *Annie, Get Your Gun*.

87. See Hampson, *After Christianity*, p. 111. Gerard Loughlin suggests that she may have fallen into such a stance, however. See Loughlin, *Alien Sex*, p. 185. Also see Coakley, *Powers and Submissions*, p. 22.

she remains open to more biologically rooted factors.[88] As Diana Fuss points out, though, 'constructionism (the position that differences are constructed, not innate) really operates as a more sophisticated form of essentialism'.[89] In any case, there seems to be something approaching the determinism that goes with essentialist accounts, so deeply does she believe the grid of patriarchy to be embedded into (at least Western) ways of thinking.[90] So when Saiving speaks of a feminine structure, Hampson would locate this in the poisonous passivity which is so ingrained into women as to seem natural.[91] And yet, we should be careful not to dismiss essentialism too quickly. Diane Leclerc rightly points out that an inability to speak of some sort of real *difference* between men and women can cause us to revert to traditional patriarchy.

> It would be an ironic twist of events if post-feminist theology, where the category 'woman' is contested, and traditional theology, where 'woman' is not taken seriously, were to become unknowing cohorts – both speechless about and apathetic toward 'woman' as a theological category.[92]

Beyond the spectre of essentialism, the problem – again, beyond a *very* general and vague sense in all of this – is that Hampson's account is itself almost without nuance. She mentions differences of race,[93] and we can hope that she would include differences of nationality, age, personality, historical and geographical locale (would seventeenth- and twenty-first-century women sin differently? what about women in the city and women in the country?) But none of these carry significant weight.[94] This is because the symbolism of gender is basic and determinate in a way that even these other factors are not.[95] Surely, for all the vital insights of Hampson's feminism, it offers an insufficient analysis in the ongoing discussion of where precisely difference lies. As an

---

88.   Hampson, *After Christianity*, pp. 117–18.

89.   Diana Fuss, *Essentially Speaking: Feminism, Nature and Difference* (New York: Routledge, 1989), pp. xi–xii; cited in Kathryn Greene-McCreight, 'Gender, Sin and Grace', *Scottish Journal of Theology* 50 (1997), pp. 415–32 (421 n. 15).

90.   See, for example, Hampson, *After Christianity*, p. 115. Hampson explicitly denies that she is a determinist, in part because she seeks to affirm that women (and men) can change.

91.   Hampson sustains an extended and insightful critique of the religious and Western construction of 'the feminine' (*Theology and Feminism*, pp. 96–102).

92.   Leclerc, *Singleness of Heart*, p. 5.

93.   Hampson, *Theology and Feminism*, pp. 76–8.

94.   Susan Thistlethwaite takes up the difference of race more effectively in Susan Brooks Thistlethwaite, *Sex, Race, and God* (New York: Crossroad, 1989), pp. 77–91.

95.   'Sex is the great cutting of humanity into two halves' (Hampson, 'The Challenge of Feminism to Christianity', p. 345). She denies that 'the difference of sex is of no more significance than the difference of race' (Hampson, *Theology and Feminism*, p. 76). Hampson poignantly points to the implication of this: 'A black man on a cross still refers to Christ, but a woman on a cross does not so refer' (Hampson, 'The Challenge of Feminism to Christianity', p. 345). Karl Barth makes the same argument about man–woman as the basic differentiation within humanity along biblical-theological lines in the section on 'Humanity as Likeness and Hope' in *CD* III/2 (§45.3, pp. 285–324).

educated, Western man, I might well have more in common with Hampson than I would with an uneducated man living in rural Indonesia.[96]

Angela West stingingly critiques the racist, classist nature of much of feminist theory and discourse. Purporting to speak on behalf of women, feminist theory (and theology) really speaks on behalf of white, modern, rich, educated, Western women. But, in its claim that women's experience (not to mention hopes and dreams) are universal, it presents a parallel ideology (and ideology it is)[97] to that of its arch-nemesis, patriarchy. For, like patriarchy with its implicit claim that the masculine is the universal (with the feminine becoming the problematic 'other'),[98] feminist discourse presents a certain *type* of woman as the universal woman, thus eliding the very real difference that exists among women and silencing or subsuming those who do not fit.[99] Thus,

96.   This, too, is not lost on Hampson. She sharply critiques naïve attempts by contemporary Western women to establish (or merely assume) solidarity with women of past centuries (in the Bible or the early church) or women in other socio-economic strata. There is a real difference here which cannot be papered over. At the same time, while differences may remain among women across space and time, *the* difference in each space and time seems to be that between male and female.

97.   West accuses Hampson of advocating 'a faith in justification by gender. Thus her project becomes a classic example of the theory of ideology – that is the disguised expression of arbitrary preference' (Angela West, 'Justification by Gender', *Scottish Journal of Theology* 51 [1998], pp. 99–105 [107]).

98.   In her ground-breaking critique of developmental psychology models, Carol Gilligan (*In a Different Voice* [London: Harvard University Press, 1993]) argues that most of the dominant models (e.g. Freud, Piaget, Erikson) have worked under the assumption that the masculine is the universal. Thus, they have looked at development in boys/men and have simply inferred, without question, that this is the pattern of development in humanity *per se*. In the process, women have been seen as children or adolescents in the extent of their development, particularly in moral reasoning. Part of Gilligan's argument is that, in failing to notice the 'different voice' in which women speak (patriarchy survives by virtue of 'the continuing eclipse of women's experience' (p. xxiv), developmental models have not simply failed to understand (and therefore have grossly misspoken in their prescriptive responses to) women. By universalizing the male experience, these models have skewed a properly *human* account of development. Hampson follows Gilligan's argument and her explication of an ethic of responsibility and care. Thus, Hampson's objection is not to pride as a good analysis of sin (how true it is of men!), but rather to its sufficiency as an analysis of human sinning *per se*. (That is, the male is not the human.) William Cahoy makes this same point in Cahoy, 'One Species or Two?', *Modern Theology* 11 (1995), pp. 429–54 (431). Also of note is Gilligan's early remark that the different voice she had heard in her research 'is characterized not by gender but by theme. Its association with women is an empirical observation...But this association is not absolute' (p. 2). This important qualification notwithstanding, Gilligan's research has come in feminist literature to refer without significant remainder to fundamental (if acquired through socialization) differences between men and women. Contrast this with Gilligan's 'Letter to Readers, 1993', which opens the newer edition of the book, in which she is explicit about the kinds of questions she is asking: 'questions about voice and relationship, not about whether there is an essential difference or who is better than who' (p. xiii).

99.   In Audre Lorde's words, 'There is a pretense to a homogeneity of experience covered by the word *sisterhood* that does not in fact exist' (West, *Deadly Innocence*, p. 45). Notably, Gilligan seems to have become more aware of (or at least devoted more time to) differences *among* women in recent years. See her 'Letter to Readers, 1993', in *In a Different Voice*, p. xxv.

West argues that feminist discourse does *not* speak for women in general and actually exacerbates many of the racist, classist forms of oppression which persecute many women.

> The 'relevance' of post-Christian feminism is largely contained in its ability to disguise from its adherents the ethnocentrism and class confinement which it shares with its liberal parents...Like all myths, it indulges our willing ignorance and permits us not to know that which we do not wish to know about ourselves.[100]

Beyond the fact that Hampson's analysis tends to be one dimensional, at points it is simply dubious. We will look at one example, which is particularly striking given its appeal to what we may think of as 'primal' male and female roles. Hampson describes the fundamentally isolating nature of the hunt or war, which 'must imply a certain disconnectedness and an impersonalization of the other'.[101] In contrast is childbirth, in which women also risk their lives, but 'in a situation of supreme connectedness to another' such that dying *here* would be 'to give one's life in giving life'.[102] Familiar are the descriptions of the isolated man and the already-related woman. But could we not read the hunt and war as unfortunate necessities moving precisely from this connectedness, as motivated by a desire to protect and provide for those with whom men are most deeply connected? Could we not also read childbirth as a particularly selfish act of self-perpetuation or self-gratification which betrays the purposes of having children in the first place?[103] Hampson seems naïve in her assumption that the 'connectedness' women experience is unqualifiedly good. Can this not be a highly cancerous, community-destroying kind of 'connectedness'? She begs all the questions here by conflating trivial relationality and right-relatedness.[104] Just because we are constantly interacting with others does not imply that we have more healthy relationships or even more true ones, as they can be just as distorted as those relationships of people who are more isolated, if in a different manner.[105]

---

100. West, *Deadly Innocence*, p. 87.

101. Hampson, *Theology and Feminism*, pp. 140–1.

102. Ibid., p. 140.

103. Such has certainly been the case with many men! Think of the obsession in many societies throughout history of producing a (almost always male) child to continue the family line and ensure a certain immortality.

104. West criticizes the 'washing-nappies-makes-you-more-relational variety' of feminist literature for its assumption that women's relationality is a *healthy* one rather than one based on protection and exclusion which sanctions violence to protect its own (West, *Deadly Innocence*, pp. 27, 59). Pertinent here is Hampson's utopian portrayal of the functioning of women's groups (including Greenham; 'Feminism', p. 97) in sharp contrast to West's dystopian account of the split *within* the Women's Peace Camp at Greenham Common (West, *Deadly Innocence*, pp. 14–19).

105. Thus, she moves between observation and judgement without signalling a shift, so that it is difficult to know whether we are to read a statement like this as an empirical observation about, for instance, how many people women see and speak to in a day or a moral judgement about the aptitude for more healthy, deeper relationships women may have:

Similarly problematic is Hampson's division between 'manly' and 'womanly' sins, which has an unfortunate effect in her treatment of *incurvatus in se*. On succeeding pages Hampson speaks of sin in Luther as pride or *hubris* and then as a being curved in on oneself. While there seems to be a rough equivocation of these two as paradigmatically Lutheran pictures of sin,[106] she does allow for a slightly wider sense of *incurvatus in se*. Thus, in the context of a discussion of inward curvature, she writes: 'Sin...is a form of egoism, a being cut off by oneself apart from God (whereas God should be the very foundation of oneself). This is true both of despair (a failing to ask for help) and of pride.' At first glance, this is a helpful (and hopeful) expansion of the category of *incurvatus in se* to include what Hampson would deem 'womanly' sins, such as self-diffusion and self-denigration. It appears, though, that she is speaking here of Kierkegaard's first form of despair, the 'male' form, which is also an independence ('a form of egoism') and a refusal to ask for help. As Hampson writes a few lines earlier, Luther 'speaks of the human as being curved in upon himself (which is egoism)'.[107] And women can scarcely be described as egoists. Indeed, they seem to be incapable of being egoists, on Hampson's account. She writes:

> Nor are they so egotistical. They are not in the powerful position[108] which should allow them to see others in relation to themselves, nor has society trained them to see themselves in this way. Of course a woman may bend the lives of others in relation to herself. But is this not more commonly through having a 'martyr complex' – which arises rather from a low self-esteem and an identity which consists in needing to be the servant of others?[109]

Egoism, pride and *incurvatus in se* seem to be equated for Hampson, such that she cannot conceive of an egoism which arises from a low self-esteem. Of course, if egoism is at its heart a truly *self*-centredness, there is every reason to include self-abasing sins with the already present self-exalting ones.[110]

'[Women] are not so isolated on a personal level.' Its context would seem at first to imply this is simply an observation, but the sentence directly following involves more of a moral judgement: 'Perhaps it is her very involvement with the everyday world...which saves many a woman from *Angst*. Women's lives are more bound up with those of others, with other women and children. They are not so isolated on a personal level. Nor are they so egotistical' (Hampson, *Theology and Feminism*, p. 139).

106. In addition to Hampson, *Christian Contradictions*, see 'On Power and Gender', where Hampson describes 'a self-enclosed self, a self which in its pride needed to be broken' (p. 240).

107. Hampson, *Christian Contradictions*, p. 37.

108. Again, the question of racism and classism arises. Rich, white, Western women are, in fact, in this powerful position in relation to all but rich, white, Western men.

109. *Theology and Feminism*, pp. 139–40.

110. Susan Nelson Dunfee argues along similar lines to Hampson, even taking as her point of departure a critique of Niebuhr. She describes the 'sin of hiding' as a paradigm for women, equating it with the virtue of self-sacrifice (Dunfee, 'The Sin of Hiding', *Soundings* 65 [1982], pp. 316–27 [321]). This is an unhelpful equivocation, but Nelson Dunfee *is* helpful in pointing out that hiding is *not* self-sacrifice at all. It is 'a hiding under the guise

The point is not the way in which one is centred on the self, but *that* one is centred on the self. Who has not been annoyed by mini-martyrs whose service and self-denial is a (sometimes only thinly) veiled appeal for love and significance? To be curved in on oneself is to make oneself the *telos* of one's thoughts, words and actions.[111] In any case, for Hampson *incurvatus in se* becomes wed to 'male' forms of sin which nevertheless fail, as we shall see, as sufficient explanatory devices when tested against the experience of many males of themselves as sinners.

A danger of such an over-simplified account of sin is that it, too, will not prove true to people's experience. Take me as an example.[112] Like many people, I have been prone to inappropriate self-regard consistently throughout my life. Often I will succumb to pride, only to lapse into some form of insecurity. Self-abasement is then over-compensated for with self-exaltation.[113] While undoubtedly many men (maybe all) are prideful, to say that there is an inverse relation between self-love and self-hate is, I think, to radically mis-diagnose the problem. I can point only to a common preoccupation with myself (whether conscious or not) in either deviation from the norm of appropriate self-regard. What's more, I can detect a not-so-subtle rejection of what I have been told by others (divine and human) about who I really am, a rejection that results not in my self-fulfilment but in 'an unresolvable self-falsification or self-negation'.[114] So, I can only conclude that Hampson's analysis of *hubris* as a characteristically

---

of self-sacrifice' (p. 322). There is still a self-concern, if its tone is different than in self-exaltation. The self-concern in this case is in the form of self-protection, in an avoidance of the call to responsibility that comes when people have been judged, forgiven and freed. Hampson similarly calls for responsibility but, for obvious reasons, refuses the crucial place of judgment and forgiveness.

111.   Not that this will always be readily apparent, to either oneself or to others around one. But such self-deception or effective veiling of the truth from others does not mean that even those acts which seem most selfless cannot often be entirely oriented towards oneself.

112.   Though slightly unorthodox in academic writing, Hampson herself uses frequent autobiographical examples in an attempt to offer her argument as *her* argument. Another example of one to whose experience this particular feminist account cannot do justice is the black woman who insisted that sloth is not a *black* woman's sin! See Thistlethwaite, *Sex, Race, and God*, p. 78. In light of this experience, Thistlethwaite wonders whether 'the desire to bond with women under an *undifferentiated* label of "sisterhood"' should not be labeled a sin'. She suggests that white feminists 'explore the *difference* color makes' and resist the rush to 'connection', which is 'a temptation all its own' (p. 86).

113.   I could argue as well from the context of a North American evangelical subculture whose adherents are socialized into the distinctly 'feminine' virtues of gentleness, passivity and docility. We read books with titles like *Sacred Romance* and sing 'Jesus, Lover of My Soul'. This is not to assert a different but still thoroughly gendered context but to point out that, for all the rich pastoral help of Saiving's work in particular, the moral psychology she offers is finally without nuance and therefore impoverished.

114.   Torrance, 'The Self-Relation, Narcissism and the Gospel of Grace', pp. 504–505. Torrance compellingly demonstrates the perils of 'any enterprise of independent self-perfection or "narcissistic" pursuit of self-fulfilment' (p. 505) as well as the complete inaccuracy and impossibility of direct self-knowledge.

'male' form of sin[115] (with its tacit assumption that men do not usually fall into 'female' forms of sin) gives me only half the picture and, in only giving me half, actually obscures the picture itself from view. In other words, I am told to look to words like 'pride', 'autonomy' and 'isolation' to understand my sin, and thus I am robbed of a grammar with which to understand (and, thereby, to work against) my self-hatred, laziness and lack of centredness.[116]

Finally, an argument from tradition. Hampson finds this mythology of sin rooted in the symbolism of the Christian myth. That is, men and women are encouraged to behave in self-exalting and self-abasing ways, respectively, by the internal logic of Christian symbols. Here Augustine is instructive. By filling out the narrative of creation and fall in Genesis 1–3 with a psychological analysis, Augustine draws attention to the fact that the narrative actually inverses our expectations. It is not the man who proudly glorifies himself, nor is it the woman who slothfully loses herself in relationship. Rather is it *Eve* who succumbs to the temptation to be like God[117] and Adam (Augustine makes this latter point explicitly) whose sin is characterized by its acquiescing self-diffusion. Here is Augustine:

> We cannot believe that the man was led astray to transgress God's law because he believed that the woman spoke the truth, but that he fell in with her suggestions because they were so closely bound in partnership. In fact, the Apostle was not off the mark when he said, 'It was not Adam, but Eve, who was seduced,' for what he meant was that Eve accepted the serpent's statement as the truth, while Adam refused to be separated from his only companion, even if it involved sharing her sin. That does not mean that he was less guilty, if he sinned knowingly and deliberately.[118]

Augustine does not seem to deny (and may be said to implicitly affirm) the existence of (at least) two forms of sin. But the gendered location of each of these forms is surprising. The central inclusion of such an inversion in the

---

115. As Mark Elliott has helpfully pointed out to me, Greek accounts of *hubris* reveal it to be by no means a boys' club. Example of women guilty of *hubris* are Arachne, Niobe, Medea and Antigone.

116. Indeed, on further reflection, there is good reason to think that laziness and self-hatred may be even more true to men's experience in general. With regard to laziness, consider the recent spate (across the ideological spectrum) of critiques of male passivity. On suicide, consider that the American Center for Disease Control (CDC) reports that men are four times more likely to commit suicide than women, though women report *attempting* suicide during their lifetime three times as often as men (http://www.cdc.gov/ncipc/factsheets/suifacts.htm – site accessed 11 October 2004). The World Health Organization (WHO) found similar trends in worldwide suicide rates in 2000, though with a 'much narrower' ratio in parts of Asia (http://www.who.int/violence_injury_prevention/violence/global_campaign/en/selfdirectedviolfacts.pdf – site accessed 11 October 2004).

117. Interestingly, seen in this light, Eve looks quite a bit like Lilith, Adam's first wife in Jewish midrash, adopted by feminists as a symbol of autonomy. See Hampson, *Theology and Feminism*, p. 110.

118. Augustine, *City of God*, XIV.xi.570.

canonical Scriptures,[119] and its treatment by the key advocate in the Christian tradition of pride understood as the paradigmatic sin, gives us one significant, even formative instance in which sin's forms are seen to transcend gender.[120]

Hampson might object that this only reinforces her point, in that women are seen in this central sacred narrative as the original culprits. Furthermore, the fact that in Eve they are labelled as proud serves to legitimize the patriarchal prescription of humility as a means of keeping women in their place. The problem with such an objection, however, is the attempt to have it both ways. Consider the alternative: what if Adam had been tempted by the serpent and given the fruit to Eve to eat? We would be told that the earliest concretions of Judaism and Christianity lock women into roles of subservience, toxic receptivity and victimization.[121] Hampson's reading of Western patriarchy seems to allow for no falsifiability, thus leaving her own feminism open to the charge of ideology (a charge which she levels against patriarchy).

Hampson's Account of Sin per se *and the Controlling Factor of Continuity*

Hampson sets up the distinction between Lutheran and Catholic structures of thought as they bear on the understanding of the self in terms of discontinuity versus continuity.[122] She finds in Kierkegaard a model for the most salutary approach to the self, precisely in that he seems to account for both of these features. His is a religion of revelation, but one that can still advocate the self's

---

119. Phyllis Trible suggests a similar reading from a feminist literary critical perspective. Adam and Eve sin in ways which subvert our expectations. Adam's 'is an act of quiescence, not of initiative. The man is not dominant; he is not aggressive; he is not a decision-maker... He follows his wife without question or comment, thereby denying his own individuality... These character portrayals are truly extraordinary in a culture dominated by men...Rather than legitimating the patriarchal culture from which it comes, the myth places that culture under judgment. And thus it functions to liberate, not to enslave' (Phyllis Trible, 'Eve and Adam', *Andover Newton Quarterly* 13 [1973], pp. 251–58 [256, 258]).

120. We note, too, the subtlety of Augustine's handling of sloth. McFadyen has pointed out that feminist redescriptions of sloth – which make significant advances in our understanding of the structure of personal as well as structural sin – emphasize the agency of slothful people. Sloth, even seen as 'self-loss' in the midst of (distorted) relationships, does not obscure (even if it does disorient) subjecthood (McFadyen, *Bound to Sin*, pp. 141–50). The situation for both feminists and Augustine is one in which the 'internal dynamic of life-intentionality (including will) is sequestered and captured by this larger dynamic; one finds one's internality "possessed", consenting to, committed to, desiring and entrapped by a pathological orientation larger than the self' (p. 196). This is a dynamic in which we are 'internally bound' by our very own willing (p. 198).

121. See Hampson's discussion of concretion in *Theology and Feminism*, pp. 81–115. 'Religion lives through its concretion. By concretion I mean the parables, the stories and the history, the images, symbols and metaphors by which it is carried' (p. 81).

122. For a trenchant critique of her characterization of Catholicism which disputes the flat continuity which Hampson attributes to it but which also seems to paper over some of the finer points of Hampson's argument, see Laurence Paul Hemming, 'A Contradiction' *New Blackfriars* 86 (2005), pp. 3–23.

'coming to itself'. Surely she has a point here. After all, for all the language of crucifixion and resurrection in the New Testament, for all the newness of this new creation, it is still *I* who have died and risen with Christ. I am a new man, but I am still called Matt. I still have a history, memories, a body. There is a basic biological and social continuity to me, even in the midst of the irruption of salvation in Christ. Hampson is concerned to not run roughshod over the identity of a person, and this drives her to pay attention to continuity. Luther would counter that this is sinful (and vain) self-preservation.[123] But Hampson has identified one of Protestantism's greatest weaknesses in the heart of its founder's structure of thought. Luther's scope is too often limited to sin and salvation (despite his own affection for the decidedly 'this-worldly' and his creating space for the secular realm), what Eugene Rogers has memorably termed merely the 'subplot' in God's larger story stretching from creation to new creation.[124] For all the merits of Luther's beginning with the person *qua* sinner (chief of which is its empirical realism), such a starting point makes it difficult for him to meaningfully relate the person *qua* creature to the person *qua* new creature. Hence the need for continuity.[125]

The problem, then, is not in Hampson's call for continuity *per se*, but in her location of continuity. One might locate continuity in God's faithfulness to his creation. That is, the God who created out of nothing will not allow his creation finally to descend into nothing but will re-create it. Similarly, the biological and social continuity which does obtain, even in the context of dying and rising with Christ (or course, there are glorious discontinuities here – transfigured bodies and resurrected communities), is one which bespeaks God's love for his creatures. Such an approach is out of bounds for Hampson, of course. Instead, she locates continuity in an unequivocal affirmation of the

123. 'But human righteousness tries first of all to take away sins and change them and also to preserve man as he is; thus it is not righteousness but hypocrisy...But when a man has not died to sin and has not been taken from it, in vain does one try to take away sin and die to it' (*LW* 25:323). Note that his concern to demolish human righteousness to make way for the *iustitia Dei* is coupled in this context (and in Luther's thought) with his fundamental distinction between person and works. It is impossible to change the works of a person without first changing the person who does the works.

124. See the section on 'Sin and Redemption as Subplot' in Eugene Rogers, 'The Stranger', in James J. Buckley and David S. Yeago (eds.), *Knowing the Triune God* (Grand Rapids: Eerdmans, 2001), pp. 265–83 (273–83). Specifically, the (at least potential) problem for sin–salvation schema is that they tend to adopt a problem–solution approach in which the solution is only as big as the problem. As a result, the love of God in Christ becomes merely antidotal.

125. We might take Gal. 2.20 as a test case in asking about the relative emphasis the New Testament places on continuity and discontinuity: 'I have been crucified with Christ; and it is no longer I who live, but Christ lives in me; and the life which I now live in the flesh I live by faith in the Son of God, who loved me, and delivered Himself up for me'. It is clearly *I* who have been crucified and now live. Paul expresses no concern to change this basic designation of selfhood. Nevertheless, we find him doubling back on himself – it is 'no longer I...but Christ'. Even this life in the flesh, which is visibly identical to my former life, is oriented to another. In this verse, there is a certain continuity which is taken for granted ('I'); but the newness of the new life is such that the continuity seems trivial.

person as person. In her critique of Reinhold Niebuhr's understanding of sin as pride, Hampson argues that the task for women is not the humility and dependence on another in faith,[126] but an appropriate self-love.[127]

> Her task it to become a differentiated self, a determinate individual, who may say 'I' without feeling guilty. To tell such a woman that it is the sin of pride to seek self-fulfilment is to reinforce her form of sin: her dispersal of herself in others, her unwarranted serving of them, her attempt to live through them, and her self-disparagement.[128]

It is clear in this context that Hampson is not arguing for the innocence of women as much as she is affirming women as centred persons who should be encouraged to develop their individuality, and to do so that they might truly be *persons* in relation. This encouragement is surely well-placed. In a similar vein, John Macmurray speaks of 'the rhythm of withdrawal and return' in which 'the withdrawal is for the sake of the return; and its necessity lies in this, that it differentiates the positive phase by enriching its content...My withdrawal from the Other is itself a phase of my relation to the Other.'[129] Nevertheless, this is a project of self-actualization.[130] And perhaps there is a certain degree of pastoral sense in this. What is more, Hampson's soteriology, which focuses on becoming whole, is not limited to women. 'Could men however but learn both to come "to" themselves and to develop a relationality with others, a violent breaking of an egocentric self would be unnecessary.'[131]

The operative word, of course, is 'could'. We might agree that *could* men and women learn to live justly and mercifully, that is, lovingly, a breaking of the self (let us call it dying to sin and being crucified with Christ) would be unnecessary. The witness of history (the last century more than any, we might think), not to mention the witness of the Christian tradition and its Scriptures, is that men and women simply *cannot*. Indeed, this is the witness of *sin*. We simply do not want to learn or develop in these ways or, if we do, we find that we cannot. Hampson's consistent use of evolutionary metaphors with their tendency towards continuity and growth (here, 'learn' and 'develop') reflects

126. McFadyen describes 'a painful awareness of the empirical consequences of the language of dependence' on the part of many feminists (Alistair McFadyen, 'Sins of Praise', in Colin E. Gunton [ed.], *God and Freedom* [Edinburgh: T&T Clark, 1995], pp. 32–56 [38]).

127. For a critique of the claim that self-love is necessary before we can love others, see Ronald F. Marshall, 'News from the Graveyard', *Pro Ecclesia* 9 (2000), pp. 19–42 (36 n. 45). Marshall's conclusion, helpful even if it is too flat: 'The fact is caring for ourselves cannot redirect our attention to others'.

128. Hampson, 'Reinhold Niebuhr on Sin', p. 49.

129. John Macmurray, *Persons in Relation* (London: Faber & Faber, 1961), pp. 90–2. And Hampson: 'What [women] need to learn is that necessary differentiation of the self from others' ('Reinhold Niebuhr on Sin', p. 54).

130. Hampson, 'Reinhold Niebuhr on Sin', p. 51.

131. Hampson, 'Luther on the Self', p. 340. Not that men are, strictly speaking, utterly inept when it comes to relating. Hampson mentions a (presumably gender-mixed) Quaker meeting in which she took part over a number of years and notes that 'such skills in inter-relating are not unique to women' ('Feminism', p. 97).

an anthropological optimism strikingly at odds with her pessimistic telling of the history of the (patriarchal) world.

The real question is about sin and its extent. In her critique of Niebuhr, Hampson writes:

> Why be constantly jumping outside oneself and denying one's past? If women's basic problem is not self-centredness, but rather lack of a sense of self, a scheme of salvation which consists in breaking the self, and in discontinuity with the past, may be unhelpful. The interrelation of love, with God and with others (by contrast with faith) allows one to feel good about oneself. One is affirmed as a self by being loved for oneself, and out of a certain centredness in oneself, loves another.[132]

Hampson's rejection of *any* discontinuity as harmful to women is misplaced. Even here, the language of a self 'being loved for oneself' subtly undermines the sharpness of the love of God. This is a God who loves sinners, that is, a God who creates worth in the very act of loving, rather than responding to the draw of one already lovely in him- or herself. Where Luther affirms that God loves sinners, precisely as sinners, Hampson is concerned that women be loved for themselves, but in such a way that does not allow for them to be called sinners.[133]

Not that this precludes any sense that women sin. According to Hampson, naming what Judith Plaskow calls women's 'failure to take responsibility for self-actualization' as sin 'is (as I have discovered when working with groups of women) very effective' in that it re-affirms women's agency.

> Whether 'the failure to take responsibility for self-actualization' should however be called 'sin' is another question...If we think of women's typical 'failings', as Saiving names them, they can hardly be said (in the way in which this is true of male pride) to be actively destructive of others. Rather have women been destructive of themselves and their own potentialities.[134]

The thrust of definition here is pragmatic. If calling something 'sin' can re-establish a woman's agency, then it serves some use. But strictly speaking, these are 'failings' which are more self-destructive. Problematic at this point is the implication that such failings have little residual effect in the lives of others. Perhaps this is just an omission, though, as Hampson is keen at other points to affirm our essential relationality. What we still have, however, is a

---

132. Hampson, 'Reinhold Niebuhr on Sin', p. 54.

133. Angela West goes so far as to say that feminists have inverted the relations of accusers and accused: 'Sometime in the mid 1970s in Britain, women were declared innocent. All charges against them were to be dropped. Women were not guilty and never had been... They took the finger that was pointed accusingly at women and pointed it back at the accusers. It is men, they declared, and not women, who are responsible for all the mortal ills of our society...It is they who stand condemned – women are innocent' (West, *Deadly Innocence*, p. xiii).

134. Hampson, *Theology and Feminism*, p. 123. Hampson is heavily indebted to Plaskow's analysis and critique of Niebuhr's and Tillich's theologies of sin and grace.

denial of any basic discontinuity. Women must change, but only in that they must recognize and live out of their own basic goodness.

It is precisely her eschewal of discontinuity that points to Hampson's inability to account for sin as anything more than an external accretion. The problem, for both men and women, seems to have come from somewhere else (our socialization into patriarchy).[135] *We* are not the problem. We may do things at times which exacerbate the problem, but we have the resources internally to solve it. What else could be said by one who denies the existence of a God who is in apposition to the world and might be said to offer a solution? Nihilism is an unattractive option, so Hampson must choose anthropological optimism and hope.

The ironic lack of seriousness with which Hampson treats sin is seen in her espousal of an ethic of *philia*. Such an ethic only works if the two parties actively love one another. Thus, it makes assumptions about the willingness (and fitness) of people to love that fly in the face of experience. Indeed, there seems to be an awareness in feminist discourse of this empirical reality which runs counter to the demands of an ethic of *philia*. Having lived long enough without true, loving mutuality, many advocates of such an ethic seek to guarantee that mutuality. That is, in asking the question, 'What if my love is not returned?', they fall prey to a commodification of the love which is to be freely given and returned. Without affirming the unconditional nature of love,[136] covenantal relationships become contracts in which the overabundant creativity and spontaneity of love dissipates.[137] But when mutuality is made conditional, it is lost.[138] In the process, an adequately *relational* anthropology

135. Hampson, 'A Reply to Angela West', p. 117.

136. I am grateful to Jen Kilps for drawing my attention to unconditionality and reciprocity as two central characteristics of hospitality in Derrida's work. See 'Hospitality, Justice and Responsibility: A Dialogue with Jacques Derrida' in Richard Kearney and Mark Dooley (eds.), *Questioning in Ethics* (London: Routledge, 1999), pp. 65–83. Derrida commends a pure, unconditional hospitality (pp. 69–70) which rejects an exchange model of the gift due to its conditionality. 'So unconditional hospitality implies that you don't ask the other, the newcomer, the guest, to give anything back, or even to identify himself or herself. Even if the other deprives you of your mastery or your home, you have to accept this. It is terrible to accept this, but that is the condition of unconditional hospitality...If, however, there is pure hospitality, or pure gift, it should consist in this opening without horizon, without horizon of expectation, an opening to the newcomer whoever that may be' (p. 70). It should be noted that Derrida wonders 'if there is such a thing' as pure hospitality (p. 71). Also see the sketch of this problematic in Simon Critchley and Richard Kearney's preface to Jacques Derrida, *On Cosmopolitanism and Forgiveness* (trans. Mark Dooley and Michael Hughes; London: Routledge, 2001), p. x.

137. See J. B. Torrance, 'Covenant or Contract?', *Scottish Journal of Theology* 23 (1970), pp. 51–76.

138. In pointing out that we do not know 'whether a friendship arose between the Good Samaritan and the man he helped', Gene Outka suggests an alternative to Hampson's mutuality of *philia*, arguing that it is best to say that 'mutuality is the internal, ideal fruition of *agape*'. That is, our love must be 'unilateral', but 'one nonetheless desires and hopes for a response' (Outka, 'Universal Love and Impartiality', in Edmund N. Santurri and William Werpehowski [eds.], *The Love Commandments* [Washington, DC: Georgetown University Press, 1992], pp. 1–130 [89]).

is compromised as well, for concern for preservation of the self continues to rule one's agenda in inter-personal relations, disqualifying one from true engagement with another person as *other* and relegating her instead to a role in which she is nothing more than a tool for the satisfaction of one's needs and desires.[138]

If sin is anywhere near as extensive as the Christian tradition teaches, then an ethic of *agape* is needed. A person who lives in light of such an ethic establishes the unconditional nature of love and trusts in the love of God mediated through (and sometimes in spite of) other people. Lesslie Newbigin notes that, while *agape* and *eros* are not finally at odds (here, he helpfully corrects Luther and Nygren), in our world 'wherein love has become self-love, God's glory can be revealed only in the form of a cross where the life-giving stream of divine love is poured out in utter self-giving in the waste-land of man's futile self-seeking'.[139] This need not imply a final stoicism in which the self is disciplined to disregard itself. Rather, it can bespeak a confidence in one's position in Christ and an eschatological suspension of gratification.[140] Indeed, it is precisely this confidence in one's being loved by God in Christ which allows for such a prolonged suspension. That is, unconditional *agape* must be theologically grounded in the God who is *pro nobis* in his unconditional love in Christ. Only this prior assurance can create a truly constructive *agape*.[141]

Thus, it does not seem that sin as pride is the entire point at issue for Hampson. It is the ambiguity with which she treats women's sin *per se*.[142] The

138.   On the closely knit concepts of eccentricity, relationality and *agape*, see Alistair McFadyen, *The Call to Personhood* (Cambridge: Cambridge University Press, 1990). It is 'through such interaction [with other personal centres] that one and others become centred' such that 'persons are what they are for others or, rather, the way in which they are for others' (p. 40). That the scaled-down expectations of an ethic of *philia* are incommensurate with a truly relational anthropology is due to the fact that, 'since personal being is ex-centric, we can only find real security by opening ourselves to God and others' (p. 236).

139.   Lesslie Newbigin, *The Household of God* (London: SCM Press, 1953), p. 130.

140.   Both of these points can be seen in relation to Philippians 2. Luther emphasizes the first ('confidence in one's position in Christ') by arguing that we have sufficiently abundant riches in faith that we need desire nothing more and can love others without thought of ourselves. Such freedom means one is '*unbound* in the desire for happiness', not having relinquished that desire but being freed by God's promise to give happiness from a slavish pursuit of it (John H. Whittaker, '"Agape" and Self-Love', in Santurri and Werpehowski [eds.], *The Love Commandments*, pp. 221–39 [236]). The second (what I have called the 'eschatological suspension of gratification') is seen in that Christ's kenotic love (and that, I would argue, of his disciples) ends in his exaltation. (See Heb. 12.2, which describes Jesus as enduring the cross 'for the joy set before him'.) Here, then, we can agree with Hampson, who writes that 'it is the person who has come to herself who can truly be in relation. Such a person neither dominates others, nor attempts to lose herself in them. The love of others promotes a rightful love of self, while a secure self is self-forgetful in delight in others' ('Luther on the Self', p. 340). It is *how* (or, in relation to *whom*) one comes to oneself that is in question.

141.   'It is when the virtues of self-giving are unplugged from the nurturing dynamics of genuine love, that they take pathological form (sloth) and fail to be genuine forms of self-presence for and orientation towards others' (McFadyen, *Bound to Sin*, p. 156).

142.   Paul Sponheim agrees (Sponheim, 'On Being and Becoming before God', p. 338).

location of the cross in the middle of the Christian life tells us that each life, not just the lives of those who are obviously proud, has been found wanting. Simply affirming such a life does nothing to transform it, and here is Hampson's problem. She wants (self-)transformation without the cross.[144]

On the Explanatory Sufficiency of incurvatus in se

Despite our critique of Hampson's insufficient account of women's sinning, that is, her hesitancy to name women's missteps 'sins', her description of the self-destructive bent of many women has widened our picture of human sinning. Again, though we take issue with her overly gendered account, that people sin differently is a point on which we can agree. Specifically, we sin in both self-exaltation and self-denigration. So speaking of pride as the paradigmatic sin, one in which all human sinning is encapsulated, is found to be insufficient. Alistair McFadyen captures the significance of such a shift:

> If both pride and its opposite are construed as sin, then, the very *sinfulness* of pride is significantly recast. What this actually indicates is a switch in the normative standard of reference underpinning the discernment of sin. The good which pride deprives one of has to be reconfigured when self-obeisance and 'self-loss' are no longer complementary *virtues* to the sin of pride, but represent instead *complementary aspects of the same pathology.* What this indicates is that feminist naming here operates by relating both pride and sloth to a more comprehensive standard of reference, which adjudicates the sinfulness of both: an understanding of the proper economy of self in relation.[145]

Given the attention being paid (rightfully so) to difference these days, it is only appropriate to ask whether *incurvatus in se* (which, as we have seen, is not to be so quickly equated with pride) can cast a wide-enough net to characterize how sinful humanity is. That is, can it carry the explanatory weight required, along with the implicit 'normative standard of reference' which underpins such an account of sin? This may ultimately be a question we can only ask on a case-by-case basis. However, given the penchant of Augustine and, more pointedly, Luther, to understand *incurvatus in se* in relation to self-exalting egoism (rather than the more self-abasing kind of egoism we have mentioned),[146] it will be helpful to look at *incurvatus in se* as applied to what we have come to see as the other side of the coin, what Hampson calls 'womanly' sins. In particular, we will look at Barth's discussion of *incurvatus in se* as it is applied

144. Hampson, 'Reinhold Niebuhr on Sin', p. 54. See also Hampson, *After Christianity*, p. 250.

145. McFadyen, *Bound to Sin*, p. 156 (emphasis his).

146. Even this picture is cloudier than it seems, however. Mary Gaebler has convincingly argued that 'the increasing failure of alleged Christians to produce "good works" apparently turned Luther's attention more and more to the sin of sloth' (Gaebler, 'Luther on the Self', p. 115).

to sloth in *Church Dogmatics* IV/2. The question we will need to continually return to throughout our discussion of Barth's work is whether *incurvatus in se* is sufficiently broad while at the same time sufficiently indicative in its rendering of various forms of sin. We have seen its explanatory power in relation to the more self-assertive aspects of egoism and will now ask whether it retains a similar power in relation to self-diffusion. Representing dipolar postures of sin (which, nevertheless, as we have seen, share much in common as 'complementary aspects of the same pathology'),[147] pride and sloth thus provide a range of meaning in relation to sin which, if covered by *incurvatus in se*, would point to an understanding of humanity curved in on itself as a useful paradigm for understanding sin.

---

147. McFadyen, *Bound to Sin*, p. 156.

Chapter 4

BROADENING THE RANGE OF THE METAPHOR:
BARTH'S THREEFOLD DESCRIPTION OF SIN

Introduction

Considering the feminist critique of using pride paradigmatically to understand how sinful humanity is, we have had to ask whether the metaphor
of being curved in on oneself possesses a wide enough descriptive range to
account for the (often radically) different experiences of people in sinning.
Clearly, gender difference demands this; but so, as we have seen in passing,
do differences of race and ethnicity, class, culture and geography. Given the
cleverly deceptive nature of sin and its sadly creative ability to take on seemingly endless new forms, we might be tempted to give up the pursuit of a
unifying, or at least characteristic, sketch of sin. After all, as soon as sin is differentiated (as in the case of Hampson, into pride and sloth), countless other
forms suggest themselves. We might think of the so-called 'seven deadly sins'[1]
or more *au courant* options such as 'anxiety' and 'despair' (the favourites of
existentialists).

Despite this proliferation, the dipolar status of pride and sloth offers us a
promising pair of test candidates. If an overarching structure can be found
which sufficiently accounts for and describes these two sins, it would be
reasonable to suggest that such a structure might serve as an explanatory
umbrella. Such an umbrella would never take the place of detailed analysis
of more particular postures of sin, nor would it provide all the resources
necessary to describe individual sinful acts, attitudes, words, systems or relationships. For this, beyond context-specific theological analysis, any number
of non-theological resources may be enlisted as appropriate.[2] Nevertheless,

---

1.   A recent series of gift books on the seven deadly sins put out by Oxford University
Press suggests the continuing relevance of and our fascination with sin as well as its marginal
place in serious thinking and living in contemporary society. The series as sign of cultural
condition is decidedly ambiguous. Does this signal a bout of collective conscience, or does it
suggest that we have finally shuffled off this moral coil of sin and attained sufficient distance
from it to write and read witty books about it?

2.   No one has attempted or accomplished such a subtle analysis of sin as Alistair
McFadyen, deft in his theological thinking-through and his handling of non-theological
modes of discourse. See McFadyen, *Bound to Sin*. McFadyen's project is very much in
keeping with Barth's methodological concerns and commitments.

a conceptual umbrella might serve as a useful organizing tool in efforts to characterize sinful humanity.

This chapter will test the metaphor of being curved in on oneself to determine its descriptive range and power as a potential paradigm for sin. There can be little question following our discussion of sin in Augustine and Luther that to speak of *homo incurvatus in se* is to refer to humanity in its pride. But Hampson's work suggests that this might be the limit of its value, and that the metaphor might not extend sufficiently to include the experiences of women. Is *incurvatus in se* tethered to pride, or can it account for the more 'feminine' sins – chief among which, according to feminist literature, is sloth? Having called into question such a strongly gendered differentiation of sin in the last chapter, we will leave that aspect to the side and address directly the question of whether it makes sense to speak of sloth as an instance of being curved in on oneself.

Karl Barth moves us beyond Augustine and Luther in explicitly acknowledging three primary forms of sin – pride [*Hochmut*], sloth [*Trägheit*] and falsehood [*Lüge*].³ At the same time, his relational anthropology, which takes its cues from Christology, leads him to suggest that sin is characterized first and foremost by broken relationships in which people live for themselves rather than for God and others. His approach shows promise, then, suggesting that one might both recognize different forms of sin and yet still speak meaningfully of an over-arching structure in all human sinning. We will move in our discussion and analysis of Barth from his Christological starting point through a brief sketch of two of the three forms of sin (as pride and falsehood) to an in-depth account of sin as sloth, asking throughout how Barth's understanding of sin squares with, is questioned by and questions feminist concerns. If McFadyen is right that pride and sloth are 'complementary aspects of the same pathology',⁴ we should expect that any comprehensive description of that pathology would elucidate rather than obscure *both* of those aspects.⁵ Our attention in this chapter will be on sloth, taking for granted the aid we have already received from Augustine and Luther in describing pride. If the metaphor of being curved in on oneself fails to illuminate the reality of sloth, it should be discarded as an umbrella concept, even if we retain it as a suitable description of certain sinful patterns. If the metaphor can be shown to effectively illuminate and maybe even *entail* sloth, then it is a good candidate to serve as a paradigm for understanding sin relationally.

A Brief Apology for Paradigms

The question of the legitimacy of seeking to establish a paradigm for sin arises in light of the sheer difference amongst sinners which feminist theologians

3.   *Contra* McFadyen, 'Sins of Praise', p. 36 n. 5.
4.   McFadyen, *Bound to Sin*, p. 156.
5.   Description of the two aspects should flesh out, in turn, our understanding of the pathology.

have described. The problem with the feminist critique of the very *notion* of
one paradigm for sin is that it assumes without question that an overarching
structural understanding of sin can only allow for a limited range of sins. In
her critique of the Augustinian tradition's emphasis on pride, Diane Leclerc
states that 'the very purpose of this entire study has been to challenge a singular, and thus limiting hamartiological paradigm'.[6] And yet, the paradigm
she critiques proves not to be limiting because it is singular, but because it is
insufficient in its descriptive range to work *as a paradigm*. Her call for mul-
tiplicity is useful insofar as it exposes the limitations of 'pride' as a label, but
she herself recognizes the value of some kind of umbrella concept. In the same
note, she admits: 'I do seek to affirm the term "idolatry" as very useful as it
encompasses both idolatry of self (pride) and idolatry of others'. The point,
then, is not that paradigms are to be rejected, but that better paradigms are
to be sought. Christian theology requires that our paradigms be *provisional*,
as Barth reminds us, with an acknowledgment of their place under the lordship and judgement of Christ. But with that *proviso* in place, the search for
a proper paradigm is nothing other than the attempt to describe how sinful
humanity is.

Sin Christologically Defined

Christology as the starting point of dogmatics

If Hampson is correct in saying that 'Christians are those who proclaim Jesus
to have been unique', then Barth must be deemed the Christian theologian *par
excellence*.[7] The uniqueness and significance of Jesus simply cannot be overes-
timated in Barth's theology. He takes with utmost seriousness the confession
that 'God was in Christ', and establishes a Christological starting point with
each turn to a 'new' subject.[8] Rather, he follows the Christological starting
point which he sees established by the Father's eternal election of the Son,
thinking after [*Nachdenken*] and, therefore, thinking theologically. More than
a starting point, Christology becomes the lens through which Barth reads each
dogmatic *locus*.

This methodological move corresponds to a material move in which Barth
not only reads all of dogmatics through a Christological lens but also reads
all of dogmatics *as* Christology. To say this is not to affirm the common criticism that Barth offers a totalizing 'Christomonism' in which all other reality
is subsumed and, the criticism usually implies, eclipsed.[9] Instead, it is precisely
in Christ that reality becomes, well, reality. Ingolf Dalferth applies patristic
Christological categories for the hypostatic union to argue that, for Barth

6.   Leclerc, *Singleness of Heart*, p. 165 n. 83.
7.   Hampson, *Theology and Feminism*, p. 50.
8.   2 Cor. 5.19 pressures Barth's reading of Scripture throughout his *corpus*.
9.   Roberts castigates Barth for his 'profound theological totalitarianism' which
serves a 'perfect illustration of (say) the Marxist critique of religion as alienation of the self'

our world of common experience is an *enhypostatic reality* which exists only in so far as it is incorporated into the concrete reality of God's saving self-realisation in Christ. Taken by itself natural reality is an anhypostatic abstraction, unable to exist on its own and systematically at one remove from the texture of concrete reality.[10]

Natural reality has no existence independent of and thus it only has its being as a being-in-relation to the very particular history of God and humanity in Christ. Thus, for Barth, it is as inaccurate to say that our world exists independently of Christ as it is that Christ's own humanity exists independently of the Word's assumption of it. But, to stay with the analogy, it is as true to say that in Christ the world does have real reality, its 'own' existence, as it is to say that Jesus is a real human being. Humanity does not lose all history and responsibility in this, becoming objects or spectators, but rather only by God's election of humanity in Christ is it made free for God. 'This one thing does not mean the extinguishing of our humanity, but its establishment...It is not for us a passive presence as spectators, but our true and highest activation' (CD IV/1, pp. 14–15). Thus the being of man is responsible thankfulness as and in community.[11]

(Richard H. Roberts, *A Theology on Its Way?* [Edinburgh: T&T Clark, 1991], pp. 56–7). Roberts has deeply misread Barth and betrays his commitment to a competitive, contrastive construal of the God-creation relationship in this comment. Barth explicitly rejects any form of 'theomonism' precisely because it makes humanity into a puppet, and '[a] puppet does not obey'. God's work is different in that 'to be quickened by the Holy Spirit is to move oneself, and to do so in obedience, listening to the order and command of God' (IV/2, p. 800). It is true that 'in relation to His action theirs will always be improper. But this action of theirs...is as such a real action' (IV/2, p. 824).

10.   Ingolf U. Dalferth, 'Karl Barth's Eschatological Realism', in S. W. Sykes (ed.), *Karl Barth* (Cambridge: Cambridge University Press, 1989), pp. 14–45 (29). Note that an anhypostatic-enhypostatic Christology was a controlling *leitmotif* in Barth's theology from his discovery of it in May 1924. See Bruce McCormack, *Karl Barth's Critically Realistic Dialectical Theology* (Oxford: Oxford University Press, 1997), pp. 327–8, 360–7. For a brief history of the anhypostasis–enhypostasis formula, see Shults, *Reforming Theological Anthropology*, pp. 140–60. Shults argues that Barth's use of the formula is an uncritical appropriation – though with Barth's ever-present doctrinal creativity – of Protestant Scholasticism's misreading of patristic Christology, though he affirms the theological judgement (if not its conceptual trappings) underlying Barth's use of the formula.

11.   Barth's claim rests on a non-contrastive, non-competitive understanding of the God–creation relation. See pages 110–12 above for Kathryn Tanner's description of such a model, which is able to 'think of deity and humanity together and still give each its due' (Eberhard Jüngel, *Karl Barth* [trans. Garrett E. Paul; Philadelphia: The Westminster Press, 1986], p. 127). John Webster's sustained argument over a number of books and articles about Barth's 'moral ontology' makes a similar point. As he writes at one point, 'Barth's apparent ontological exclusivism is in fact an inclusivism: *solus Christus* embraces and does not suspend or absorb the world of creatures and actions' (Webster, *Barth's Ethics of Reconciliation*, p. 29; cited in David W. Haddorff, 'The Postmodern Realism of Barth's Ethics', *Scottish Journal of Theology* 57 [2004], pp. 269–86 [280]). Also see Webster, *Barth's Moral Theology*.

Trevor Hart points out that Catholic and Protestant accounts of justification have been trapped in an 'ontology of the actual' in which what is real is identified with what is actual.[12] In contrast, Barth works from an 'ontology of relation to Christ' where reality is identified with *'the concrete history of the one man Jesus of Nazareth'*.[13] This is a relational ontology which defines humanity primarily in terms of its relationships rather than appealing to substance, qualities, capacities or states.[14] It is also a particular ontology actualized in a history, and it is this delimitation – relationship to one man being basically constitutive of humanity – that most clearly sets Barth's own brand of personalism apart from someone like John Macmurray.[15] As relational and particular, this is a covenantal ontology.[16] In Barth's 'carefully worked out alternative ontology',[17] the real is often set in explicit *contradiction* to the actual. This is not to punt to idealism or the nominalism of a 'legal fiction'. Rather it is to highlight the *relational* determination of humanity as a being-with-Christ. That is to say, when the real and actual are set in opposition as, for instance, when Barth speaks of 'real man' (i.e., Jesus and us in him) versus the actual 'man of sin', he means to articulate our being *extra nos* in Christ versus our sinful, futile being *in* and *pro se*. But Luther's negative category of extrinsic being is not quite right. While Barth can on occasion speak in this way, he is more interested in making the corresponding positive point – that

12.   Trevor Hart, *Regarding Karl Barth* (Carlisle: Paternoster Press, 1999), p. 56.
13.   Ibid., pp. 60, 58.
14.   Though note Donald Mackinnon's excellent article, in which he gives a deftly rounded account of the role substance plays in Christian theology as well as the 'enlargement' that such a term from the analytic philosophical tradition undergoes when it encounters the *novum* of God in Christ. See D. M. Mackinnon, '"Substance" in Christology', in S. W. Sykes and J. P. Clayton (eds.), *Christ, Faith and History* (London: Cambridge University Press, 1972), pp. 279–300.
15.   See Macmurray, *Persons in Relation*. Macmurray argues that the self is not a substance (as in a Cartesian/Hobbesian model); nor is it an organism (as in Rousseau and Hegel). Rather, the self is a person in relation (pp. 15, 17). This is why Macmurray views the self not in terms of subjectivity or mind but as agent (the subject of the first volume of his 1953–54 Gifford Lectures, *Self as Agent*, of which *Persons in Relation* is the second volume). Note the connection between a relational ontology and a certain understanding of personal agency. If Macmurray is right (and, for what it is worth, Tony Blair thinks he is, having modelled much of his public policy on Macmurray's philosophy), then a relational anthropology lends itself well to an account of humanity's being-in-the-world that dovetails with the recent recuperation of and emphasis on notions of practice, habits and embodiment.
16.   Bruce McCormack writes that it would be more accurate 'to express Barth's ontology *theologically* as a "covenant ontology" since it is not in "relationality" in general that God's being is constituted but in a most concrete, particular relation'. As covenantal, Barth's ontology is historical and actualist rather than essentialist. See Bruce McCormack, 'Grace and Being', in John Webster (ed.), *The Cambridge Companion to Karl Barth* (Cambridge: Cambridge University Press, 2000), pp. 92–110 (99, 108–9). On covenant as the ruling or 'root metaphor' (ruling precisely because it follows the logic of the incarnation) in Barth's theology and the notion of a 'covenantal ontology', see Stuart D. McLean, *Humanity in the Thought of Karl Barth* (Edinburgh: T&T Clark, 1981), pp. 6, 20, 56, 61.
17   Hart, *Regarding Karl Barth*, p. 59.

we really do find our being, and find it in relation. That is why Barth prefers the language of *enhypostasis*.[18]

Christology as the starting point of anthropology

Barth begins everything with Christology. That is, he consistently seeks to think from the triune God's self-revelation in Christ. So we should not be surprised, despite the relative infrequency of such a move in modern theology, when he commends 'the founding of anthropology on Christology'.[19] Pilate was more right than he knew: '*Ecce homo*' (p. 44). Thus first of all we must look to the nature of man in the concrete, particular instance of Jesus and only then at the nature of man as that of all men (p. 46). But there are problems here. We can make no direct equation of 'human nature as we know it in our-selves with the human nature of Jesus' (p. 47). *However*, due to God's merciful judgment, 'there now remains only the pure and free humanity of Jesus as our own humanity' (p. 48). Jesus is the original; we are the copy (p. 50). Christ, in other words, is our mediator: 'It is either through Him that we know what we truly are as men, or we do not know it at all. Our self-knowledge can only be an act of discipleship. But as an act of discipleship it can be a true and estab-lished and certain knowledge' (p. 53). The consequence of all of this is that, 'although we are dealing with our existence, we are dealing with our existence in Jesus Christ as our true existence, that we are therefore dealing with Him and not with us, and with us only in so far as absolutely and exclusively with Him'.[20] The method of theological anthropology is indirect. Nevertheless, this is the only approach to true (that is, theological) knowledge of humanity.

The problem with an 'anthropology which is independent of theology'[21] is its tendency to *remain* independent of theology.[22] In taking the experi-

---

18.   Note, too, that while the enhypostatic assumes the anhypostatic as its necessary counterpart, Barth articulates reality according to the former more than the latter in keeping with his doggedly faithful insistence on starting with reality *as it is in Christ*. In this light, even the anhypostatic, given too much attention or autonomy, can become speculative.

19.   *CD* III/2, p. 44. The quotations in this paragraph are from *CD* III/2, with page numbers in parentheses in the body of the text.

20.   *CD* IV/1, p. 154. Barth's structural polemic against liberal Protestantism can be seen in his shuffling of the doctrine of election in *CD* II/2 to begin with the election of Jesus Christ, then move to the election of Israel and the Church and only then to that of individual Christians. This move is paralleled in *CD* IV/1-3, where Barth begins reconciliation with the incarnation, followed by descriptions of the Church and individual Christians.

21.   *CD* III/2, p. 21. Schleiermacher illustrates this general anthropology for Barth, deriving the being of Jesus Christ from the being of man in a 'topsy-turvy' manner (IV/1, p. 49). This movement from general to particular runs afoul of Barth's commitment to a reverse direction, pressured not so much by a philosophical commitment to particularity as by a theological commitment to the priority of God's self-revelation in Christ. On Barth's particularism, see George Hunsinger, *How to Read Karl Barth* (Oxford: Oxford University Press, 1991), pp. 32–5.

22.   Though surprisingly scarce in this discussion, Descartes does come in for critique earlier in the *Dogmatics*. Despite Descartes' stated attempts to move from doubt to reflexivity

ence of individual Christians as its starting point, liberal Protestant theology (from Schleiermacher's *Glaubenslehre* to Herrmann's *The Communion of the Christian with God*) betrayed its commitment to taking the experience of individual Christians as its endpoint as well. For Schleiermacher and those of his ilk: 'Theology in general and with it the doctrine of the atonement could only be the self-interpretation of the pious Christian self-consciousness as such, of the *homo religiosus incurvatus in se*' (IV/1, p. 153).[23] Barth does not intend to avoid this problem of religious man, but he notes that 'faith and love and hope are relative concepts. The being of Christians indicated by them is a being in relation. Faith lives by its object, love by its basis, hope by its surety. Jesus Christ by the Holy Spirit is this object and basis and surety' (IV/1, pp. 153–4). It is this continual attending to the object of faith, to the Christian's eccentric existence in Christ that safeguards theology against solipsism. And with this proviso in place, Barth can retrieve a category as tainted by liberal Protestantism as 'experience'. Despite his 'non-pietist' stance, as Joseph Mangina calls it, Barth allows Christian experience a place in his theology.[24] After all, how can God's creatures know him but experientially (that is, in all the spatio-temporal contingency of their existence as creatures of God)?[25] But Barth is nevertheless continually clear that Christian experience is true only 'to the extent that it lives entirely by Him and cannot curve in upon itself in self-sufficiency [*sofern sie ganz und gar von ihm lebt*

---

to God's existence, 'the circle of the *cogitare* is never broken through. He never penetrates to the region of the *esse*' (III/1, p. 359; discussion on pp. 350–63). Superficial similarities aside, Descartes and Anselm construct antithetical proofs, the one beginning with anthropocentric doubt, the other with theocentric confession. On Anselm's proof, see Karl Barth, *Anselm* (trans. Ian W. Robertson; London: SCM Press, 2nd end, 1960).

23.   The irony, of course, is that it is the priority given to the self in Schleiermacher that brings about an eclipse of the self. For an account of Schleiermacher's understanding and rediscovery of the embodied self, see Thandeka, 'Schleiermacher's Dialektik', *Harvard Theological Review* 85 (1992), pp. 433–52. As Thandeka notes, the self that he found was indistinct from the rest of reality, a 'nonindividuated part of the natural world', or simply itself 'the world' (p. 448). This is hardly the picture of a creature distinct from God and others who, because of this real distinction, can live in covenant partnership with God and others. That is, despite the appearance of relationality in Schleiermacherian monism, it cannot allow for *persons* in relation. This, despite Schleiermacher's own rich relational life, the spirit of which can be seen in Schleiermacher, *Christmas Eve*.

24.   Joseph L. Mangina, *Karl Barth on the Christian Life* (New York: Peter Lang, 2001), p. 31. On Barth's retrieval of experience, see pp. 32–45. On the early Barth's relation to Pietism, see Eberhard Busch, *Karl Barth and the Pietists* (trans. Daniel W. Bloesch; Downers Grove, IL: InterVarsity Press, 2004).

25.   Mangina, *Karl Barth on the Christian Life*, p. 37. It seems likely that, in his zeal to resist any interpretation of creaturely reality that would speak of the creature 'possessing' God or anything good in a way that renders God's continued activity unnecessary, Barth failed to sufficiently account for the various ways in which creatures relate to Jesus. *That* to be human means to be always already related to Jesus was his anthropological *leitmotif*; but his description of *how* this relation is embodied in the Christian community, while clearly showing signs of deepening over the course of his career, has been roundly and probably rightly criticized.

und gerade nicht sich selbst genügend in sich selber kreist]' (*CD* IV/1, p. 249; *KD* IV/1, p. 274).

Despite superficial similarities with and an obvious indebtedness to Luther's use of *incurvatus in se* as an organizing scheme for understanding sin and countering the anthropocentrism of mediaeval theology, Barth criticizes Luther for a similar self-enclosure. This can be seen most strikingly in Barth's early lectures on the Reformed confessions. In comparing Lutheran and Reformed theology, Barth argues as follows: Where Reformed theology speaks of God, Lutheran theology speaks of faith.[26] While Luther is insistent that Christ is present in faith, Lutheran theology on the whole threatens to turn faith into a pseudo-work, or at least veers towards subjectivism. In the Reformed insistence on starting and staying with God, we hear that faith (as well as works!) is a gift of God. Where Reformed theologians argue that *God* saves through faith, Lutherans hammer home the fact that God saves through *faith*. The former ask *who* saves us, the latter *how* we are saved.[27] Barth argues that for Luther 'faith is somewhat hypostatic; it functions in some ways like a mythological intermediary'.[28] Often for Luther, faith becomes 'a god that tolerates nothing next to it', not even obedience.[29] Because of these varying emphases, Barth argues, Reformed theology has always done a better job of speaking of faith and obedience, justification and sanctification together. Further, and this is key to Barth's point, speaking of faith focuses our attention on the human agent.[30] The gospel becomes a message that is *first* about

---

26.   At the end of his life, Barth will speak of 'invocation' as the form of the Christian life. See the comparison of faith and prayer as the 'leading motifs of Luther's and Barth's moral ontologies' in Webster, *Barth's Moral Theology*, pp. 151–78 (176). The theocentric thrust remains in prayer, but a subtle shift has taken place. Barth now sees the 'anthropological correlate of grace' as 'not only dependence or contingency but also our *specification* to be active in the space and within the limits allotted to us by God. Grace limits, but in limiting grace *shapes*'. It is as if Luther's implicit anthropocentric orientation has handcuffed him into seeing humanity as pure passivity while Barth's theocentric stance has freed him to articulate a real, if derived (and *just so* real) activity.

27.   See Karl Barth, *The Theology of the Reformed Confessions* (trans. Darrell L. Guder and Judith J. Guder; London: Westminster/John Knox Press, 2002), pp. 72, 78, 81, 150. The difference between these two approaches explains why Barth considered the confession of Christ rather than justification the *articulus stantis et cadentis ecclesiae*. It should be said, though, that he thought that Luther would probably agree (IV/1, pp. 527–28). Jüngel's diatribe against Barth's move (arguing that 'this is precisely the function of the doctrine of justification: to convey the being and work of Jesus Christ for us, to us and with us') is more a disagreement about Luther and the extent to which his theology tends toward the uniting or cleaving of Christ and faith than it is a material difference over the content of justification. (Jüngel, *Justification*, pp. 18–31 [28–29]).

28.   Barth, *The Theology of the Reformed Confessions*, p. 98. For an important connection of this point with Feuerbach's theory of projection, see Barth, 'An Introductory Essay' (trans. James Luther Adams), in Ludwig Feuerbach, *The Essence of Christianity* (trans. George Eliot; New York: Harper & Row, 1957), pp. x–xxxii (xxii–xxiii).

29.   Barth, *The Theology of the Reformed Confessions*, p. 100.

30.   It might be objected that Scripture itself speaks of the power of faith without reference to its object, and not just in the Pauline epistles. In the story of the ten lepers who

us and only then about God. While its content is clearly twofold, for Barth, the gospel is only heard aright as first a proclamation about God which only then makes possible a word about humanity. The upshot is this: Lutheran theology (and this in relative, if not complete continuity with its namesake) is insufficiently concerned with theology and succumbs to anthropology, falling prey to the very thing against which Luther fought so rabidly.

But is Barth right, and if he is, is it Luther's fault? Tuomo Mannermaa has argued persuasively for the importance of the 'Christ present in faith' in Luther's theology, such that to say 'faith' is always also to say 'Christ'.[31] As Barth himself notes, the language of faith should run throughout good theology, provided we simply remember that faith is a 'relative concept' which 'lives by its object'.[32] The danger is in forgetting this relation, relegating it to a matter of secondary importance or simply failing to call attention to it. It is arguable that Luther did not extend his critique of anthropocentric religion far enough, instead replacing a crass anthropocentrism with a more subtle, more 'religious' (in all the ambiguity of that term) anthropocentrism. Might Luther's not represent, on one level, a theology *curvatum in se* for just this reason?

At the very least, a trajectory of Lutheran interpretation can be traced along these lines. This can be seen in changing understandings of faith. Luther rightly criticized mediaeval notions of faith as mere assent which left people spectators rather than believers, in the full-orbed sense of the word. Luther countered by placing an unprecedented emphasis on faith as *fiducia*, or trust; but he naturally continued to assume a sense of faith as assent (*fides*) to the teaching of Scripture and, derivatively, the creeds and ecumenical councils. Furthermore, the believer's trust was always to be in an external

---

were cleansed (Lk. 17.11-21), Jesus says to the one Samaritan leper who returned, 'Rise, and go your way; your faith has made you well' (v. 19). There is no word here about *God* saving. But the context clearly ties this healing faith to its object. The incident begins when the ten lepers cry to Jesus at a distance to have mercy on them (v. 13). Then this one whose faith made him well returns, falling at Jesus' feet and giving glory to God (vv. 15-16). So when Jesus says that the man's faith made him well, he simply uses a shortened version of 'faith in Jesus/God as the one who is Lord and can make people well'. Luther uses a similar shorthand, by and large, in his talk of faith.

31.   See Mannermaa, *Christ Present in Faith*. Arguing the centrality of union with Christ in Luther, Mannermaa goes as far as to say that the personal union between Christ and the believer is such that the Christian's life '*is*, in an ontologically real manner, Christ himself' (p. 39). The two form one person, and so we can follow Luther in saying that 'faith makes a [person] God' (p. 43). Similarly, Joest points out that 'in faith a daily *adventus Christi* occurs'. Christ's presence in faith allows us to hold together the 'forensic' and 'effective' aspects of justification together such that the Christian's righteousness '*remains* alien righteousness and that *nevertheless* the beginning of a new life and concrete works of faith can be spoken of' (Joest, *Ontologie der Person bei Luther*, pp. 369, 376).

32.   'New Testament faith does not curve in upon itself or centre on itself as *fides qua creditor* [*Der neutestamentliche Glaube kreist nicht als* fides qua creditor *in oder um sicht selber*]' (CD IV/1, p. 248; KD IV/1, p. 273).

Word of God (Scripture and sacraments), never a false internal one.[33] But the characteristic verve with which Luther emphasized *fiducia* (at times to the apparent exclusion of any concern with assent) left an (at least) affective mark on later Protestant theology, whose concern continued to be *fiducia*, and increasingly *fiducia* alone, divorced from its object. Such a historical sketch both exonerates Luther and implicates him. He is surely not responsible for Schleiermacher, but Barth's point is that attending to the human subject (*faith in God*) before attending to the divine subject (faith in *God*) always leads to a godless, relationless theology.[34] Thus an internal contradiction threatens in Luther's theology, which despite its theocentric thrust betrays a simultaneous inclination to curve in on itself.[35]

And yet, this cannot be the last word on Luther. His unfortunate tendency at times to speak at length about faith with precious few explicit references to Christ needs to be read in the context of one who seeks to witness to the freedom of a new life in Christ entered into by the sheer gift of faith. It also needs to be balanced by Luther's own adamant insistence on an eccentric understanding of human personhood that is fundamentally relational. Indeed, Mangina insists that 'the *force* of the reference' of the *pro me* (which is correlated with *fiducia*) is 'eccentric' such that 'statements about the self are finally Christological statements'.[36] While Barth is right to correct (and at times maybe even over-correct) the later divorce of faith from its object, this error can only very provisionally and parenthetically be place at the feet of Luther.[37]

33.   On the importance of sacramental theology for Luther's 'discovery' and its marking a 'turn toward the very heart of the catholic tradition' rather than away from it, see David S. Yeago, 'The Catholic Luther', *First Things* 61 (1996), pp. 37–41.

34.   This is why Barth 'plays down justification by faith alone as the "subjective side" of justification' in favour of its objectivity in Christ (Wolf Krötke, *Sin and Nothingness* [Princeton: Princeton Theological Seminary, 2005], p. 86).

35.   Barth mentions, not without sympathy, Feuerbach's claim that theology had become anthropology since Protestantism, 'and especially Luther, emphatically shifted the interest from what God is in himself to what God is for man' (Barth, 'An Introductory Essay', p. xix). Feuerbach wrote a book on *The Essence of Faith in Luther*. Herrmann, too, saw himself in continuity with Luther. Note the subtitle of the work for which he is known, *The Communion of the Christian with God: Described on the Basis of Luther's Statements*.

36.   Mangina, *Karl Barth on the Christian Life*, p. 55.

37.   Still, Luther's failure to make this tie explicit with due frequency sped along the theologically lazy (not to mention heretical) severance of faith from its object. At the same time, and without commenting in depth on the debate about the relation between Luther and Lutherans in general and Luther and Melanchthon in particular, it may be more appropriate to point to Melanchthon's claim in the 1521 edition of the *Loci Communes* that we are to know Christ according to his benefits as the main source of the severance of faith and its object. And yet, Melanchthon does not posit any split between the person and work of Christ and he is abundantly clear in a chapter on the word 'faith' in the 1555 edition of the *Loci* that faith is a reliance upon Christ. He does not separate faith and its object (*Melanchthon on Christian Doctrine* [trans. Clyde L. Manschreck; Grand Rapids: Baker, 1982], pp. 158–59). Mangina, following Hans Joachim-Iwand, points to Kant's distinction between pure and practical reason, and his restriction of our knowledge of God to the latter as the culprit (Mangina, *Karl Barth on the Christian Life*, p. 56).

A second problem of general anthropology is that it only yields the phenomenon of the human ('symptoms'), not real humanity. Speaking about these ambiguous phenomenal observations of humanity apart from the context of real man (who is always in relation to God) is like speaking 'about knives without edges, or handles without pots, or predicates without subjects'.[38] Theological anthropology, on the other hand, treats man *himself*.[39] Thus, for knowledge of real man, our self-understanding 'must be reversed and refounded, being changed from an autonomous into a theonomous self-understanding'.[40] With this proviso in place, Barth can accommodate and even enthusiastically make use of insights from non-theological accounts of humanity, which can be genuine as long as they presuppose the theological.[41] There is no place for self-confidence in non-theological anthropologies, which must remain provisional and partial in the service of theology.[42]

But there is a still more pointed reason for Barth's beginning of anthropology with Christology. Barth envisions nothing short of the complete displacing of humanity by and in Christ. Consider the following statements:

> Jesus Christ as very man and very God has taken the place of every man. He has penetrated to that place where every man is in his inner being supremely by and for himself. This sanctuary belongs to Him and not to man. He has to do what has to be done there. What is man in relation to Him? One who is dispossessed, expelled, a displaced person. He has no more say even in this home of his.

This is what it means to say: 'He is radically and totally for us, in our place'.[43]

> His [i.e., Jesus'] existence, therefore, is the decision who and what they are and are not with what they do and do not do; the decision as to their whence and whither. Thus the decision is taken wholly and once for all out of their hands. It is no longer a matter of what they themselves think.[44]

At the cross, according to Barth, there was a 'complete replacement [*Beseitigung*]...of the man of sin'.[45]

---

38.   *CD* III/2, p. 76. John Macken puts Barth's point well, recognizing the value of such phenomenal observations when they are put in service of revelation: 'Everything which can be thought and said about man reads like a commentary on an unseen text which must first be read before the commentary makes sense' (Macken, *The Autonomy Theme*, p. 54).

39.   *CD* III/2, p. 25.

40.   *CD* III/2, p. 125.

41.   *CD* III/2, pp. 199–202.

42.   *CD* III/2, pp. 22–6. Theology, it should be noted, must itself remain provisional and partial in the service of the Word of God.

43.   *CD* IV/1, p. 232.

44.   *CD* IV/2, p. 395.

45.   *CD* IV/2, p. 400. *KD* IV/2, pp. 448–9. See also the editors' comment on '*Stellvertretung*' as more radical and comprehensive than its English equivalents of 'representation' and 'substitution' (IV/1, p. vii).

Our dis-placement by Christ is not the final word, however. We have been re-placed by him, both in the sense that he has taken our place and in the sense that he has given us a new place. Christ is the one who squeezes us out and, precisely in so doing, creates space for us to live.[46] Barth radicalizes Augustine's concept of the *totus Christus*.[47] For both, to say 'Christ' is to say 'Christ and his members'. Barth's expansion is in (1) his holding to the assumption of *all* of humanity (i.e., each human) in Christ and (2) the sheer thoroughness with which he applies the *totus Christus* to Christology, ecclesiology and anthropology. The universality of the scope of the *totus Christus*[48] carries with it the ethical implication that we are to look on other people 'with hope'.[49] God gives new being to all people in Christ. Christians exist in Christ as examples, representatives and predecessors of all other men and women. The new being is reflected in the Christian, but not (or not yet) in the non-Christian. They do not lack the new being; they lack the obedience to his Holy Spirit.[50] There is a *de jure*, if not a (in the weak sense) *de facto* participation of all of humanity in Christ's new humanity which requires that all statements made of the man Jesus Christ be extended to include those who are in him.

Barth's deference to an *analogia relationis* (following Bonhoeffer)[51] grounds the *totus Christus* in the life of the triune God.[52] There is an analogy between the relation within God (Father–Son) and the relation between God and humanity (Son–disciples). The second term in this analogy 'follows the essence, the inner being of God. It is this inner being which takes this form *ad extra* in the humanity of Jesus.'[53] Just as one cannot speak of the Father without speak-

---

46.   The only place left for us to stand is in 'that of the One who expatriated us by becoming ours' (IV/1, p. 75).

47.   Most of Augustine's references to the *totus Christus* are in his sermons on the Psalms and 1 John. To take one example: 'And today it is still one person who speaks in all nations and all tongues, one man, Head and body, one person who is Christ and the Church, a perfect man, he the bridegroom, she the bride' (Augustine, 'Exposition 2 of Psalm 18', in *Expositions of the Psalms 1–32*, vol. 1 [trans. Maria Boulding; Hyde Park, NY: New City Press, 2000], p. 210). Barth's references are scattered throughout Volume IV in particular of the *Church Dogmatics*. See, e.g., IV/2, pp. 675–6, 679 (where he speaks of a 'christologico-ecclesiological concept of the community'), p. 835.

48.   'God from all eternity has chosen man (all men) in this One' (IV/1, p. 91).

49.   CD IV/1, p. 58. Note that even here Barth is clear: 'But if we do not look exclusively to Jesus Christ and therefore to God we lose the capacity on this basis to think inclusively'.

50.   CD IV/1, p. 92–3.

51.   See Dietrich Bonhoeffer, *Creation and Fall* (trans. Douglas Stephen Box; Minneapolis: Fortress Press, 1997), pp. 65–6.

52.   Douglas Farrow notes that 'the *totus Christus* idea obviously serves as a powerful brake on individualism'. Hence its natural fit with the *analogia relationis*. The danger with such a concept, according to Farrow, is that the Church comes to be seen as an extension of the incarnation in Augustine and, despite his own protestations against such an extension, as a secondary form of the incarnation in Barth. As a consequence, the Church improperly usurps Christ's mediatorial role as priest. See Douglas Farrow, *Ascension and Ecclesia* (Grand Rapids: Eerdmans, 1999), pp. 122, 253. At the same time, Barth is clear that, while 'Jesus Christ is the community', 'the community is not Jesus Christ' (IV/2, p. 655).

53.   CD III/2, p. 220.

ing of the Son (as the Cappadocians would put it), so one cannot speak of the Son without speaking of his disciples, the head without his members.[54]

Christology as the starting point of hamartiology

Apart from his methodological concern to begin anthropology with God's self-revelation in Christ, Barth also acknowledges a pragmatic problem with beginning at any other point: 'To "start from man" can only mean to start with man of the lost *status integritatis*, that is, of the presently existing *status corruptionis*'. Such a starting point will yield only humanity in its sin, not as it was created.[55] The consequence is clear: 'There is a way from Christology to anthropology. There is no way from an anthropology to Christology'.[56] Barth goes a step further, though, in his insistence that knowledge of *sinful* humanity is found only in Christ. The sweep of the grand reconciliation narrative of *Church Dogmatics* IV, which is structured according to the parable of the prodigal or lost son, can be seen programmatically summed up in a passage from the opening part-volume of his dogmatics nearly twenty years earlier:

> The knowledge that 'I have sinned...and am no more worthy to be called thy son' (Luke 15:18f.) is not the discovery of an abstract anthropology. Only the son who has already recalled to mind the father's house is aware that he is a lost son. We are first and only aware of being God's enemies, because God has actually established intercourse with us.[57]

It is hardly surprising from this early statement that Barth denies a discrete locus to sin in his dogmatics, one which traditionally would be found between the doctrines of creation and reconciliation. Instead, sin is placed *within* the doctrine of reconciliation, and in each of the three part-volumes even the paragraph dealing with sin begins with a consideration of 'The Man of Sin in the Light of' Jesus Christ.

Barth realizes the novelty of such a move, and yet he insists that such novelty hides a deeper faithfulness to the *old* story of God's redemptive work in Christ. That is, it is not the novelty of heresy but a re-hearing of the gospel that shows up the heretical orientation of other hamartiologies.[58] Looking for another source for the knowledge of sin is itself sinful.[59]

54.   The central role of Jesus' high priestly prayer in John 17 is the background of all of this, of course.

55.   This runs parallel to Luther's mocking critique of the philosophers who assume that creation can be sufficiently accounted for without recourse to eschatology, as if its present state of 'groaning and waiting' were the whole story. See page 74–5 above.

56.   CD I/1, p. 148 (trans. Thomson).

57.   CD I/1, pp. 466–7 (trans. Thomson).

58.   He realizes that he has to do so 'carefully, because we are on a way which has hardly been trodden before; but resolutely, because from what we have seen there is no other way open' (IV/1, p. 397).

59.   CD IV/1, pp. 389–90.

And yet, the question stands: 'Why have we not followed the example of the dogmatics of all ages, Churches and movements and begun with a doctrine of sin?'[60] Why not take the customary problem–solution–appropriation approach? First, the knowledge of sin is a part of the knowledge of God and is therefore an article of faith (p. 359). As an article of faith, sin is not something man can know 'of himself, by communing with himself, or by conversation with his fellow-men, any more than he can know in this way that he is justified and comforted by God' (p. 360). We *may* be able to come to a knowledge of ourselves as limited, deficient, imperfect, but such knowledge is 'not by a long way' a knowledge of ourselves as sinners (p. 360). We lack this knowledge precisely because we are sinners. We are 'crooked even in the knowledge of [our] crookedness' and thus 'can only oppose the Word of God which enlightens and instructs [us] concerning [our] crookedness' (p. 361).

But there is a further problem with the traditional dogmatic location of sin. It presupposes a split between law and gospel and a division in the knowledge and Word of God. This approach works in abstraction, with an abstract notion of God *in se* and his claim on humanity, when in reality 'a division of God in Christ and a god outside Christ is quite impossible' (p. 363).[61] As a result, God is turned into an idol, and his 'real Law is emptied of content' (p. 365). So Barth attacks philosophical approaches to the knowledge of sin, but he also attacks biblicist ones. For all their commitment to the Scriptures as the revelation of God's Word, the Reformers did not sufficiently allow their reading of Scripture to be ruled by and orientated to its centre and *skopos* in Christ (p. 366). Had they done so, they would have found sin and the law within the contours of the gospel.[62]

This is not a matter of choosing one set of categories and commitments over another for Barth, as though a prior commitment to 'unity' or even 'Christology' in abstract constrained his reading of Scripture and his critique of tradition on this point. What is the controlling element, then? Why does he feel compelled here?

---

60.   *CD* IV/1, p. 359. The following quotations are from *CD* IV/1, with page numbers in parentheses in the body of the text.

61.   Though he fails to mention this, a similar division between creation and covenant would result. For Barth, the covenant is the internal basis of creation and creation the external basis of the covenant (see *CD* III/1). So in seating the doctrine of sin within the covenant's fulfilment in reconciliation, Barth establishes sin's vanquishing as the vindication of creation. In light of this close connection between creation and covenant, David Kelsey's suggestion that Barth's theology evidences a 'migration' of sin from its traditional home in the doctrine of creation to a new home in Christology is misleading (even if his description is helpful) (Kelsey, 'Whatever Happened to the Doctrine of Sin?', *Theology Today* 50 (1993), pp. 169–78).

62.   Luther and Melanchthon are critiqued for just such a failure (IV/1, pp. 396–7). In the background here is Barth's inversion of Luther's ordering of law–gospel, his rejection of any 'natural' theology that refuses to begin with revelation, and his broader critique of an *ordo salutis*.

> Not because we can find and produce another and better method, the christological, but because Jesus Christ Himself is present, living and speaking and attesting and convincing; because in this matter we need not and cannot and should not speak to ourselves...We hear Him and we hear this verdict. We see Him, and in this mirror we see ourselves. (pp. 389–90).

It is the presence of the crucified and risen Lord, his own authoritative speaking, which precludes any autonomous word on our part. His speech constrains ours, and so even hamartiology is Christological. When Jesus speaks, we hear God's verdict on him and us in him. It is in this verdict, which God issued in raising Jesus from the dead, that God 'unmasks this old man, showing what every man is before God, and therefore what I myself am before Him, the man who is judged and put to death and destroyed' (pp. 390–1). Here 'we learn what God knows about us, and therefore how it really is with us' (p. 391). This is what it means to call Jesus the 'mirror' in which we know ourselves as sinners judged, killed and raised to new life in him.[63]

Were we to accord a discrete place to sin in dogmatics, were we to attempt to see it apart from Christ, we would be giving it far too much credence and denying Jesus' true witness to us of sin's vanquishing. This would be to give sin a power which it does not have: 'It is neither a creature nor itself a creator...it is quite unproductive'.[64] Besides, giving autonomous place to sin would be to fail to correspond to Scripture – 'For what is the ontological place of sin in the Bible?'[65] And, in that we have bypassed grace in so doing, 'is not this necessarily to sin again – theologically!'[66]

But is Barth *right* to begin hamartiology with Christology? Might the doctrine of sin not present a special case wherein we can in all propriety begin someplace else? Does the Christian confession of the sinlessness of Christ not give sufficient justification to look elsewhere? What can a sinless God-man tell us about sinful humanity? Consider the objection of Robert Williams:

> If the meaning of sin is entirely generated out of the symbols and concepts of soteriology, no real insight is obtained into sin and evil as aspects of human experience. It was precisely its genuine existential and phenomenological insights into the human experience of evil that made the Augustinian tradition so persuasive and powerful... Moreover, [Augustine's and Aquinas'] discussions of concupiscence can be appreciated to a considerable extent apart from soteriology and Christology.[67]

---

63.   On Christ as 'mirror', see *CD* IV/1, pp. 390, 397, 413.

64.   *CD* IV/1, p. 139.

65.   *CD* IV/1, p. 139. Also see III/2, p. 37.

66.   *CD* IV/1, p. 141.

67.   Robert R. Williams, 'Sin and Evil', in Peter Hodgson and Robert King (eds), *Christian Theology* (Minneapolis: Fortress Press, 1994), pp. 168–95 (210). Stanley Hauerwas (whose critique drew my attention to Williams' article) critiques Williams' claim that sin is any easier to know and describe than *God* and argues that Augustine's account of sin under a supposed general anthropology is in reality Augustine following Paul back through Christ to understand humanity in Adam. That is, it is a hamartiology developed from soteriology. He further objects to the notion that sin is any less a confession of faith than is Christ.

Williams' objection, and his conclusion that Christian theology must remain 'committed to an anthropological account of evil',[68] amounts to the judgement that speaking directly of Jesus Christ and only indirectly of humanity *en masse* fails to provide adequate resources for a proper understanding of what it means to be human. As such, it can be read as a rejection of Barth's particularism in favour of a universal or general anthropology. Surely this is heightened by the Christian confession that Jesus is sinless and thus the *form* of his particularity (which, of course, is not exhausted by his sinlessness), whether or not Williams himself personally subscribes to such a view. But the more basic claim seems to be that one person (particularly *this* one person) cannot tell us enough about humanity *per se*.

As Barth himself would confess, the only answer to such an objection is a re-description of the man of sin as seen in the light of Jesus. How far this suffices is a question of the phenomenological richness of the description, and so we will have to consider whether Barth has delivered an account of sin that is both theologically proper and phenomenologically potent. But we must heed the caution of Barth and not become so concerned with (apologetic?) description of sin that we lose sight of its vanquishing in Christ.[69] Indeed, if Barth is correct, it will only be in a seemingly irrelevant attending to Christ's victory that the sin he defeated will come in to focus.

Humanity Through a Christological Lens: A Closer Look

What do we see, then, when we look at Christ? Barth answers this question through a portrayal of the life and death of Jesus as the one, true human ('*Ecce homo!*') who provides the pattern for humanity.[70] From this perspective, 'to sin is to wander from a path which does not cease to be the definite and exclusive path of man even though he leaves it' (III/2, p. 227).

From the outset of his explication of Jesus as the one, true man, Barth highlights the constitutive relationality of the humanity of Jesus. Jesus is

See Stanley Hauerwas, '"Salvation even in Sin"', in *Sanctify Them in the Truth* (Nashville: Abingdon Press), pp. 61–74. Bernard Lohse agrees, arguing that 'the Christian doctrine of sin, as well as the Christian doctrine of grace, were developed in their decisive aspects from the perspective of Christology' (Bernard Lohse, *A Short History of Christian Doctrine* [trans. F. Ernest Stoeffler; Philadelphia: Fortress Press, 1985], p. 101).

68. Williams, 'Sin and Evil', p. 211.

69. Barth railed against apologetics throughout his career, seeing in it a capitulation to a logic foreign to the gospel, a failed attempt to establish a point of contact for the gospel or, as he called it early in his career, 'anxiety concerning the victory of the Gospel' (Karl Barth, *The Epistle to the Romans* [trans. Edwyn C. Hoskyns; Oxford: Oxford University Press, 6th edn, 1933], p. 35).

70. There are a number of angles from which Barth approaches Christ as the true human to which we cannot afford attention at this point. The most significant of these are the perspective of the passion of Christ, which reveals the sinful humanity whose reconciliation 'requires' such radical suffering, and the resurrection of Christ, which reveals the sinful humanity justified in Christ as God raises him from the dead.

Emmanuel, God with us.[71] And he is us with God. He is the eventful history in which God helps and humanity is helped, in which God establishes and confirms humans as his covenant-partners and they in turn live lives of free, joyful, grateful partnership with him. Jesus simply *is* 'man for God' and 'man for other men', and it is as such that he is 'real man'.[72] The Christian message is a 'common statement' which essentially includes a statement about humanity, but which is *primarily* a statement about God (IV/1, p. 3). Because God in Christ is with and for humanity, humanity in Christ can be and is with and for God. There is not, nor can there be any neutrality on God's part towards humanity or on humanity's part towards God. The 'original thing' about God and man, that 'I shall be your God' and 'Ye shall be my people', breaks out in Jesus; and this is the basic determination of God and humanity as seen in him (IV/1, p. 42).

To begin with, then, Jesus is 'man for God'. We are to understand this historically, not statically. Jesus' being for God is an activity, a continual movement or series of movements in one direction (III/2, p. 57). Jesus' determination to be for God is thus not to be sought for 'behind' the text of the Gospels; rather is it to be equated with his acts as recorded by the Gospels. Any quest for a 'historical' Jesus immediately forsakes him *in his very history*, which constitutes him, which he *is*.[73] Being and act, person and works are identified here.

It is worth noting in passing Barth's divergence from Luther on this point. Luther distinguishes person and works for the sake of clarifying that the one who sins is already a sinner (works growing out of the person, like fruit from a tree).[74] His polemic is against those who would treat sin as extrinsic and not in *some* way determinative. He also wants to affirm the bondage of a will which can only confirm in sinful actions a person's (at least logically) prior status as sinner. Barth takes a more radical step in insisting that we can make no distinction between person and works, emphasizing the role of sinful action in the (un-)making of the human person. Who we are is nothing more or less than what we do.[75] That 'all have sinned' points to the utter reality that all are

---

71.   'What unites God and us men is that He does not will to be God without us', such that 'we ourselves are in the sphere of God' (IV/1, p. 7). '"God with us" carries with it in all seriousness a "We with God"' (p. 14). As a result, human 'godlessness' is strictly impossible (III/2, p. 136), as is God's 'manlessness' (IV/1, p. 480). Note that Barth assumes humanity's structural openness to God, a common theme in theologians from Schleiermacher to Rahner which we might expect him to dismiss as 'semi-Pelagian' or 'anthropocentric'. But he grounds this openness and the knowledge of it radically *extra se* in Christ. See Wolf Krötke, 'The Humanity of the Human Person', in Webster (ed.), *The Cambridge Companion to Karl Barth*, pp. 159–76 (160).

72.   Barth titles sections of CD III/2 'Jesus, Man for God' (§44.1) and 'Jesus, Man for other Men' (§45.1).

73.   CD III/2, p. 57. 'Jesus does not merely have a history but is Himself this history' (p. 60). He is a Way, not an idea (p. 56).

74.   See pages 63–5 above.

75.   In this, humanity corresponds to God, whose being in act is a being as the one who loves in freedom.

sinners. He rejects the notion of hereditary sin communicated by propagation (an 'extremely unfortunate and mistaken' idea) not because it shuts humanity up in sin or is too pessimistic, but because it obscures the acknowledgment that 'it is still his *peccatum*, that act in which he makes himself a prisoner and therefore has to be a prisoner'.[76] Barth departs from Luther, Calvin and the vast majority of Protestant theologians at this point, though not from an underestimation of sin, as one might think.[77] In fact, Barth critiques the notion of hereditary sin for not taking sin seriously enough. If anything, it offers a way out, an Adamic alibi in the face of which our guilt loses its sharpness and can hardly be damning (IV/1, pp. 499–501).[78]

Returning, then, to Jesus' existence 'for God', Barth offers a negative definition in his claim that to say that Jesus and, therefore, humanity exists for God is to say that he does not exist for himself (III/2, p. 133). God is the one who loves in freedom. Indeed, 'so seriously is love self-giving that [the life of the one who loves] is an "eccentric" life, i.e., one which has its centre outside itself. This is what God does when He loves us' (IV/2, p. 788).[79] The true human life of Jesus is one in which God accomplishes his work of 'turning man away from his sin and to Himself, and summoning him to obedience to His will' (IV/2, p. 772). This obedience takes the form of joyful, grateful response in a life lived in correspondence to God's free, self-giving love.[80] As such, Jesus' being-in-act 'for God' is a life turned towards God, one which follows his direction. We are those who have been set in a definite direction in Christ,[81] a direction which has the geographical character of indication, the critical character of warning or correction and the positive character of instruction (IV/2, p. 362). Thus an analogy obtains: 'Yahweh Himself has turned to His people, thus taking up its action into fellowship with His own, determining and qualifying it from the very first as an action which responds or corresponds to His own, being the "analogue" of His own "Logos"' (IV/2, pp. 780–81). Humanity's 'Yes', its grateful affirmation of God's Word, can only have 'the force and reach of an echo' (III/2, p. 188). But it can and may

76. '"Hereditary sin" has a hopelessly naturalistic, deterministic and even fatalistic ring' (IV/1, p. 501).

77. Barth follows Calvin, though, in his eschewal of speculation vis-à-vis original sin and 'the nature of pre-fallen humanity' and offers a consequently 'minimalist' account of original sin (Allen Jorgenson, 'Karl Barth's Christological Treatment of Sin', *Scottish Journal of Theology* 54 [2001], pp. 437–62 [447]).

78. Barth eventually follows Calvin in using the language of imputation, estimation, attribution and adjudication to describe our being in Adam (IV/1, p. 511). He is clear, though, that our being in Adam can only be understood in light of our being in Christ (IV/1, pp. 512–13).

79. See further the discussion of 'Ec-centric Existence and the Centrality of Hope', in William Stacy Johnson, *The Mystery of God* (Louisville, KY: Westminster/John Knox Press, 1997), pp. 176–83.

80. As Nicholas Healy puts it, we 'turn cheerfully away from ourselves' (Nicholas M. Healy, 'Karl Barth's Ecclesiology Reconsidered', *Scottish Journal of Theology* 57 [2004], pp. 287–97 [299]).

81. See §64.4 on 'The Direction of the Son' (IV/2, pp. 264–377).

and must have such a reach. To say that Jesus, and humanity in him, lives for God is also to say that he does not live for himself.

But that he does not live for himself also means Jesus is 'man for other men'. The direction we have received in him is towards other men and women as well as God. 'When we think of the humanity of the man Jesus, humanity is to be described unequivocally as fellow-humanity' (III/2, p. 208). This is why there is no interest in the 'private life' of Jesus in the Gospels.[82] Even his private life with God (as Father and Son) is *for others* (III/2, p. 209). The incarnation is strictly of soteriological significance (cf. the 'for us and our salvation' of Nicea [III/2, p. 210]); the *pro nobis* does not follow on (after) the *in se* of Jesus (III/2, pp. 210–11).[83] 'If we see Him alone, we do not see Him at all.' And yet: '"Selfless" is hardly the word to describe this humanity. Jesus is not "selfless." For in this way He is supremely Himself...What emerges in it [the New Testament] is a supreme I wholly determined by and to the Thou' (III/2, p. 216). Here, then, is the correspondence between Jesus' being for God and his being for man (III/2, p. 219), the *analogia relationis* between the relation within God and the relation between God and humanity (III/2, pp. 220–2).

Humanity, christologically defined, is fundamentally *relational* in its constitution. Whatever else we may say, humanity cannot be thought of as self-enclosed but must be seen in some sense as 'open and related to God Himself' (III/2, p. 72). The fact that in Jesus God is with us means that, like it or not, we are with God. Our fellowship with Jesus means a confrontation with the divine other such that 'to be a man is to be with God' (III/2, p. 135). The same applies horizontally. To be human is to be with other women and men. We do not see man at all if we see him 'in and for himself', in isolation, or in opposition or neutrality towards others – or if we see him as only accidentally related to others (III/2, pp. 226–7). 'In the Christian Church we have no option but to interpret humanity as fellow-humanity. And *si quis dixerit hominem esse solitarium, anathema sit*' (III/2, p. 319). But is this self-evidently Christian? It is if we understand the logic of the incarnation. And it is if Nietzsche was right about Christianity.[84] Nietzsche is the prophet of 'humanity without the fellow-man. He did not merely reveal its secret; he blabbed it out.' He was the

---

82.   This is also, presumably, why certain moments receive thick description (e.g., Passion Week) while other long stretches of time are passed over completely (e.g., Jesus' childhood).

83.   Rom. 8.31 ('If God is for us, who is against us?') summarizes the entire New Testament, according to Barth (III/2, p. 213). So Jüngel describes God's essential 'outgoingness' and Jenson speaks of his 'roominess' (Jüngel, *Karl Barth*, p. 132; Robert W. Jenson, *Systematic Theology 1* [Oxford: Oxford University Press, 1997], p. 226).

84.   For all his castigation of Nietzsche, Feuerbach, Schleiermacher and Bultmann (to name a few of his favourite targets), Barth maintains a remarkable attentiveness and openness to learning from them. His reading of them often (though not always) embodies a true 'encounter' in which he listens and speaks with respect as well as criticism. So, in this instance, Nietzsche proves an ally who 'got the point' of the gospel's relational mandate, even though his violent reaction to it must be rejected. For a subtle reading of Barth in relation to Schleiermacher, see Johnson, *The Mystery of God*.

consummate projectionist, only ever talking about himself. Nietzsche's commitment to individualism was the very *basis* of his rejection of Christianity, according to Barth (III/2, p. 232; discussion on pp. 231–42). Yet Barth commends him for having 'hurled himself against the strongest and not the weakest point in the opposing front' (III/2, p. 242). That he could not stand the God who is for us does not mean that he did not grasp the significance of that *pro nobis*.[85]

In contrast to Nietzsche stands Jesus, whose humanity 'consists in His being for man'. We cannot be for others in quite the same way as Christ, as to be 'for' allows no reciprocity. But we can begin with 'the fact that the humanity of man consists in the determination of his being as a being with the other' (III/2, p. 243). Furthermore, we *can* be for another in a secondary, analogous sense and 'the preposition "for" augments the preposition "with"'.[86] 'We can support but not carry him, give him encouragement but not victory, alleviate but not liberate.'[87]

What does it mean to be with and for another? Here Barth draws heavily on Martin Buber.[88] To be human is to be related to another. 'The word "Thou," although it is a very different word, is immanent to "I." It is not a word which is radically alien, but one which belongs to it.' So, 'I am as I am in a relation'. This relation is not a state but a history of encounter between two people, such that '"I am"…may thus be paraphrased: "I am in encounter" [« *Ich bin* » … *ist also zu umschreiben: Ich bin in der Begegnung*].' Or more simply: 'I am as Thou art' (*CD* III/2, pp. 245–8; *KD* III/2, pp. 292–6).[89] Humanity's being-in-encounter involves (1) looking another in the eye (including openness to others and letting oneself be seen) (III/2, p. 250), (2)

85. In a sense, Nietzsche's allergic reaction to the social implications of the *Deus pro nobis* is more to the point than a cheap utopian picture that might arise of easy, comfortable community. For an account of the *pro nobis* in relation to participation in God in Barth, see Mangina, *Karl Barth on the Christian Life*, pp. 51–89. For a stringent critique of the (mis)appropriation of the *Deus pro nobis* in contemporary America's therapeutic culture (which sees it as one of two 'sources of the nice god'), see D. Stephen Long, 'God is Not Nice' in D. Brent Laytham (ed.), *God is Not…* (Grand Rapids: Eerdmans, 2004), pp. 39–54.

86. Stuart D. McLean, 'Creation and Anthropology' in John Thompson (ed.), *Theology Beyond Christendom* (Allison Park, PA: Pickwick Publications, 1986), pp. 111–42, (112). On the analogy of Christ's 'forness' and ours, see McLean, *Humanity in the Thought of Karl Barth*, p. 41.

87. McLean, *Humanity in the Thought of Karl Barth*, p. 41.

88. For a helpful outline of Barth's relationship to Buber, see Suzanne Selinger, *Charlotte von Kirschbaum and Karl Barth* (University Park, PA: The Pennsylvania State University Press, 1998), pp. 126–34.

89. Despite the emphasis here on reciprocity, there is an internal tension in Barth's thinking between such absolute reciprocity and a series of irreversible orders (e.g., man–woman). As a result of giving priority to the ordering of man and woman, the freedom of the *imago Dei* is compromised. It becomes a 'structure' rather than an 'event' in encounter. See Elouise Renich Fraser, 'Jesus' Humanity and Ours', in Marguerite Shuster and Richard Muller (eds.), *Perspectives on Christology* (Grand Rapids: Zondervan, 1991), pp. 179–96 (180–2, 184–5).

mutual speaking and hearing (III/2, p. 252),[90] (3) mutual assistance (III/2, p. 260) and (4) mutual gladness ('the secret of the whole') throughout (III/2, p. 265).[91] It is gladness which speaks of the component of relative autonomy (an autonomy which corresponds to God's autonomy) and an appropriate self-positing/self-determination (III/2, pp. 268–9). Gladness is therefore the form of human freedom in encounter.

The programmatic emphasis Barth places on encounter leads him to think of human relationality more in 'dyadic' than 'communal' terms, with the references to the communal tending towards 'abstract collectivities'.[92] Thus, while Barth's anthropology (and theology as a whole) is unprecedented in its relational form and content, the scope of this relationality remains unnecessarily limited by the I–Thou of encounter.[93] In particular, we might ask how the dyadic encounter between a believer and Jesus Christ offers a model for a more structurally complex encounter amongst believers in the Church. To reduce relations within the Church to a collection of dyadic encounters would be to do an injustice to the depth at which the Church represents a *social* and not merely *inter-personal* encounter.

We should be clear that Barth's is a *description* rather than a *prescription* of encounter. Given that Christ is real man and that all of humanity is elect in him, Barth's anthropology takes on a descriptive rather than idealistic cast.[94] He will present his vision of humanity not as something towards which we should strive but as something which is already true of us and to which we must correspond in daily life.[95]

> What is demanded is simply that man should not wander away but be himself in the best sense of the term, keeping to the determination which he has been given as a man. It is to be noted that at the place and in the form in which Christian anthropology sees him man cannot make the favourite excuse that too much is expected of him, that he is given too high and holy a destiny. On the contrary, all that he has to do is simply to

90.   With Luther and against Augustine, Barth privileges the verbal over the visual. See McLean, *Humanity in the Thought of Karl Barth*, p. 13.

91.   Barth notes that all this is not restricted to Christians. The 'children of this world' may know more about humanity and be more human than 'the often very inhuman and therefore foolish Christians' (III/2, p. 276).

92.   Selinger, *Charlotte von Kirschbaum and Karl Barth*, p. 136.

93.   For a comparison of the relational anthropologies of Barth (in terms of 'I–Thou encounter') and Pannenberg (in terms of 'exocentricity'), see Shults, *Reforming Theological Anthropology*, pp. 117–39.

94.   John Webster is right to remind us that 'Barth's anthropology is non-theoretical and non-utopian. He is not about the business of expounding an anthropological ideal, for to do so would simply repeat the error of thinking that human beings are at liberty to constitute themselves in ways of their own choosing. His aim is *descriptive*' (John Webster, 'Rescuing the Subject', in Geoff Thompson and Christiaan Mostert [eds.], *Karl Barth* [Hindmarsh: Australian Theological Forum, 2000], pp. 49–69 [57]).

95.   Note that 'a failure to understand the meaning and significance of Barth's conception of correspondence [*Entsprechung*] leads to errors of interpretation all along the line' (Kimlyn J. Bender, *Karl Barth's Christological Ecclesiology* [Aldershot: Ashgate, 2005], p. 177).

see himself in the situation in which he actually finds himself, keeping to this situation, and not trying to adapt himself to any other. (III/2, pp. 264–5)

No excuses are left because we have already been exalted to fellowship with God and one another in Christ. This is the freedom in which we have been set, where space has already been cleared for true (the only true) human action. Barth can say that our being is both gift and task, but it is only the latter as it is the former (III/2, p. 180). This is what must be said of us because it is true of Jesus.

In light of this, sin is defined not as the failure to realize or reach an abstract ideal of humanity but rather as the failure to conform or correspond to humanity's pattern and reality as it is given in Christ.[96] Sin is any attempt to be otherwise than who we are, that is, those who are with and for God and others. This attempt is always vain, accomplishing nothing. Not only are we morally wrong, but we are simply in error about what it means to be human.

> The error of man concerning himself, his self-alienation, is that he thinks he can love and choose and will and assert and maintain and exalt himself – *sese propter seipsum* – in his being in himself, his self-hood, and that in so doing he will be truly man. Whether this takes place more in pride or in modesty, either way man misses his true being. For neither as an individual nor in society was he created to be placed alone, to be self-controlling and self-sufficient, to be self-centred, to rotate around himself. Like every other creature he was created for the glory of God and only in that way for his own salvation...He is a man, himself, as he comes from God and moves towards God. He is a man as he is open to God, or not at all. If he chooses himself in any other way, *incurvatus in se*, in self-containment, then he misses the very thing that he seeks. (IV/1, p. 421)

Sin is the self-contradiction in which we live for ourselves in self-enclosure rather than for God and others. To sin is, for Barth, to be *homo incurvatus in se* and thereby attempt to be 'relationless man'.[97] Indeed, this phrase describes the total orientation of one's life, 'my determination for evil, the corrupt disposition and inclination of my heart' (IV/1, p. 500).[98] Barth sums up faithful God and faithless humanity as 'God utterly self-giving and man always turned in upon himself' (III/2, p. 35). Note that this is the case in the passage above 'whether this takes place more in pride or in modesty'. Incurvature is not to be equated without remainder with pride but includes its opposite.

---

96.   As Stacy Johnson points out, the danger of abstraction is just this sort of extrication of something from its context: '"To abstract" is to draw or pull something away from something else. To view something abstractly is to view it in disconnection from other things that are properly a part of it' (Johnson, *The Mystery of God*, p. 60).

97.   Barth rejects both naturalistic and idealistic/ethical approaches to the knowledge of man, because they see man as 'a self-contained reality' (III/2, p. 109). Fichte turns out to be the poster boy of an absolute idealism which treats of 'relationless man' and exhibits 'the lack of a limit, the fundamental lack of a counterpart' (III/2, pp. 96–109).

98.   This is Barth agreeing with Melanchthon's description.

Because sin is directed against a person rather than an abstract law of nature, relational rather than juridical categories are the fitting conceptual tools to describe it (IV/1, p. 140). The metaphor of incurvature, which carries with it the implication of having curved away from a relationship or relationships, fits well this relational character of sin. Sin is the refusal to conform to our determination in Christ to be relationally constituted and relationally directed. And the fact that even in the isolation which the metaphor conveys one cannot escape the reminder of the relationships which have been shunned underscores Barth's point that sin can only ever be self-contradiction, stopping short of self-transformation or the realization of a real, alternate possibility. Sin can only be an 'impossible possibility' (IV/1, pp. 409–10; IV/2, p. 495; IV/3.1, p. 463).[99]

As a case in point of sin as failure to conform to the pattern of humanity in Christ, and without anticipating too much of our discussion of sloth, we can take Barth's description of two false forms of encounter. The first occurs when we lose ourselves in the other and become property. This is an 'active subjection' which amounts to an erasure of otherness. Note that the harm here is done to the One *to whom* we are subject, not (or not only) to the one subjected (III/2, pp. 269–70). The second error is in seeking ourselves in the other. This is a 'passive subjection'. 'If in the other I seek myself at a higher or deeper level, the Thou is for me merely my extended I' (III/2, p. 270). What both misunderstandings have in common is an eliding of the distinction between self and other, which must be maintained even in an affirmation of the relationality of persons.[100] And this is harmful to both parties, for neither can be human apart from the real encounter of two people. Rather than being an encounter of two people with and for one another, each false form contradicts the truth of humanity in Christ by reducing the bi-polar nature of the relationship to one or the other pole.

It is a fair question to ask at this point whether, for all his methodological insistence on understanding humanity and sin christologically, Barth actually does so. After all, the relationality which he places at the heart of humanity

---

99.   Krötke notes that, whereas Barth had applied 'impossible possibility' to our knowledge of God in his earlier writing, by the time of his book on Anselm he limits its use to the description of sin and speaks of real knowledge of God (Krötke, *Sin and Nothingness*, p. 8). At times, Barth is forced to use extremely paradoxical language which some have criticized as nonsensical. However, terms like '"nothingness" and "impossible possibility" mean simply – and no more – that evil and sin, though they do exist inexplicably and factually, have no right to exist because they have been treated that way in Jesus Christ. Barth challenges someone to think of a better term' (Ron Highfield, *Barth and Rahner in Dialogue* [New York: Peter Lang, 1989], p. 158).

100.   So encounter is characterized by a freedom 'in which both keep their distance because they are so close, and are so close because they can keep their distance' (III/2, p. 272). Similarly, Volf highlights the need for an embrace which begins with an open-armed waiting and concludes with a letting go, that is, a refusal to engulf the other person even in the closeness of encounter. See Miroslav Volf, *Exclusion and Embrace* (Nashville: Abingdon Press, 1996).

and its violation in sin bears a striking resemblance to Buber's work, as well as overlapping significantly with personalism. Is he merely riding the wave of a particular (general?!) anthropology in vogue in the mid-twentieth century? That he was influenced along these lines cannot be doubted. But similarities, superficial or otherwise, with other schools of thought do not make Barth guilty of inconsistency vis-à-vis his stated methodology. It is as likely, and Barth would likely answer, that he found in personalist categories and Buber's notion of encounter categories which fit the gospel. Furthermore, he might suggest that the confluence of his and Buber's reflection is due as much to their reflection on the God of the Scriptures and his ways with the world as it is due to certain philosophical commitments. That this was Barth's *intention* can be seen explicitly in his replacing an *analogia entis* with the *analogia relationis*. Furthermore, despite what is viewed often as a harshly exclusive commitment to theological over against other modes of (secular) discourse, Barth used non-theological sources constantly and freely. Of course, to say that he did so *freely* is to say that he did so in the freedom which is the life lived in the direction given and commanded by God in Christ. That is, Barth's freedom in drawing from various sources involves (1) an *ad hoc*, eclectic employment of those sources (2) in service of, and in obedience to the logic of the Word of God.[101] The test of consistency, which falls outwith the scope of this chapter, must entail a detailed examination of the fittingness of the categories of relationality and encounter with the Scripture's witness to Christ.

Beyond this methodological point is one about the *character* of humanity's being in encounter as it is in Christ. Barth's is not a philosophical personalism without consequences, some golden vision of effortless communion. Nor is it the cautious conditional mutuality seen in many communitarian utopias. It is an unconditional commitment to be for others regardless of their stance towards oneself. That the triune God aims at (and accomplishes in Christ) the creation of covenant-partners to be in true relationships of mutual love with himself does not mean that these relationships are purchased cheaply. No, God being 'for us' means death – both his and ours in Christ. In turn, our being for and with others takes the form this side of the eschaton of a continual dying (and, by God's grace, rising) for the other's sake.[102] Rather than underwriting a vapid fantasy of everyone 'just getting along' (to use Rodney King's now-famous phrase), Barth casts a vision of a community founded on *crisis*.[103] To know our

---

101. See, e.g., *CD* III/2, pp. 199–202. While agreeing that this is probably the best approach which safeguards theology from being co-opted by philosophy, Bultmann's charge that Barth 'leaves his conceptual scheme unexplained' highlights the manner in which an *ad hoc* approach can tend to smuggle in the Trojan horse of philosophical ideology. See Krötke, *Sin and Nothingness*, p. 11.

102. Stacy Johnson highlights the importance of Barth's distinction between 'relationality' and 'fellowship'. 'Relationality' speaks of God's being with us and our being with one another and God, where as 'fellowship' articulates the 'forness' of this. 'Whereas relationality is our nature, fellowship is our destiny' (Johnson, *The Mystery of God*, p. 87).

103. This is a 'critical reconciliation' which 'takes place in the form of a real *conflict* of God with sin and sinners' (Eberhard Busch, *The Great Passion* [Grand Rapids: Eerdmans, 2004], p. 206).

fellow humanity with Christ is first to know ourselves made obsolete. Thus, rather than finding in God's being-in-act on our behalf a therapeutic crutch, it is the *Deus pro nobis* (hardly the sentimental moniker it might initially appear to be) who we in our sin so doggedly try to escape.[104] Indeed, Lessing's ditch and the nineteenth- and twentieth-century's obsession with the 'problem' of faith and history is just this kind of evasion.[105] It is a delay tactic which springs from 'the need to hide ourselves (like Adam and Eve in the garden of Eden) from Jesus Christ' (IV/1, p. 292).[106] 'The assault this makes on us is too violent and incisive.' And so Barth comments on 'the catastrophe which...the knowledge of the *Christus pro nobis praesens*, would mean for us'.[107] 'The "for us" of His death on the cross includes and encloses this terrible "against us."...It is something that we have to see and read like an opened page which we have no power to turn...Judgment is judgment. Death is death. End is end' (IV/1, pp. 291–92, 296).[108]

Barth is adamant that it is precisely the God who is 'for us' whom we should fear, as this being-for-us takes the form of a being-against-us as we are judged in Christ. A further word about the character of this *Deus pro nobis* is necessary in light of Stephen Long's recent argument that the 'pro nobis' is one of two sources of the 'nice god' which God is emphatically *not*.[109] Long fails

---

104.   In Rusty Reno's words, *'pro nobis'* are 'words we do not want to hear' (R. R. Reno, *In the Ruins of the Church* [Grand Rapids: Brazos Press, 2002], p. 47).

105.   And it is not a real problem at all, but one which 'is soluble and has actually been solved' in that Jesus lives and *is* present (IV/1, p. 292).

106.   Andrew Delbanco puts it bluntly: 'our primal parents run from God with all the dignity of roaches fleeing the kitchen when the light switch is thrown' (Andrew Delbanco, *The Death of Satan* [New York: Farrar, Straus and Giroux, 1995], p. 155).

107.   Note the unexpected, unwelcome way in which Christ acts as our Mediator. Even as he mediates between God and humanity, he *is* God-with-us, allowing no 'safe' distance in the relationship.

108.   The frequency of statements like this render dubious the common criticism McGrath articulates that 'although Barth concedes that predestination includes a negative element, this has no bearing upon man whatsoever' (McGrath, *Iustitia Dei*, p. 367).

109.   See Long, 'God is Not Nice'. Long's critique is pointed at Melanchthon's claim in the 1521 edition of the *Loci Communes* that we can know only the benefits of Christ, not Christ *in se*. Melanchthon's comment is in keeping with the Reformers' concern to avoid any speculation that leaves God at an existential distance. It is also a critique of a philosophically determined theology that skirts around God's own self-revelation in Christ. What it is not is the opening up of a breach between the person and work of Christ. Of course, there is certainly an unfortunate history of theological decline in liberal Protestantism in which such a split becomes a veritable *ditch* and the *Christus* is eclipsed in favour of and/or limited to the *pro nobis*. But in misreading and countering Melanchthon's claim and its co-opting by a therapeutic culture, Long falls into the opposite trap of speaking of a God/Christ *in se* separate from the one who is *pro nobis*. Barth, and to a great degree Luther and Melanchthon before him, by refusing to differentiate between *Deus in se* and *Deus pro nobis*, never collapses into the anthropocentrism of a soteriology which ceases to be always already Christology. As Luther and Barth would have it, God being for us means that we may no longer be for ourselves but must be for others, 'even to death on a cross'. Frankly, Christian *eudaemonia*, with its daily dying and rising, is the farthest thing imaginable from therapy.

to draw a distinction between the *Deus pro nobis* and its misappropriation, implying that attending to God as the one who is 'for us' amounts to or leads to egoism. He reads a therapeutic rendering of it back into the original concept, which if anything carries the very sober application of a *theologia crucis* to the Christian life. It is the very claim that the *Deus pro nobis* is not – and must not be construed to be – a mere therapeutic projection that undergirds Barth's continuous talk of the stubbornly contrarian God who is for us despite our desire that he would be anything but for us. We want to be alone, but the God we meet in Christ relentlessly (and that is the sort of modifier required) gives himself to us, unwilling to let us be ourselves by ourselves. What Barth castigates is a co-opting of God for our own agenda, an identification of our cause with God's:

> There is, however, a desecration of the name of God which in comparison to that in atheism and that in the religions is even worse. This is the attempt of the world to exalt its own cause as God's or, conversely, to subject God's cause to its own, to make it serve it. In both forms one might call this an attempted 'nostrification' of God.[110]

Note that Barth attacks our making our cause God's, but he does not attack God's making our cause his own. Indeed, he sees the latter as the sum of the gospel, even as he sees the former as the essence of sin. The nostrified God is ranged *against* the God who is for us, with the key question of differentiation being that of *who* – *who* is making our cause God's? The problem with humanity doing so, beyond the obvious greedy egoism motivating the act, is that humanity continually fails to know what its own cause is. That is, despite an obsessive self-attention, we do not know what is good for us; and our projects of sinful self-exaltation, beginning in deicide, always end in suicide.

Having looked at length at Barth's methodology, particularly his Christological starting point in the knowledge of sinful humanity, we will turn now to a brief description of two of the three primary forms of sin which are revealed in the mirror and light of Jesus Christ – pride and falsehood. This sketch will be useful to help us compare Barth's insights with those of Augustine and Luther on similar points and will set the stage for an extended discussion of Barth's treatment of sin under the form of sloth and the question of the feminist critique of *incurvatus in se*.

Sin as Pride: CD IV/1

Readers of Barth need to keep constantly in mind the unity of each volume of the *Church Dogmatics*. Volume IV treats the doctrine of reconciliation from three different angles, but each angle is on one and the same movement. It would be easy to take Barth's adoption of the so-called Parable of the Prodigal

---

110. Karl Barth, *The Christian Life* (trans. Geoffrey W. Bromiley; Grand Rapids: Eerdmans, 1981), p. 130.

Son as a narratival structure for the doctrine of reconciliation to speak of two movements. In Jesus' parable, the son leaves his father's house for the 'far country', squandering his father's gifts and his own life, only to return destitute to the welcoming arms of the father, whose prodigality is even greater than his son's.[111] But Barth's adoption of this narratival structure involves an adapting of the parable. Rather than two movements (there and back), stages or states (humiliation and exaltation), the incarnation according to Barth is one unified being-in-act.[112] The atonement, which Barth extends to include all of Jesus' life, not merely his passion or the event of the cross, is a history, 'the very special history of God with man [*die höchst besondere Geschichte Gottes mit dem Menschen*]' in which God is humbled and humanity is exalted (*CD* IV/1, p. 157; *KD* IV/1, p. 171). But even these categories are read dialectically, so that God's humiliation *is* his exaltation and humanity's exaltation in him *is* its humiliation.[113] The subject and content of all of this is, of course, Jesus Christ. In the unity of his being-in-act, Jesus is God, man, the God-man. And 'we must always learn from Jesus Christ. He defines those concepts: they do not define Him' (IV/1, p. 129). Accordingly, Barth begins each section on sin with Christological sub-sections and only then moves to sub-sections on the sin of the man of sin and on the consequences of that sin.

Just as the incarnation is one movement, the three forms of sin can be seen as the same rejection of that movement taking different shape. They are three forms of a nonetheless formally identical counter-movement. They are formally identical because they all represent a movement away from and against God, in direct opposition to God's movement towards and for us. In the highly complex synthesis of dogmatic categories in Volume IV, Barth coordinates these counter-movements with God's movement towards us in Christ under the rubric of Christ's threefold office (*munus triplex*).[114] To each aspect of the office there is a perverse parody. The humble priest is mocked by his proud counterpart. The exalted king is contrasted with the man of

---

111. Already we can see Barth's ever-present contention that grace is simply *bigger* than sin. The 'Yes' outweighs the 'No', even when it is hidden under the 'No'. Grace is of grander scope and consequence than sin, whose reality is secondary, transient and futile.

112. See *CD* IV/1, pp. 132–3.

113. It is one of the most striking virtues of Barth's account of the incarnation that he finds in his willingness to be immanent in humiliation a 'proof' of God's transcendent exaltation. Indeed, this is what makes him *God* rather than just another (false) god. 'In this act He is this God and therefore the true God, distinguished from all false gods by the fact that they are not capable of this act, that they have not in fact accomplished it, that their supposed glory and honour and eternity and omnipotence not only do not include but exclude their self-humiliation. False gods are all reflections of a false and all too human self-exaltation. They are all lords who cannot and will not be servants, who are therefore no true lords, whose being is not a truly divine being' (IV/1, p. 130).

114. See *CD* IV/3.1, pp. 369, 373, for a brief recapitulation of sin in light of the threefold office.

sloth. The true witness ('prophet') is opposed by a liar.[115] The significance of this for our analysis of Hampson's gendering of sin is that 'the doctrines of reconciliation and sin are linked in such a way that "sin" cannot be divided up and parcelled out, this sort to these individuals and that to those…And here, of course, comes the rub for feminist hamartiologies.'[116] And yet, the non-gendered unity-in-diversity of sin can be a salutary insight for feminist theologies concerned to disable patriarchy and empower women. To take just one example, consider the near-heroic cast of pride in contemporary society, even when it is acknowledged as sin. It is something acceptable to men, part of 'boys being boys'. But what if it were seen under the guise of sloth as well as the supremely 'unmanly' timidity of one who refuses to 'play the man'? The refuge which pride has become is thus rooted out as its slothful underbelly is exposed.

The first counter-movement, then, takes the form of pride. There is a logical priority here, for, while we cannot separate the humiliation of the Son of God (the Lord as servant) from the exaltation of the Son of Man (the servant as Lord), the former establishes the latter.[117] Under this first form, we see 'the man of sin in light of the obedience of the Son of God'. Jesus' obedience was an obedience unto death, even death on a cross. It is the extent of this obedience which reveals the radical corruption of sin.[118] In contrast to 'what in the light of the being and activity of Jesus Christ we can only call the humility of God' stands the pride of man (IV/1, p. 418).[119] While sin is fundamentally unbelief, such a definition requires concretion, which pride provides (pp. 414, 417).[120] Barth looks at 'the human disorder which is the antithesis of the

---

115. Ever concerned with following the structure and logic of the gospel, Barth switches the traditional ordering of the *munus triplex* (prophet–priest–king becomes priest–king–prophet) in part to counter a liberal Protestant tendency to read Christ's role as prophet in isolation from his roles as priest and king, often enough marginalizing or simply eliminating the other two. His situating of Christ as prophet at the end re-integrates that role within Christ's person and work, which remains a unity even in its threefold character.

116. Greene-McCreight, 'Gender, Sin and Grace', p. 425. Greene-McCreight makes the interesting suggestion that it is the universal rejection of Jesus on the part of fallen humanity as well as, of course, his enduring that rejection and God's redemption of rejecting humanity, that equalizes humanity. In comparison to the difference between Jesus and all other humans, other forms of difference (e.g., gender) are relativized, if not trivialized (pp. 427–8).

117. The hymn in Phil. 2.5-11 illustrates this well, even as it calls into question Barth's strict refusal of any two-stage view of the incarnation. The temporally consequent exaltation of Jesus, following as it does on his obedience, would seem to point to at least some kind of double-movement. What Barth wants to protect, and rightly so, is the notion that it is in no way ill-fitting for the Lord to become a servant. Rather, this is what it means to be God, the one who loves in freedom (IV/1, p. 134).

118. See *CD* IV/1, p. 412.

119. The following quotations under the discussion of the form of sin as pride will be from *CD* IV/1 unless otherwise noted.

120. As Jorgenson notes, in identifying pride and unbelief (something which Luther also does), Barth effectively brings together the positive and privative aspects of sin (Jorgenson, 'Karl Barth's Christological Treatment of Sin', p. 450).

divine order of grace' from four standpoints under the form of sin as pride
(p. 418). At each standpoint, he notes the concealing character of sin. He also
includes a brief reflection on Genesis 3 in each and a longer exposition of an
Old Testament concretion of the particular form of pride.

The first of these standpoints is the acknowledgment that the Word became
flesh. 'He became man...man not only in his limitation but in the misery
which is the consequence of his sin, man like us. This is how God is God.' On
the other hand, and in contradiction, 'we want to be as God is, we want to
be God' (p. 418).[121] This attempt to be as God on our own terms parodies the
wondrous exchange (*admirabile commercium*) of our sinful and Christ's perfect humanity. In our attempted robbery, seeking to usurp the place of God, a
'mad exchange [*tolle Verwechslung*] takes place' (*CD* IV/1, p. 422; *KD* IV/1,
p. 468). The end of our self-deification is, of course, unattainable. Indeed,
while for God to be a man is consistent with what it means to be God, for a
man to want to be God is self-contradictory:[122] 'Man ceases to be a man when
he wants this'. So in seeking to exalt himself, man debases himself.[123] That this

---

121. Modern theology is one long 'undercover apotheosis of man' in which theology is
transformed into anthropology. See Barth's introduction to Feuerbach, in which he concludes
that Feuerbach is 'entirely right' in his interpretation of religion, even (especially) as it applies
to the Christian religion! (Barth, 'An Introductory Essay', pp. xxii, xxix).

122. While it is proper for God to be man (proper because Jesus is the God-man), it is
improper for man to be God (as this reverses the logic of the incarnation and threatens the
freedom of God's self-giving love).

123. Barth's polemic against deification is an exercise in 'denying the divinity of humanity
on the basis of the humanity of God' (Eberhard Jüngel, 'Humanity in Correspondence to
God' in *Theological Essays* [Edinburgh: T&T Clark, 1989], pp. 124–53, [152]). Besides
embodying an inappropriate self-arrogation of divinity, deification too often makes the
mistake of thinking of God undialectically as one exalted to the heights instead of knowing
him as he is in Christ, in his exaltation to the depths of humiliation. Furthermore, deification
is characterized by what Barth calls a 'dissipated' dissatisfaction with limits which bemoans
a God-established creatureliness. In the background of Barth's rejection of deification is his
rejection of a Lutheran understanding of the *communicatio idiomatum* which threatens to
confuse divinity and humanity by speaking of their union without paying sufficient attention
to their union in the *person* of Christ. The union is *hypostatic* rather than *natural*, as is the
case with many of Luther's metaphors (iron in fire being one prominent example). Squarely
within the Reformed tradition on this point, Barth sees Lutheran theology as falling afoul of
Chalcedon's condemnations of confusion and change in Christ's two natures and threatening
to invert God and humanity (see 'An Introductory Essay', p. xxiii; IV/1, p. 181; IV/2, pp. 82–
101). For all the vigour of this critique, however, Barth gives one of the richest accounts of the
exaltation of humanity in Christ imaginable, certainly as rich as any in Protestant theology.
Mangina calls the wonderful account of Jesus as the royal man 'a classic instance of Barth's
seeking to outbid his liberal precursors' (Mangina, *Karl Barth on the Christian Life*, p. 66).
Barth speaks the language of participation in our representative and substitute, however, not
that of deification (IV/1, 8). Barth uses this strategy to safeguard the mediated character of
our exaltation (rather than, for example, the anti-Trinitarian sense of immediacy in Pseudo-
Dionysius and some mystical theologians) and to ensure this is a fully *creaturely* exaltation.
Speaking of the exaltation of humanity *as* divine establishes a glass ceiling for humanity,
beyond which it morphs into something else, thereby ironically *under*valuing the new life and
fellowship of humanity with God in Christ. His instincts are right here, though his semantic

is not strictly a possibility for man *as man* demonstrates the absurd, purely negative character of sin. 'It cannot be deduced or explained or justified. It is simply a fact', a fact in which man 'makes himself impossible'. Given that sin is a surd, description rather than explanation is the mode of discourse appropriate to it (p. 419).[124]

Concealment occurs here in that humanity thinks it is only choosing one amongst a number of possibilities for its existence as humanity. It simply wants to exist on its own, *in ut pro se* (p. 420). And its error is in thinking that it will be humanity in its self-deification. However, 'neither as an individual nor in society was he created to be placed alone, to be self-controlling and self-sufficient, to be self-centred, to rotate around himself' (p. 421). It is only the gravity of sin that moves humanity to think otherwise and to make a corresponding error about God. Humanity assumes that 'the God [it] wants to be like is obviously only a self-sufficient, self-affirming, self-desiring supreme being, self-centred and rotating about himself. Such a being is not God. God is for Himself, but He is not only for Himself. He is in a supreme self-hood, but not a self-contained self-hood' (p. 422). Barth finds a concretion of this first aspect of pride in the golden calf incident of Exodus 32 (pp. 423–32).

The second standpoint from which Barth examines sin under the form of pride is the affirmation that 'the Lord became a servant. His rule consists in the fact that He became a subject. His power works itself out in His own obligation and binding – the obligation of the Son to the Father, and His binding to us men.' 'But the man for whom God is God in this way in Jesus Christ is the very opposite – the servant who wants to be lord' (p. 432). Of course, such a man can never *be* lord. The concealment here is the use of power under the guise of a respectable humility and 'the inevitable and ordained coming of age'. The subtlety of sin is why the 'Word of God is always needed to bring evil to the light' (p. 434). Barth mocks the vain attempt at self-exaltation of man, 'as though the exercise of his lordship could ever be anything but the most ridiculous failure, the most frightful blundering of a self-seeker, a usurper, a parvenu, a vain and evil and snobbish *nouveau riche*' (p. 437). This second form of sin as pride is seen concretely again from the Old Testament in the story of Saul in 1 Samuel 8–31 (pp. 437–45). Saul begins by playing his role as king exactly like the judges. Sadly, 'instead of overcoming in his own person the wrong that Israel had done with its demand for an autocratic king, he granted it a new lease of life' (p. 444).

Barth's third standpoint from which to examine the sin of man as pride is that of Jesus as the judge who judges by being judged. Jesus accuses us 'by turning and taking to Himself the accusation which is laid properly against

polemic is misguided. Indeed, Barth conveys much of the traditional insights of a doctrine of deification and divinization without using the terms themselves. On the complementarity of deification language and participation language, see the recent spate of deification research. In relation to Augustine, see pages 9–13 above.

124. While sin is inexplicable, the incarnation is inconceivable. At the same time, unlike sin, the incarnation is *not* absurd (I/2, p. 160).

us'. In his very taking this judgement on himself, he reveals us as those who
desire to judge themselves rather than bear the judgement of God (p. 445).
Of course, as in each of these standpoints, we are not strictly *capable* of
judging ourselves. We can 'only play the judge'.[125] Concealment here is seen
in the apparently laudatory desire to distinguish right from wrong (p. 447);
and with his promise of *Eritis sicut Deus*, 'what the serpent has in mind is
the establishment of ethics...The only trouble is that it is an analysis, i.e., a
dissolving or unraveling, of the divine commandment' (p. 448).[126] Here we
see the exegetical basis for Barth's divine command ethic.[127] There is pride *in*
ethics as self-judgement.[128] Moral behaviour is not an autonomous deciding
for oneself, but a 'repetition of the divine decision' (449). 'As judge of good
and evil, man wants to stand at God's side in defence of the cosmos.' But 'he
lets hell loose by doing it. Why and how? Because he is not the man to cut this
figure' (p. 450). The Old Testament concretion of this standpoint is found in
Ahab's injustice towards Naboth (pp. 453–8).

The fourth and final standpoint from which Barth looks at the form of
sin as pride is the aspect of the cross, 'the final depth of His humiliation' and

125. 'He thinks he sits on a high throne, but in reality he sits only on a child's stool,
blowing his little trumpet, cracking his little whip, pointing with frightful seriousness his little
finger, while all the time nothing happens that really matters. He can only play the judge. He
is only a dilettante, a blunderer, in his attempt to distinguish between good and evil...' And
yet, 'on the little stool which he thinks is a throne, man does create facts' (pp. 446, 447).

126. Judas comes in for a similar critique in his desire to decide for himself what
constitutes discipleship. See II/2, p. 463. And yet, it must be said that where Judas over-
appropriates the role of judge, Barth offers impressionistic sketches of 'attitudes' at best.
This 'rather frustrating vagueness' can be attributed to his 'suspicion of moral rules and their
proclivity to become the legalistic heart and soul of ethics' (Biggar, *The Hastening that Waits*,
p. 114).

127. Nigel Biggar has helpfully pointed out that Barth is obviously lampooning a
certain *kind* of ethic here, one based on autarchy. Barth's divine command ethic does not
preclude moral deliberation, even if it can veer towards the voluntaristic. Biggar suggests
thinking of Barth's divine command as 'personal vocation' and calls ethics an 'aid to hearing'.
See Biggar, *The Hastening that Waits*, pp. 7–45, especially pp. 25, 44. For Stacy Johnson,
the paucity of prescription in Barth's ethics is a function of the freedom of the mysterious
God who commands which issues in an 'open-ended', 'radically contextual' ethic that
eschews principalization and any other form of anticipation of the divine command and the
corresponding human response. See Johnson, *The Mystery of God*, pp. 153–75 (154). While
right to attend to the 'counter-melody' of theocentrism in Barth's thought, with its emphasis
on the uncircumscribable God, Johnson pays insufficient attention (with the exception of
his strictly formal account of the God who is 'for others') to the fact that, for all God's
surprising, ever-new Trinitarian dynamic, we can still speak of his faithful character. That
is, while even God's faithfulness will take continually surprising shapes, there *is* a sense in
which we know what to expect of God – that is, faithfulness. And so there are certain ethical
parameters of which we can speak confidently.

128. Hence Barth's continual refusal to separate dogmatics and ethics. While there is
good reason to question the adequacy of Barth's specific prescriptions in ethics, the common
critique that he *lacks* any substantial ethics is to miss entirely his weaving of ethics throughout
his work for the express purpose of acknowledging both that ethics is theological and that
theology is ethical.

the cry of dereliction (p. 458). 'This helpless man was the almighty God' (p. 459). The contradiction of Jesus under this standpoint is humanity's arrogant, if futile attempt at self-help. We even enlist God in this (p. 461), and our sin is concealed from us under the form of a perfectly understandable self-preservation. We ask: 'If I do not care for myself, then who will?' (p. 462) As Augustine saw so well, in seeking to help ourselves we aim to take for ourselves what can only be received as a gift. 'He loses himself, his soul, his life, by undertaking his own cause, by trying to defend and maintain and save himself' (p. 464). The remarkable (to our eyes) thing is that Adam and Eve actually *lost* their independence and individuality as they helped themselves. The Old Testament concretion of this final form of pride is seen in Jeremiah's account of the king and people in Jerusalem on either side of its fall in 587 BCE (pp. 468–78).

Following sub-sections on the Christological light in which we read sin and on what sin is (in this case, pride), Barth turns to a sub-section dealing with 'who and what the man is who commits sin'. Proud man is *fallen* man (and these are two corresponding determinations of humanity, or two sides of one determination), 'fallen to the place where God who does not and cannot fall has humbled Himself for him in Jesus Christ. He is the man who exists in the depths where God visits him in Jesus Christ and takes His place with him. He is that which God became in Jesus Christ to be his Saviour' (p. 478). The light of Christ will look like a pessimistic darkness to the world on this point, and indeed it is in the rejection of the 'darker' convictions of the Reformers that the origins of the Enlightenment are to be found (p. 479). That being said, Barth is careful to make a restriction on our use of the term 'fall': 'we cannot say that man is fallen completely away from God...He cannot make himself another being or destroy the being that he is. Again, he has not ordained and established the covenant, and it is not for him to dissolve it' (p. 480). Barth rejects any suggestion of ontological transformation through sin for theocentric reasons. To say that sin now determines humanity in a more fundamental way than God's good grace in creation and covenant is to suggest that victory has been swallowed up by death rather than death by victory.[129] It is to suggest that God 'has not merely suffered death but fallen a prey to it.' On the contrary, 'God does not allow Himself to be diverted by the sin of man from addressing His Yes to him. He carries through His original Yes by reconciling him to Himself' (p. 481).

Barth then considers three propositions in relation to the corruption humanity experiences as fallen. The first is that humanity stands in a relationship of debt to God (p. 484). Accordingly, there is no place for pride. In his contradiction of the giving of God, man 'has to bear the fact that the same good will of God now contradicts him' (p. 489). This is God's wrath, though as wrath it is always oriented to mercy as 'the redemptive fire of His love' (p. 490).

---

129. The question of whether this amounts to an over-realized eschatology is simply the question of whether Barth gets the gospel right.

The second proposition starts from the death of Jesus in the place of all of humanity. That is, his death was total in its substitution, in the sense of including all women and men and also in that it encompassed the totality of each and every person. This reveals that our corruption is both 'radical and total'. Barth robustly defends the doctrine of total depravity, arguing that it is 'the whole man [*der ganze Mensch*]' who 'is caught in this turning away from God and has to exist as turned away from Him [*in dieser Abwendung von Gott begriffen ist, in dieser Abgewendetheit von ihm existieren mu*]' (*CD* IV/1, p. 492; *KD* IV/1, p. 548). When it comes to original sin, Barth repeatedly affirms that 'there never was a time when he was not proud' (p. 495). Too, he shares Luther's commitment to a holistic (*totus homo*) anthropology in which humanity is *simul totus iustus et totus peccator*.[130] We are 'not just partly but altogether "flesh"' (p. 496). Again, though, the totality of humanity's depravity cannot be allowed to undo creation. 'The Bible accuses man as a sinner from head to foot, but it does not dispute to man his full and unchanged humanity, his nature as God created it good, the possession and use of all the faculties which God has given him.' Moreover, given Barth's understanding of the *imago Dei* as co-humanity, 'we cannot even speak of the loss of his divine likeness' (p. 492). At the same time, speaking of corruption rather than the loss or alteration of humanity (the parallels with Augustine are striking here) does not represent a mitigation of the effects of sin. Rather the situation is *worse* in that humanity cannot rest in a sinful state in which it is at least consistent with itself but instead lives in an unbearable environment of self-contradiction.

Finally, Barth considers the proposition arising from Rom. 11.32, that all are 'concluded' in disobedience. Every woman and man stands in 'two great contexts, or unities', one prospective with reference to our future being, the other retrospective with reference to our past being. The latter is our divine conclusion, and both 'meet and intersect in the present of all men' (p. 501). In reference to the retrospective reality about us, we can only describe the man of sin as 'the one that we were, or had been, not the one that we can be or will be again' (p. 502). This is a reality which is true of us, but only as a reality which cannot continue to be true of us. Following a critique of the methodological naturalism of biblical scholarship and a finely nuanced discussion of Genesis 1–3 as saga, Barth goes on to detail what it means to say we are 'in Adam'. He offers a representative rather than hereditary picture of this relationship, such that 'the successors of Adam are…those who are represented in his person and deed' (p. 510). Barth is very careful to avoid the 'how' question regarding the transmission of sin, or at least he refuses to give an anthropological answer to that question. All we can say is that all of humanity *is* (and 'is' needs to be heard in the primary sense of 'was')[131] in Adam, and that it is God who has made this conclusion.

---

130. 'The whole man in all his actions is a sinner, sinful flesh' (p. 498). Also see pp. 596, 602–3.

131. 'To be exact, what we have had to say concerning him [i.e., the man of sin] can only be put in the perfect [i.e., 'he has been'/'I have been a sinner'] or even the pluperfect tense [i.e., 'he had been'/'I had been a sinner']' (p. 502).

Adam is not a fate which God has suspended over us. Adam is the truth concerning us as it is known to God and told to us. The relationship between him and us, and us and him, is not, therefore, one which is pragmatically grounded and demonstrable, nor is it one which can be explained in terms of a transmission between him and us. It is God who establishes it. It is the Word of God which gives this name and title to mankind and the history of man. It is God's Word which fuses all men into unity with this man as *primus inter pares*. (p. 511)

Sin as Falsehood: CD IV/3

Under the third aspect of the doctrine of reconciliation, Barth deals with the promise of the Spirit and Christ's prophetic office.[132] He begins here, as in the other two sub-sections, with Christology. Jesus is the 'true Witness' and is himself 'the truth which unmasks' the man of sin (p. 375). How does the true Witness encounter us? 'What takes place, then, is simply that the truth reveals itself as such to man, that he does not want it, that he advances against it his untruth, that it shows this to be what it is, that man is thus shown up as a liar and stands unmasked as such' (p. 375). Having sketched the outline of our encounter with truth, Barth backs up to ask Pilate's question: What is the truth that encounters us? It is not any ideal, system, principle or doctrine (p. 375).[133] No, truth is a person; and doctrine can at best only participate in the truth by teaching the one who is truth. 'Jesus Christ in the promise of the Spirit as His revelation in the sphere of our time and history is the truth' (p. 376). For Barth, revelation is always effective, such that it includes within it the response of humanity in the Spirit to God's self-disclosure. So, the revelation of God and the reception of that revelation by humanity in confession belong together. Truth happens, then, when Jesus witnesses to himself and we, by the power of his Spirit, respond in joyful acknowledgment of his witness. The Christian's witness is thereby both relativized and established.[134] Barth further clarifies the nature of the truth of revelation, which is Christ: 'The meeting of this revelation of God and this confession of man is truth in the full sense of the term. For both, i.e., both God as He is and man as he is, are the one, whole truth' (p. 380). So where Augustine takes Jesus' claim to be the

---

132. The following quotations under the discussion of the form of sin as falsehood will be from *CD* IV/3.1 unless otherwise noted.

133. 'It cannot try to be itself this Word. Even though it be the purest doctrine, it is not this Word...It is good or bad to the degree that as genuine *doctrina* it points beyond itself and summons us to hear, not itself, but Him...In every case, then, He Himself replaces it.' God's Word is that 'which in its reality transcends all the words of human indication, which leaves them behind and judges them, yet also heals and orders them' (pp. 419–20). Doctrine's function can only be *iconic*, pointing towards the one who is truth. But it is precisely the incarnation which frees doctrine to truly be (always in the freedom of the Spirit's direction) iconic rather than prematurely representational or hopelessly apophatic. For more on this 'third way' between 'the violence of positivist kataphatics and the silence of apophatics', see Smith, *Speech and Theology*, p. 129.

134. Webster, *Barth's Moral Theology*, p. 144.

truth to mean that *God* is truth, Barth takes it to mean that *God-and-man* is truth.[135] The incarnation reveals both God and humanity in the one mediator, and Barth insists upon this *duplex cognitio* as the only faithful reading of Emmanuel.

Barth states explicitly that Job was the source for this section (p. 384). He is a type of the true Witness, even a type of Jesus Christ, a witness to the true Witness (p. 388). Job serves as an apt figure in his character as a *suffering* witness, corresponding to the one whose true witness took on passionate form. Such is our world that the mediator between God and humanity lived a life that led to death, in which his very being for us took the shape of one who is against us. Yet even here on the cross we do not have to do with some *opus alienum* but with God's very proper being-in-act (p. 414).[136] While the cross is God's *opus proprium* (can his work be anything else?), it is hidden *sub contrario*. And so our knowledge of Jesus Christ, whose form and content correspond to his being in the world, is *sub specie aliena* – that is, it is indirect. 'Indirect knowledge is that which arises when the person or object to be known makes itself known' (p. 389).

We turn now to the man of sin who is 'unmasked' by the truth (p. 375). To live in falsehood is to refuse to participate in the truth which is *this* truth, the truth of God-with-us, the truth of Christ. It is to deny the true Witness with our own counter-witness. Falsehood is 'the specifically Christian form of sin', by which Barth means that it is the sin with which we have to do in the present, post-resurrection age in that it involves a denial of Jesus the true Witness (pp. 435–6). We seek to oppose the truth of our being reconciled to God in Christ. But it is 'quite useless' to resist directly the truth of Jesus' witness, so we turn to the indirect movement of evasion (p. 435). Man seeks to evade the truth

> by changing or transposing it into a translation of his own, into an improved edition, in which it looks most deceptively like itself...but has become the truth which is mastered by him instead of the truth which masters him, being given a pretty but very effective muzzle, so that it can still give a muffled bark but can no longer bite. (p. 436)

Like all sin, our falsehood is a form of self-preservation, one in which we seek to avoid the questioning and ultimate judgement that comes to us even in (only in!) Christ's truthful word of reconciliation. Yet the very blandness and unoriginality of sin demonstrates its impossibility, its futile attempt to create

---

135. For Augustine's reading of Jn 14.6 ('I am the way, and the truth, and the life'), see p. 22 above.

136. An implicit critique of Luther stands behind this remark. While Luther binds God's *opus alienum* and his *opus proprium* closely together, it is characteristic of Barth to identify them and speak of two aspects, forms or angles from which to view one unity rather than any sense of a sequence. Barth rejected any sequencing of law and gospel, something he saw in Luther.

a reality that can never be, its fundamentally *passé* hopes and dreams.[137] For all this, though, human falsehood is a *fact*. Yet given the subtle concealment of falsehood – Jüngel speaks of sin's 'pseudonymity' – the question remains: how are we to differentiate such falsehood from truth?[138] We must be very careful not to presume to differentiate them ourselves, but instead allow them to be differentiated for us by Jesus Christ (pp. 438–9).

Barth gives a vivid picture of human falsehood as he turns once more to Job, this time to consider his three friends (pp. 453–61). His insistence on the freedom of both revelation and witness, the freedom of God for humanity and of humanity for God as covenant-partners, is central at this point.[139] Job's friends are not wrong in their counsel. What they say is good doctrine, through and through. Indeed, it is shared by Job, for all the latter's protestations. Where they epitomize the falsehood of man is in their presumption to speak *for* God. Moreover, they speak about God and Job in 'unhistorical' terms, proving their ineptitude as witnesses (p. 457). This discussion is one of the highpoints of Barth's discussions of Scripture in the empathic way he connects exegesis, dogmatics and pastoral theology. Job's friends 'preach timeless truths', hoarding theological manna from the past rather than listening for the voice of truth in present encounter with God (p. 457).[140] These are 'truths which cost nothing and are worth nothing, which neither wound nor heal and which therefore involve genuine torture, which do not have to be confessed but may simply be stated'. Job's friends 'speak as those who are totally unaffected by the despairing struggle for the knowledge of God into which Job finds himself plunged by what has befallen him' (p. 458). They seek to evade encounter with the living God by constructing closed systems which, for all their orthodoxy, give place to neither God nor humanity in their freedom (p. 460). Job, on the other hand, sees a living, active and speaking God uniquely confronting a living man in his unique existence and responsibility (p. 459).

Finally, Barth describes the condemnation of man. It will be helpful at this point to note the nature of the relationship between the three aspects of the doctrine of reconciliation and the sins which correspond to them. Where the humiliation of the Son of God in his priestly office and the exaltation of the Son of Man in his kingly office speak of an (in some sense) already enacted

---

137. Falsehood affords us simply 'another indication of how feeble and inferior and unoriginal he is in relation to the prophecy of Jesus Christ, and how far ahead of him this is' (p. 437).

138. Pseudonymity fits sin's parasitic, privative character. See Jüngel, *Justification*, pp. 113–14.

139. 'God's sovereign grasping of man is not an act of force to induce a *sacrificium intellectus et voluntatis*. On the contrary, it evokes and establishes the *intellectus* and the *voluntas fidei*' (p. 447).

140. This is similar to Elisabeth Moltmann-Wendel's comment that women's sin 'is not pride, but persistence', what Daniel Migliore calls 'the temptation to hold on to the past'. See Elisabeth Moltmann-Wendel, *The Women around Jesus*, p. 72; quoted in D. L. Migliore, 'Sin and Self-Loss', in Walter Brueggemann and George W. Stoup (eds.), *Many Voices, One God* (Louisville: Wesminster/John Knox Press, 1998), pp. 139–54 (145).

history, a *past*, Christ's work as the mediator–prophet brings that past alive into the *present*. The effect of this is to make even that past, finished work 'not dead but living history'. And so the charge that Barth's soteriology is *merely* retrospective can be dismissed.[141] What Barth is concerned to do at this point is to emphasize with equal force (and in this order!) that salvation happened and that the saviour continues to make a claim on us, demanding the acknowledgment of worship and obedience.[142]

Pride and sloth represent our counter-movement to this (not really) *past* history of our atonement in the humiliation and exaltation of Christ, but falsehood is our very *present* counter-movement to the Word of God which comes to us in the power of the Spirit.[143] So falsehood's 'specific function' is 'to be the common exponent in which they [i.e., pride and sloth] both necessarily betray and express themselves as sin'. It is the guise under which they attempt to conceal themselves (p. 372). The consequences of this are dire, and the sense of sin's threat is far more palpable here than in Barth's previous two discussions of sin. Consider the following: 'To lie is to try to substitute for the election of man fulfilled by God a rejection which is not God's will for him and which according to God's Word is averted by His act.' As the rejection of God's word of pardon and life, lying is the equivalent of cursing oneself (p. 464), and 'it does not mean nothing to say: "Well, I'll be damned!" even though it is God's affair whether or when He will take seriously and put into effect this insane desire' (pp. 465–6).

Barth is clear that falsehood, like all sin, has no transformative power. It cannot substitute one reality for another or tweak a reality beyond all recognition. Its only power – and this is given it by God – is 'to be man's punishment as well as his sin' (p. 468). So, in attempting to substitute a lie for the truth of the Spirit's promise in Christ's resurrection, the Christian 'is betrayed, or relapses, or causes himself to relapse, into the same situation as that from which he had to be redeemed as Jesus Christ encountered him and as he could thus perceive and accept the divine pardon' (p. 466). This situation is one in which we are threatened and one in which, as a consequence of our sin, the true reality of God's being *pro nobis* as well as of our own being encounters us *sub specie aliena*. It is something akin to the experience of standing on one's head in which, while reality remains the same, our sensation of it becomes distorted and disorienting. The condemned man 'exists in a subjective reality alien to and contradicting his objective reality'. The truth 'punishes the man who tries to subject it to this process by representing itself and the reality of his being in such a way as to correspond to the untruth into which he seeks to transform it' (p. 469). That is, the truth asserts itself as a contradiction of this man who seeks to live in contradiction to it.

---

141. See Mangina, *Karl Barth on the Christian Life*, pp. 76–7.
142. For Barth's understanding of acknowledgment, see Mangina, *Karl Barth on the Christian Life*, pp. 39–43.
143. Barth calls pride and sloth the 'works' and falsehood the 'word of the man of sin' (p. 373).

At the same time, 'man can stand on his head, but he cannot make the truth do so. He can only attempt to change it into untruth' (p. 475). And, 'the truth is on the offensive against the falsehood of man' (p. 476). 'The falsehood of man is ultimately only his falsehood' (p. 474). That is, we may imply, it is not *God's* falsehood. The man of falsehood has not turned God's truth into a lie and can never do so. These kinds of comments seem to pressure the conversation towards certain eschatological judgements and conclusions, leaving us with a question: Is the threat, finally, *real*? Barth concludes his discussion of falsehood with a brief excursus on universalism (pp. 477–8). This is an eschatological question, he points out, and must be left to its proper place. Nevertheless, two comments are in order. First, 'God does not owe eternal patience and therefore deliverance' to humanity. Therefore, we may not prematurely assume an *apokatastasis* 'even though theological consistency' might seem to lead in this direction. Furthermore, and this is his main point, any *apokatastasis* would be nothing but a gracious gift of God, not something to be grasped or taken for granted. At issue is faithfulness to the *person* of Christ, not a Christological *principle*; and this person refuses domestication.[144] Second, we have no good reason not to be open to this possibility of universal salvation. Indeed, while we cannot presume, we can and must pray and hope for it.

Barth makes another point in relation to the very real threat before humanity in the argument of Volume IV as a whole. His concern, as we have seen, is to see humanity always already in the light of Christ. A humanity which resists such an outlook and seeks to live in contradiction to it finds that it *is* threatened. What's more, the threat facing sinful humanity has grown teeth and is now a promise. The promise is strange, though, in that it first looks backward. It is a promise that we will be judged in all the vileness of our sin because we already have been judged in Christ. Barth is clear, too, that the judgement is definitive and destructive. It is one in which we really die – only we die in Christ. So the threat which we have always taken sin to render – that we are in danger of losing ourselves – has been accomplished. What Barth does is to offer gospel even in this difficult word of law. It is actually the good news of the threat-made-promise that escorts us into a new life in which sin has no future. Hence, while the threat is real, it is redefined from a predominantly future, anthropocentric orientation to a primarily retrospective, Christocentric one.[145] 'But it is even more true that there is said to [humanity] with overriding definiteness and all the power of a once-for-all act of God: "The Lord is at hand. Be careful for nothing"' (IV/2, p. 478). The final word is not sin. Nor is it even judgement. And so, writes Daniel Chua, 'the real

---

144. See Highfield, *Barth and Rahner in Dialogue*, p. 154.

145. Not that Barth dismisses the eschatological judgement, though it must be said that in his constant reminder that the *parousia* is really a threefold event in which the first aspect (Christ's incarnation) is accomplishment with the remaining two serving as (mere?) revelation of that accomplishment he risks marginalizing the final judgement.

question is whether humanity can face up to redemption'.[146] Now the threat is not hell so much as Christ, specifically that Christ, the one true human, has taken our threat on himself and given us the promise of life in exchange. 'What is man in relation to Him? One who is dispossessed, expelled, a displaced person. He has no more say even in this home of his' (IV/1, p. 232). And this remains *threat* because of the coming together of two thoughts: (1) our new life in Christ is taken care of and (2) we do not like it.

Sin as Sloth: CD IV/2

We turn now to an extended discussion of sin under the form of sloth.[147] Before we trace Barth's argument, though, it will be salutary to look briefly at the role of paradigms in describing sin. Consider the following statements by McFadyen:

> In regarding pride as the paradigm of all sin, the tradition suggests both that all sin is pride and that any form of pride is sin. This over-emphasis is addressed, not by the substitution of a new term, but by naming the corresponding dissipation of self as also sin...Simply in naming a complement to what is traditionally claimed to be *universally* extensive and *omni*competent, feminist theology achieves a shift in the way that sin is being understood; a shift which is as radical as it is subtle. For naming sloth as sin fundamentally alters the normative frame of reference that underpins the identification of pride as what sin essentially is...[which issues in] the suggestion that, if self-loss is sin, then not all forms of what we term pride in normal discourse are sinful. Pride itself therefore undergoes a reinterpretation once it is drawn into the orbit of the complementary sin of sloth, now referring to a more particularly defined and restricted range of self-assertions than traditionally. Self-assertion, self-protection, self-esteem are not sins in all forms or in all circumstances. Indeed, *failing* to assert, protect and esteem oneself might also prove sinful.[148]

> If both pride and its opposite are construed as sin, then, the very *sinfulness* of pride is significantly recast...The good which pride deprives one of has to be reconfigured when self-obeisance and 'self-loss' are no longer complementary *virtues* to the sin of pride, but represent instead *complementary aspects of the same pathology*. What this indicates is that feminist naming here operates by relating both pride and sloth to a more comprehensive standard of reference, which adjudicates the sinfulness of both: an understanding of the proper economy of self in relation.[149]

The extension of sin to include a second primary form forces one to pay attention to context in speaking of sin. Formal description becomes insufficient and demands explicit *material* comment as well. That is, self-assertion is no longer a sin *per se* but only in relation to a particular context

146.   Daniel K. L. Chua, *Absolute Music and the Construction of Meaning* (Cambridge: Cambridge University Press, 1999), p. 290.
147.   The following quotations under the discussion of the form of sin as sloth will be from *CD* IV/2 unless otherwise noted.
148.   McFadyen, *Bound to Sin*, pp. 155–56.
149.   McFadyen, *Bound to Sin*, p. 156.

and a certain set of relationships. Conversely, self-denial is no longer a virtue *per se* but only insofar as it fulfils certain conditions (e.g., denial for the sake of another). A woman's refusal to enable her husband's lazy behaviour by continually picking up after him and excusing his neglect, her insistence that *he* contribute something, might (given the context and relationships at play) constitute a virtue. What's more, such self-assertion might actually embody a form of self-giving love even, ironically, self-denial. Conversely, self-denial might *require* self-assertion, such that the self-denial of silence on the part of a man who is repeatedly verbally abused by his wife will more appropriately be deemed vicious than virtuous – and in the process call into question its status as self-denial.[150]

This is the point at which the limits of language strain our discussion. We have a problem that allows for two solutions. Take the example of self-denial. It would seem that certain forms of 'self-denial' can be vicious, though it has typically been taken to represent a clearly virtuous action or disposition. How do we respond to this ambiguity in our theological formulations of sin? Do we admit it into the concept of self-denial itself by speaking of various forms (both virtuous and vicious) of self-denial? Or do we insist instead that vicious self-denial is really no denial of self but a particularly subtle form of (sinful) self-assertion and reserve the application of the term 'self-denial' to virtuous acts? McFadyen seems to take the former approach, though he is cautious about speaking of virtuous forms of pride or sloth, preferring instead to speak of the ambiguity of 'self-assertion' and 'self-denial'. We might think that Hampson and feminist theologians in general take the former approach as well, but the over-determination of humanity according to gender in many feminist theologies is more rigid than that. It would seem that, rather than speaking of various forms of self-denial in various contexts, Hampson would more simplistically state that self-denial is always appropriate for men and never for women. McFadyen's approach has merit, chiefly in his insistence that we pay attention to the context of self-denial and not give it such a wide conceptual berth. Barth tends to adopt the second approach, though he is not for that reason less cautious in his concern for full-orbed, context-specific description.[151]

McFadyen insists that, for all his structural adjustments to the traditional doctrine of sin in expanding the discussion to include three characteristic forms of sin, Barth still treats sloth under the paradigm of pride.[152] In Barth's hands, sloth represents 'a less active way of idolizing the self, one that could be construed as another, less obvious, form of pride'.[153] The danger of this,

---

150. The (probably jarring) use of a male as a victim of spousal abuse is intended to underscore the descriptive insufficiency of Hampson's hard differentiation of masculine and feminine forms of sin.

151. At the same time, Barth is not averse to speaking of sinful self-denial, thus adopting the first approach. He writes at one point: 'Sin is man's denial of himself in face of the grace of his Creator' (IV/1, p. 140).

152. McFadyen, *Bound to Sin*, pp. 139–40.

153. McFadyen, *Bound to Sin*, p. 139.

according to McFadyen, is that a self-denigration or humility *for its own sake* rather than a vision of the self in right relation with others will operate as a 'normative standard of reference'. Of course, one's picture of reality exercises considerable power in the shaping of one's life. So the importance of a proper norm in relation to which sin is defined is vital. The question we will have to pose of Barth is this: From which normative standard of reference does he understand sin?

Of course, the first answer will be (and Barth is relentlessly consistent on this) that the normative standard of reference for understanding sin is *neither* pride nor sloth nor the third option of falsehood, but Jesus Christ, in whom the man of sin is revealed. And of course, to say 'Jesus Christ' is to say 'God with and for us' *as well as* 'us with and for God and one another'. This is surely to fulfil McFadyen's requirement of 'a more comprehensive standard of reference, which adjudicates the sinfulness of both [pride and sloth]: an understanding of the proper economy of self in relation'. While we have dealt with this in detail above, it is worth returning to. Pride and sloth are, in the end, far too abstract on their own to define humanity's sin. 'Whose pride?' we might ask, adapting Alasdair MacIntyre's justly famous words. The very breadth of semantic range of such terms calls into question their ability to carry the theological weight of sin. McFadyen puts this point well:

> Yet pride and sloth are not intrinsically theological terms. In themselves, they do not point to ways of relating to God. They have to be given this meaning through use. Otherwise, they function as ways of naming disorders of selfhood unplugged from the ecology of relation to God.[154]

In tethering pride, sloth and falsehood to their revelation in Christ, Barth makes them truly *theological* terms. 'Whose pride?' we repeat. The pride of the person for whom the Son of God humiliated himself, taking on the form of a servant. The pride of the person for whom Christ fulfilled his priestly office.

Sloth in the Son of Man's shadow

And whose sloth? The sloth of the one for whom the Son of Man was exalted, fulfilling his kingly office. Indeed, the one who was exalted with and in the Son of Man's exaltation, like it or not. This one 'who would not make use of his freedom, but was content with the low level of a self-enclosed being' has already been overcome at the cross (IV/2, p. 378). In light of this, this one is

> no longer unfree to let himself be exalted and to exalt himself. The existence of this One, and the fact of the direction of the Holy Spirit which He gives, is equivalent in practice to a *Sursum corda! Sursum homines!* which is called out, and applies and

---

154. McFadyen, *Bound to Sin*, p. 164.

comes, radically and objectively to all men, even though they may be at the very lowest point and have never so much as heard of Him. Because this man exists, there is no man who does not exist under the sign of this *Sursum!* For this man is not a private person. (pp. 382–83)

The call to lift up our hearts which comes in Jesus and is the Spirit's direction shames us, revealing our revulsion at the thought of royalty (p. 384). There are four things which the Christian to whom this is revealed knows of herself and of all humanity. First, it is really the case that *all* men and women encounter the exalted Jesus from a place of humiliation (p. 389). If one were to object that there are relatively few truly base people, Barth responds with the assertion that humiliated humanity is, more than anything, *average, mediocre* humanity (p. 391).

But a second question arises: Can such mediocrity really be termed 'evil'? 'Is triviality real corruption?' (p. 391) Backing up, Barth reconsiders that Jesus is in no way a 'private person' apart from whom we can live in peace. Rather, 'what He is necessarily includes in itself our true being as it is ascribed and given us by God'. And so 'the ground is cut away from under our feet' and we are now 'new men who are lifted out of this ordinariness and separated from it' (p. 392). So Barth must answer his question about the badness of being ordinary in the affirmative, as triviality reveals at heart an 'undeniable ingratitude' which flies in the face of reality in Christ, one in which man is like 'a prisoner who when the doors are opened will not leave his cell but wants to remain in it' (p. 393).

Third, Barth considers how far the individual is implicated in relation to Jesus. It could be that 'man of sin' is an epithet mitigating human freedom, thereby saying more than is warranted. A person's sloth is his own, and any sense of determinism or an 'automatic' sinning is out of bounds. Sin is 'a new and responsible work, and it is in contradiction to his nature, so that when he does it he is a stranger to himself' (p. 393). But the danger in avoiding the terminology of 'sinner' (that is, 'man of sin') and speaking only of 'sins' is that sin becomes accidental, something which happens to me rather than something which I commit.[155] Or at least, if I can be said to have committed it, I myself am unstained by it. And so, robust responsibility is again avoided.[156] But man cannot say this; 'he has no alibi and cannot find one…he himself is really mean as the doer of these mean actions'. This is actually gospel, though, for the man of sin's 'whence' and 'whither' are given 'in the existence of this man' (p. 395). 'If he is not prepared to be such, to be a man of sin, this can only mean that he does not want to be one of those whom God has taken to Himself in this one man' (p. 396). Here Barth affirms Luther's sense of the *totus homo incurvatus in se* with gusto, but again places it far more deeply in a Christological context.

---

155. It is thus strange that Highfield claims Barth 'rarely speaks of the subject of the act of sin' in *CD* IV/1–3 (Highfield, *Barth and Rahner in Dialogue*, p. 126).

156. 'I do not have any direct part in its loathsome and offensive character. In the last resort it has taken place in my absence. I myself am elsewhere and aloof from it' (p. 394).

Finally, Barth asks if this situation of sin is 'necessary'. Is this somehow humanity's destiny, God needing a 'shadow', some Hegelian 'harmony of being in which he is affirmed as well as negated' (p. 397)? On the contrary, for Hegel provides a safe house for the sinner, when Jesus has already taken his place such that no place (and every place) is now safe.[157] Jesus has effected a 'radical delimitation of sin and man as its doer' (p. 399), which means that 'in sin man strikes a chord which cannot be taken up into any melody' (p. 400). So the necessity of Hegelian antithesis and any dualism which posits evil or sin as a necessary counterpart to or stage in the development of God are seen to be another attempt to steer clear of encounter with Jesus Christ, with all the freedom and obedience that comes with it.

The sloth of man

As we turn now to Barth's section on the sloth of man, his standpoint bears repeating. The knowledge of Jesus as *this* man gives us knowledge of ourselves in sinful contradiction. But this knowledge is itself 'set under the sign of the great *Sursum!*, the Forward! and Onward!' (p. 383) And so even this discussion of sloth bears within it the spurs of hope prodding us to participate in the homecoming and exaltation of the Son of Man whose 'royalty does not exclude, but includes, us'.[158]

Barth states explicitly at the outset of his discussion of sloth that Protestantism and Western Christianity have generally overlooked sloth and focused on pride. 'We are missing the real man', he insists, 'if we try to see and understand his sin consistently and one-sidedly as hybris, as this brilliant perversion of human pride'. He seems to anticipate feminist concerns directly and struggles to articulate an appropriate sense of sin's unity-in-diversity. Sin has 'different dimensions and aspects, but it is a single entity'. Yet that being said, it is difficult to locate a 'common denominator'. Barth considers whether pride might be subsumed under the rubric of sloth, but then notes that it could work the other way around. However things are understood formally, there is a *material* necessity at play: 'The important thing is that we have every reason closely to scrutinise this second form'.

> The sin of man is not merely heroic in its perversion. It is also...ordinary, trivial and mediocre. The sinner is not merely Prometheus or Lucifer. He is also – and for the sake of clarity, and to match the grossness of the matter, we will use rather popular expressions – a lazy-bones, a sluggard, a good-for-nothing, a slow-coach and a loafer [*ein Faulpelz, ein Siebenschläfer, ein Nichtstuer, ein Bummler*]. (*CD* IV/2, p. 404; *KD* IV/2, p. 454)

157. There is 'no framework within which he may finally be secure as a sinner' (p. 399).
158. Jüngel, *Karl Barth*, p. 128.

And yet again, we can say that the slothful man *is* the proud man (p. 405). At this point, one wonders whether Barth is not more committed to an abstract unity (a concern which can be seen throughout the *Dogmatics*) than a meaningful, phenomenologically rich description of sin. Or maybe he is simply another exponent of pride as the universal form of sin. But *if* Barth is methodologically consistent, there must be something more to his concern for unity. In his remark about different 'aspects' of the 'single entity' of sin, he is taking his cues from the reconciliation of God and humanity in Christ. Recall that Barth treats reconciliation under three 'aspects' of one unified being-in-act.[159] Pride is the 'counter-movement [*Gegenbewegung*] to the divine condescension', while sloth is the 'counter-movement [*Gegenbewegung*] to the elevation which has come to man from God Himself in Jesus Christ' (*CD* IV/2, p. 403; *KD* IV/2, p. 453). Sin is our refusal of God's coming to us and our refusal of our going to him in Christ. As such, it is characterized by our attempt to isolate ourselves from Christ. Slothful man 'wants to be left alone' and withdraws into himself (pp. 407, 455).[160] Sloth represents a maintaining of a 'continual reserve', a falling back upon or sinking back into oneself (p. 455). It is an inaction which is itself a robust form of action (pp. 404–5). Barth recognizes that sin can never be pure inaction, that for something to be called 'sin' it must involve some form of intentional action, some real human willing and agency. He calls sloth 'culpable negligence' (p. 470).

Sloth is still a self-assertion of the 'man in contradiction', against whom God offers a 'superior contradiction' and 'another refusal' (pp. 408–10). Nevertheless, this is a very different self-assertion. Rather than speaking the language of expansion which corresponds to assertion (think of the common counsel to 'put yourself out there'), slothful self-assertion paradoxically involves a retraction which represents a *certain* kind of passivity. Barth may be overestimating the plasticity of 'self-assertion' at this point, but if so it is in the service of Christology. Living in the direction of Jesus means living a life with and for God and others, and so the disobedience of living in and for oneself, even in this slothful form of refusing to 'step up' rather than the more familiar over-stepping of pride, amounts to self-assertion.

In a striking image, Barth writes that slothful man 'turns his back on God, rolling himself into a ball [*in sich selbst zusammen zu rollen*] like a hedgehog with prickly spikes' (*CD* IV/2, p. 405; *KD* IV/2, p. 455). Here we see the resolute refusal of the *Deus pro nobis* which is also a refusal of the others toward whom our being in Christ is oriented. This refusal characterizes sloth-ful man as 'turned in upon himself and finding his satisfaction and comfort in his own ego [*in sich selbst verschlossene, sich in seinem Ichsein genügende und vergenügende*]...He wants to be left alone' (*CD* IV/2, p. 407; *KD* IV/2, pp. 457–8). In fact, a 'life which moves and circles around itself, which is self-orientated but also self-directed, seems to hold out far greater promise

---

159. See IV/1, pp. 132–3.

160. Recall Nietzsche and Fichte, epitomes of the futile attempt to constitute oneself as 'relationless man'.

than one which is lived in this fellowship'. The rejection of this fellowship is a refusal of the freedom promised to us in the man Jesus. As such, it is also a self-refusal (p. 408). There are four aspects to this contradiction on the part of humanity. Barth begins each of these with a Christological premise, namely that the Word became flesh, a premise which points to the fundamental futility of each of our attempts at evading freedom. And he notes in each of the four that these aspects of our refusal are conducted in a concealment which leads to their 'repetition and confirmation and concentration' in hypocrisy (p. 458). Each of these aspects of refusal, or disruptions of man's right relationships (p. 475) is also coordinated with the other three, as they bear on one another. Each is both cause and consequence of the other three.

First, in our relationship with God, our refusal of freedom in Christ is seen in our stupidity or foolishness vis-à-vis the knowledge of God – that is, in our godlessness (pp. 409–32). Here the character is the atheist. The sharpness of this folly is that it cannot be overcome by education (p. 411). Rather, what is needed is revelation; and fools are simply those who do not think they need revelation (p. 412).[161]

Second, humanity's refusal of Christian freedom is seen in its relationship with fellow-man, in its inhumanity (pp. 432–52). Here the character is the inhuman man. Barth reminds us of what he is assuming from the outset:

> In the actualisation which it has found in Him humanity means to be bound and committed to other men. In Him, therefore, man is turned not merely to God but to other men. In Him he is quite open and willing and ready and active for them. (p. 432)

Furthermore, Jesus Christ is 'a summons to participate' in this humanity, and receiving the Spirit is receiving this summons. And yet: 'we remain in our isolation...in our inhumanity' (p. 433). Surprisingly, when it comes to a critique, Barth accuses philanthropy with its commitment to various 'causes' for its hypocritical interest in an abstract and anonymous humanity rather than one's very concrete neighbour. In such abstraction, though appearing to be fundamentally with and for humanity, we manage to escape being with our neighbour and maintain an attention to ourselves rather than the needs of others. There are strong parallels with the feminist description of sin as self-loss in this discussion. Self-loss can be seen as a form of philanthropy ideologically committed to abstract, universal ideals of love while at the same time remaining blind to the particularities of the neighbour to be loved and therefore clumsy at best and often destructive in its demonstrations of that 'love'. Think of the downtrodden man who continues to enable his boss's manipulation and abuse of him in the name of 'service'. Any avoidance tactic can look like love. After all, what do we like more than avoiding conflict? Take a very different, though typical example. A woman is so involved in activities of service and love – organizing a blood drive at church, say, on top

---

161. For a stark contrast between salvation by education and salvation by revelation, see Kierkegaard's *Philosophical Fragments*.

of overseeing a homeless shelter – but nevertheless misses any real encounter with *people*.[162] Barth sees in such situations an evasion: 'I can so easily escape this being with [my neighbour] in the prosecution of a mere cause' (p. 438). Even here, humanity is *incurvatus in se*:

> I can apply myself to a human cause, and give myself wholeheartedly to the prosecution and success of the relevant programme and enterprise, yet always have my own activity and therefore myself in mind rather than the other man, thus thinking and speaking and acting with a complete disregard for his questions and needs and expectations, for his existence generally, and proving myself to be quite inhuman. (p. 438)

It is not that the causes of philanthropy are deficient, but rather that 'the inhuman element in all of us...finds particularly effective concealment' therein (p. 440). What is most deeply disturbing is that there is a form of love which is 'mere philanthropy' in which we master and use our neighbour. This is a love in which,

> however sacrificially it is practiced, the other is not seized by a human hand but by a cold instrument, or even by a paw with sheathed talons, and therefore genuinely isolated and frozen and estranged and oppressed and humiliated, so that he feels that he is trampled under the feet of the one who is supposed to love him, and cannot react with gratitude. (p. 440)

Sadly, this finds expression in the institutions of Christianity more often than in the world's loves (p. 440). And yet it may also fit the sin feminist writers have described as 'self-loss', which at its heart betrays an abstract notion of love inattentive to (or at least misreading) the context. That is, a woman who loses herself dysfunctionally in her family fails to love her family as they need to be loved. Rather than finding herself in relationships of mutuality in an encounter with each of her family members, she evades all encounters with them and thus lives an inhuman, anti-social and finally self-enclosed life. By treating (or using) them as objects of philanthropy, she denies their subjectivity and in turn denies them access to herself as a subject with whom to relate.

The third form of our withdrawal into ourselves is 'a life of dissipation' in relation to the created order (p. 452, section is pp. 452–67). Here the character is the vagabond. We exist as wanderers, not because we cannot find a home but because we are discontent with the home which has been given us.[163] As vagabonds, we continually reject the limits of our creaturely existence – limits which in reality mark off the territory of our freedom – in an effort to be something else. Dissipation is our living as if we were purely spirit or purely flesh, our living in self-contradiction of our determination as

---

162. This is not to downplay the importance of organization and, in its place, bureaucracy, but rather to unmask the self-serving orientation of even our most virtuous of activities.

163. As such, we are like the prodigal son whose story shapes Barth's treatment of the doctrine of reconciliation.

the soul of our body (p. 453).[164] The indisciplined man 'regards himself as the supreme court' and wills 'to be without spirit' and on the way to soullessness and bodilessness (p. 454). There is a real disintegrative power at work which 'leads to a disarmament of man and therefore to a supreme disinclination...It is our pleasure – and this is the awful positive element in what we have called our indiscipline – to decompose our human nature' (p. 456).[165]

The classic act of dissipation is David's sin against Bathsheba and Uriah (pp. 464–7). The opening of this narrative in 2 Samuel makes the point with great subtlety: 'In the spring, at the time when kings go off to war, David sent Joab out with the king's men and the whole Israelite army. They destroyed the Ammonites and besieged Rabbah. But David remained in Jerusalem' (2 Sam. 11.1, NIV). The beginning of David's dissipation was surely justified. He had a long and storied career, even before ascending to the throne. That he would send his nephew as deputy to lead his army is understandable. And yet, this is the beginning of his sin. It lies in David's simple refusal to do what all kings do, his treating of himself as a man apart. But rather than an august figure at this point, David is merely lazy.[166] Sloth means that 'we are too lazy to follow the movement of God which lifts us up, that instead we let ourselves sink and fall. Fall into what? Into our graceless being for ourselves [*unser gnadenloses Sein für uns selbst*]' (*CD* IV/2, p. 458; *KD* IV/2, p. 516). Such gracelessness involves one in a 'habit of self-forgiveness [which] spoils his taste for a life by free grace' (p. 461). We want 'simply to live: to live but not to be converted' (p. 458).

These themes of self-forgiveness and a life without conversion perfectly fit Hampson's pastoral suggestions for women, with her emphasis on continuity and self-actualization rather than crucifixion and resurrection through identification with another, namely Christ, and in her comment that women are better described as 'once-born'. All of this is predicated on a denial of women's sin, or a restriction of sin to describe women's failure to love and accept themselves as they are. And yet for Barth, these various emphases compose 'our graceless being for ourselves'. They are in no way salutary but instead betray the sin of sloth in its character as dissipation. Is Barth falling back into the old paradigm of pride at this point?

Consider that it is in this small subsection that Barth offers a compelling discussion of the ramifications of sin as a type of self-loss in our relationships with others. He writes:

164. 'Man is soul of a body and therefore necessarily both soul and body' (III/2, p. 373). On 'Man as Soul and Body', see *CD* III/2, §46, pp. 325–436. Note that, in addition to employing it in speaking of humanity's total depravity, the *totus homo* underscores the inseparability of soul and body for Barth so that one cannot speak of one without the other.

165. Decomposition and disintegration imply diminishment, and so Allen Jorgenson can write that 'smallness is the sin of humans as sloth' (Jorgenson, 'Karl Barth's Christological Treatment of Sin', p. 452).

166. Barth calls dissipation 'indiscipline' at one point (p. 454).

In the measure that we abandon and assert ourselves we are useless for society, refusing our responsibilities in relation to our fellows, our neighbours, our brothers. The destruction of the I in which we are involved necessarily means that there is a vacuum at the point where the other seeks a Thou to whom he can be an I. The dissipated man becomes a neutral, an It which is without personal activity and with which the other cannot enter into a fruitful personal reciprocity. (p. 462)

Note that Barth refers explicitly to self-loss and self-seeking in this passage, but finds them two sides of the same coin. In either case, they dash any hope of encounter, precisely in that they destroy us and eliminate one of the two poles necessary for the mutuality of encounter. The destruction comes in humanity's dissipated refusal of itself as it is in the exaltation of the Son of Man, and it removes humanity from the realm of the personal, which is never neutral but always *for others*.[167] In Barth's description, he recognizes and effectively diagnoses self-loss, that characteristically 'feminine' sin, yet sees in it not a failure to accept oneself but as another form of being for oneself (speaking of 'losing himself in his attempt to assert himself' [p. 408]), living in contradiction to one's humanity which is determined in Christ as a being for and with others. At the very least, this is a failure to be for others which carries an implicit being for oneself.[168] Barth's ability to argue in such a way is due to his conviction that any form of failure to live truly for others amounts to a living for oneself. And he would seem to be right in this. What's more, such a description has the pastoral effect of unmasking the sinful losing of oneself in others. No matter the motivation and intention of the person who loses himself in another, precisely because the being-in-act of that person is not truly one of self-giving love, it can only be called what it is – self-serving love.

The fourth and final form of sloth Barth considers is 'human care' in man's relationship with his time in its historical limitation. Here the character is the unhappy man of care or the discontented man. This temporal component of sin is something we have seen little of in Augustine and Luther and is one of Barth's greatest strengths. Indeed, he takes human spatio-temporality as seriously as any modern theologian.[169] To be in time is so essential to our being

---

167. This refusal of relationship with God in Christ and with others highlights the missional character of union with Christ in Barth's theology. On this, see Johnson, *The Mystery of God*, pp. 147–8, 176–83.

168. Of course, Barth is, as always, careful to remind us that, because we find in Jesus a once-and-for-all 'normalisation of our nature', there can be no 'absolute contradiction' of who we are in him (p. 453).

169. The critiques of him on this point have been harsh and not without some warrant. The loudest voice is Richard H. Roberts. See his essay on Barth's doctrine of time in Roberts, *A Theology on Its Way?*, pp. 1–58. Without delving into the difficult questions and the often intractable prose in Barth's treatment of time and eternity in the *Dogmatics* (not to mention the *Römerbrief*), suffice it to say that his doctrine of eternity as the simultaneity or coinherence of past, present and future threatens to eliminate the pastness of the past and the futurity of the future. In Alan Padgett's words, Barth's eternity is '*the fullness of time without the defects of succession*...What Barth's doctrine does in effect is to call into

per se that Barth can write: 'Humanity is temporality' (III/2, p. 522). 'I am not only what I was, I am already, even if only *in nuce*, what I shall be' (III/2, p. 541). This sort of continuity is not self-evident, however (III/2, p. 542). Rather the guarantee of this, of the meaningful connection of my time(s), is God, the very fact that *he* was and is and will be establishing us and the continuity of our identity. And 'He was never not our Creator, Father and Redeemer' (III/2, p. 545). So this temporality which humanity simply *is* is a particular kind of temporality, what Barth calls 'given time'.[170]

As sinful humanity we take care when 'we will not thankfully accept the limitation of our existence where we should hope in the light of it, and be certain, joyously certain, of the fulfilment of our life in the expectation of its end' (IV/2, p. 468). Accordingly, in taking care, we suffer from perpetually bad timing (pp. 413–14). We either get lost in the past or over-anticipate the future. Whatever our attitude towards time, it is marked by an attempt to shake off our mortality, and our time's particular allotment. Part of our taking care is due to viewing our time as abstractly limited rather than limited by God (III/2, p. 563). Such abstraction regards our final frontier 'as a threat rather than our hope' (p. 470). This is because we see death as something without God, not seeing that this 'illusionary opponent...has already been routed' (p. 471). But for Christians, death must *now* mean hope. God has defeated death and raised Jesus from the dead in the power of the Spirit, and so our death has lost its sting and must be seen, somehow, as part of 'the good order of God'.

It might be tempting to dismiss care as a natural, if regrettable aspect of humanity's composition. But it, like all sloth is marked by 'refusal and negligence' in the face of humanity's exaltation in Christ. It can thus be called '*the* human sin' from a temporal perspective (p. 472). Care's concealment takes many forms, which can be brought under the rubric of activism (how unlike sloth it *appears*!) and passivism (pp. 472–4). The reason Barth speaks of the concealment of each of these forms of sloth is his concern to highlight its *reality* and *power* precisely in their concealment, even if this reality is finally relative as God has given Jesus to this very man of care, such that redemption is 'even more true' than his sin (p. 478). Barth turns to Numbers 13–14, the story of the spies who went to canvass Canaan, to 'give concretion to our analysis' of care (pp. 478–83, [478]). The story provides a vivid example of the care which 'destroys human fellowship' in that it 'not only does not gather us but disperses and scatters us' (p. 476). These are people on the cusp of the Promised Land who fall into fear, accusations and division into

question the reality of process' (Alan G. Padgett, *God, Eternity and the Nature of Time* [New York: St. Martin's Press, 1992], p. 143). It may be here that he is most open to charges of idealism. Furthermore, Barth departs sharply from the biblical conception of eternity as endless duration. I am thankful to Mark Bilby for making this second point clear to me. And finally, rejecting succession threatens to render meaningless the notion of God's own becoming in Christ (Padgett, *God, Eternity and the Nature of Time*, p. 145).

170. See his discussion of 'given time' in *CD* III/2, pp. 511–53.

splinter groups. Refusing the word of promise of Yahweh, they take care and alter their course to the point of slaughter at the hand of the Amalekites and Canaanites. Barth is clear about the order of isolation which occurs when we take care. In taking seriously and fearing a godless death, we isolate ourselves from God and thereby from one another. Against Hampson's view that it is *only* and *precisely* by isolating ourselves from a transcendent God who is 'wholly other' that we can be rightly ourselves in relation with one another, Barth counters by assuming that it is only by being rightly related to the God who is wholly other that we can be rightly related to one another. It is only by refusing to take care, that is, it is only by trusting God that we can live in fellowship with one another as those who are gathered together (i.e., the Church) rather than scattered in our isolated corners of care.

The misery of slothful man

Even given what is true of us in Jesus, given that he ventured out into the far country as the Son of God 'in order that He may return home as the Son of Man, not in isolation but as our Lord and Head and Representative, bringing us with Him' (recall the *totus Christus*), we create ourselves a situation in which we are miserable:

> Instead of being those who are exalted in and with Him, as we are in truth, we are revealed in His light as those who lead a false existence, remaining in exile and therefore in misery as though the true God had come to us in vain, as though He had not taken us up with Him, as though we were not already at home in and with Him, sharing His royal freedom. (p. 483)

The miserable man of sloth lives 'as though'. The force of Barth's rhetoric and his strategic employment of prepositional phrases like this effect the reversing of the traditional Protestant rhetoric of justification. It is not 'as though' I were no longer a sinner, but rather 'as though' I were *still* a sinner. The 'legal fiction' in this case is the man of sin, not his justification. This man lives quite literally in the past, in a life which is no longer his.[171] Think of the man who excelled in school sports and continues to regale friends with stories of his exploits thirty years later. What passes for nostalgia often deteriorates into a hopelessly backwards orientation, hopeless precisely because such a man cannot look outside himself and cannot look to the future. This is *homo incurvatus in se*, caught somewhere between tragedy (in the depths of his misery) and absurdity (in the sheer impossibility which marks his enterprise). The man of misery 'remains below where he does not belong, and is not at home, but where he irrevocably has his place [*ist...da drunten, wo er nicht hingehört, wo er nicht daheim ist, wo er aber...unwiderruflich seinen Ort hat*] – so long as his corrupt will is not broken by the direction of Jesus' (*CD* IV/2, p. 484; *KD* IV/2, p. 547).

---

171. Sloth causes our 'tarrying in the past' (p. 493).

But we remember that this is still an 'as though', and man's location in his misery is truly a utopia, a no-place.[172] Nor can he make such a *topos* into a home in the future: 'As he has not created himself, he cannot disannul or transform himself'. The facts of the incarnation, resurrection, Pentecost, etc., are all just that – 'facts. As man has not brought them about, he cannot reverse them by anything that he does.' We simply cannot undo ourselves. In fact, 'it is these very facts which make the misery of man so severe...The very thing which limits his misery – the fact that in it he belongs to God – is also the very thing which makes it so sharp' (pp. 484–5). We cannot find any rest in our desire to be alone, so we are miserable.

What is the misery resulting from sloth? It is three things, all of which are learned from the reconciliation of man in Jesus. First, it is a mortal sickness whose end would have been our death were it not for Jesus taking our place. And yet: 'It does in fact end with our death to the extent that Jesus, burdened with our sickness, suffered our death' (486). Barth wants to talk about 'perversion' rather than 'transformation' or 'destruction', because humanity always remains God's good creature. But he also wants to speak of a kind of total depravity, though characteristically speaking of the *event* or *history* rather than *state* of our perversion or corruption (pp. 488–9).

Humanity both is what it does and does what it is. So, and this is the second point, unless a new birth, a totally new beginning with a new subject be made in Jesus, we will be caught in the circle of our misery (pp. 490–93).[173] Barth wonders about the usefulness of categorical distinctions such as sins of omission and commission, but besides their value as a 'penitential mirror', they help point out the inescapability of God's judgment on all sin and also the particularity of his judgment on each sin (p. 492). He rejects the distinction between mortal and venial sins as assuming a 'quantitative concept of sin' which is not taking seriously the judgment on every sin. Voluntary and involuntary sins are rejected for the same reason (p. 493).

Finally, our misery is our will's determination as a *bound* will (pp. 493–4). Barth notes that the bondage of the will must be established christologically, not empirically or abstractly. And further, it need not and cannot imply a commitment to determinism (or indeterminism, for that matter) nor that man has no will at all. If such were the case, we would cease to be human. He then discusses freedom: 'Freedom is not an empty and formal concept...It does not speak only of a capacity...The free man is the man who can be genuinely man in fellowship with God. He exercises and has this freedom, therefore, not in an indefinite but in a definite choice in which he demonstrates this capacity' (p. 494). So the free man *cannot* sin. Barth and Hampson could not

---

172. We must be cautious with the language of home, as Barth consistently maps references to 'place' on to the *history* of Jesus Christ. That is, our place which has been taken by Jesus, in whom we find in turn a new place is more accurately spoken of in terms of direction than location. It is a story rather than a state. For the relevance of this to justification, see Hart, *Regarding Karl Barth*, pp. 62–3.

173. Hampson comes to mind here, with her explicit rejection of conversion for women and parallel (if implicit) denial of women's sin.

stand further apart in how they conceive of freedom. Hampson's freedom is radical autonomy, self-determination which entails a libertarian's freedom of choice. Any determination by another disqualifies the terms 'autonomy' and 'freedom' from use. This is truly and properly named a freedom 'for oneself'. Barth's freedom is always freedom 'for another' and as such has one direction and one direction only. That is the direction of the Son, whose way is towards God and others. The Son's direction is a freedom for obedience in which all of humanity may and does participate. Thus, Barth describes the sinner as failing to make use of his freedom rather than freely choosing another valid direction (p. 495).

Barth's pattern is well-established in the doctrine of reconciliation. First he describes sin. Then he reminds us that sin is futile, transient and unnecessary because God is creator and redeemer and is fundamentally *pro nobis* in Christ. But then Barth turns around again and, the former *proviso* being in place, acknowledges the very real, if only provisionally so, character of sin. As Robert Cushman puts it: 'We *can* be sinners just because, as creatures of God and with our creation, we are called to existence with him in Jesus Christ'.[174] In the section on the bondage of the will, Barth adapts Luther's *simul* (without explicit reference) in writing that even the sanctified are 'not only in Jesus' but 'also' in themselves (IV/2, p. 496). The similarity with Luther is clear – humanity between the first and second advents of Christ is bilocal. According to Barth, there are two 'qualitative determinations [*Bestimmungen*] of the one undivided being of man'.[175] Two different dialectics are in play with Luther and Barth, however. As Michael Beintker has shown, in Barth's thinking our being 'in Christ' and our being 'in sin' or 'in Adam' form a 'supplementary dialectic'. Beintker contrasts this more Hegelian mode of dialectic which moves in an irreversible direction with a Kierkegaardian complementary dialectic in which the two poles abide in tension.[176] Luther employs a complementary dialectic, particularly in the way he applies the *simul iustus et peccator* to the *totus homo*. Of course, Barth reads the *simul* holistically as well, but the weight of what has happened in Christ simply overwhelms what was in Adam such that they cannot remain equally valid and forceful poles determining the Christian's life.[177]

Trevor Hart helpfully points out Barth's resistance of any notion of progress in the *simul*. We are not gradually becoming more righteous and less sinful *in se*, contrary to Augustine's view which continues to hold sway

---

174. Robert E. Cushman, 'Barth's Attack upon Cartesianism', in *Faith Seeking Understanding* (Durham, NC: Duke University Press, 1981), pp. 118–19.

175. IV/1, p. 494 (cited in Highfield, *Barth and Rahner in Dialogue*, p. 126). The 'qualitative' rather than 'quantitative' points to a holistic anthropology in which these are determinations of the *totus homo*.

176. On the distinction, see McCormack, *Karl Barth's Critically Realistic Dialectical Theology*, pp. 162–5. On the Adam–Christ dialectic, see pp. 266–9.

177. Barth is critical of the tendency of the Reformation *simul* to lead to 'a stabilization of life under a double bookkeeping' (Busch, *The Great Passion*, p. 202).

in Roman Catholic thinking.[178] As we have seen, despite a holistic anthropology which thought of sin in terms of postures of the self, Augustine could not affirm the *totus* aspect of the *simul* and instead thought of it in terms of a *via* along which growth occurs.[179] And yet, while rejecting a process of change, an 'imbalanced proportionality in which we are *in ourselves* gradually more *iustus* and less *peccator*', Barth's thinking in terms of histories rather than states moves him to think of justified sinners as 'in transition'.[180] Right now, 'as [man's] past as a sinner is *still his present*, so his future as a righteous man is *already his present*'.[181] It is precisely this historical orientation of Barth's thought that, while not succumbing to a crassly empirical notion of growth in righteousness, nevertheless moves him beyond Luther's strictly dialectical (in the Kierkegaardian sense) approach.[182] The past is the sinner's present, but its very outdatedness and futility circumscribe its power as his present. For Barth, Adam is passé, hopefully out-of-date and stripped of his power. The future is also his present, but its loud proclamation of the victory of Christ drowns out the past.[183] This is not to suggest a denial of sin or any intrinsic, non-participatory ideas of Christian perfection on Barth's part. It is, instead, to see in Barth even more than in Luther the defeat of sin and the death of death.

Hampson and Barth: A Tale of Two Sloths

How, then, do Hampson and Barth compare in their portrayal of sloth? Their diagnoses are strikingly similar. Consider again Valerie Saiving's classic description of women in sin, which Hampson takes on without remainder. According to Saiving, women 'are better suggested by such items as triviality, distractability, and diffuseness...in short, underdevelopment or negation of the self'.[184] Saiving and Hampson contrast this sharply with the self-assertion of pride. Barth's adjectives run parallel:

> The sin of man is not merely heroic in its perversion. It is also...ordinary, trivial and mediocre. The sinner is not merely Prometheus or Lucifer. He is also – and for the sake of clarity, and to match the grossness of the matter, we will use rather popular expressions – a lazy-bones, a sluggard, a good-for-nothing, a slow-coach and a loafer. (IV/2, p. 404)

178. Hart, *Regarding Karl Barth*, pp. 53–5.
179. See pages 51–3 above.
180. Hart, *Regarding Karl Barth*, pp. 54, 55.
181. IV/1, 55 (quoted in Hart, *Regarding Karl Barth*, p. 55).
182. *Contra* Hart, *Regarding Karl Barth*, pp. 53–5. A biography of Barth could never be called *Barth: Man Between God and the Devil*, whereas the title of Oberman's biography of Luther captures the ethos of the Reformer well.
183. Barth makes a related point in concluding a careful discussion of Romans 5: 'our relation to Adam is less essential than our relationship to Christ' (Karl Barth, *Christ and Adam* [trans. T. A. Smail; New York: Harper & Brothers, 1956], p. 86).
184. Hampson, 'Reinhold Niebuhr on Sin', p. 50.

A laziness, passivity, lack of focus, distraction, unwillingness to *move* characterizes sloth in both accounts. Both agree, too, that this involves a negation of the self, though to Saiving's 'underdevelopment' Barth might add a dialectical 'overdevelopment concealed within underdevelopment'.[185] But clearly, after our long discussion of sloth in *Church Dogmatics* IV/2, Barth has anticipated many of the concerns of feminists to broaden the scope of our understanding of sin. The extent of agreement is striking.[186]

Except, of course, when it comes to the remedy for sloth. In Hampson's words, 'Feminists believe, not in the undoing of the self, castigating a person for her pride, but rather in building up what is already given. Feminists will therefore look askance at a doctrine which advocates turning away from the self to God.'[187] For Hampson, then, the remedy for sloth is a radical autonomy vis-à-vis God rather than a dependence on him. Here we notice that her account of sloth, for all its phenomenological similarity to Barth's, lacks *theology*.[188] Sloth and its antidote, in her account, is entirely self-referential – it is a matter of coming to oneself. For Barth, on the other hand, sin is fundamentally a failure to be for and with God and others, with the humanity of Jesus as the 'normative standard of reference'. So the remedy for sloth is anything but a greater attending to oneself. It is a more faithfully, lovingly (and always freely) attending to God and others.

The question remains, however, about the pastoral implications of conceiving sloth under the umbrella of sin as incurvature. Hampson's objection is pointed. By telling a person (hopefully it is well-established by now that this may be just as true of men as it is of women) guilty of the type of sloth in which the self is dissipated that he needs to live eccentrically in God and others, are we not perpetuating sinful relational cycles? By calling even the self-loss of sloth 'self-centred' we draw attention to the personal responsibility of the one who is lost, thereby removing the last remaining refuge for the sinner. And it is in its ability to name self-loss as *sin* that *incurvatus in se* possesses the conceptual resources to fight against and such self-loss, thereby regaining the self through confession, forgiveness and reconciliation. Hampson, on the other hand, is powerless to counteract such self-loss precisely because she lacks these conceptual resources found in the language of sin and salvation. Strangely, it is *Barth* who comes across as a true 'feminist', an advocate for women (and

185. Really, such an overdevelopment is regressive, not progressive, and so hardly counts as true development.

186. Gene Outka also gives a rich account of sloth: 'And so a life dominated by sloth acquires no discernible shape. In describing such a life, one is at a loss to find abiding aims, or definite views, or permanent loyalties. One who lives such a life lacks particularity, some characteristic personal center' (Outka, 'Universal Love and Impartiality', pp. 53–7 [53]).

187. Hampson, *After Christianity*, p. 282.

188. McFadyen's comment about feminist theologies of sin certainly applies to Hampson: 'In its lack of clarity concerning the sense in which sloth and pride are sins against God and not just against self or "right-relation", one wonders whether sin is here a functioning theological language' (McFadyen, *Bound to Sin*, p. 165). Of course, Hampson explicitly denies any conception of God as a personal other over against me with whom I relate.

any perpetrators of sloth) in his refusal to either reduce sloth to pride (thereby making it a 'manly' sin) or excuse sloth as a pure phenomenon of victimization (thereby taking away its status as sin).[189] To say this is not to deny the structural and broader social dynamics of sin, which we have only lightly touched upon. Nor is it to put the entire blame for sin at the feet of the sinner. As Daniel Migliore cautions, 'We must be careful in stating this point, more careful than Barth himself was. The danger is that we might engage in blaming the victim.'[190] The one who sins knows himself as both guilty sinner and helplessly entrapped victim of a fallen matrix of relational dynamics.[191] Both Barth and the better feminist theologies of sin (Hampson's is unfortunately not one of these) recognize this double-bind, and feminists better than Barth. Thanks to the feminist re-drawing of the hamartiological boundaries, as well as their attention to the interplay of subjectivity and oppressive systems, 'sloth is rather named as a continuing mode of personal agency, which may yet itself by characterised in terms of "self-loss"'.[192] For a hamartiology to be *Christian*, it must speak of humanity's wilful (hence culpable) disobedience. No matter how our understanding of sin is nuanced to account for difference, if these two simple features disappear, our understanding has ceased to be Christian. Hampson does not ask us to be more properly Christian by naming sin with greater precision and attention to particularity. Rather, she asks us to limit the set of sinners to something less than all of humanity.

Where feminist hamartiologies consistently miss the mark is in their rejection of a straw version of an eccentric model of personhood and an egocentric model of sin. To love another well requires one to be a loving person. That is, a certain centredness is *necessary* for one to live eccentrically. There must

---

189. Not that Barth is consistently 'feminist'. One failure is his declaration that woman exists *only* as the 'Thou' to man's 'I' (which also keeps man from being a 'Thou'), a failure which evacuates the active subjectivity of woman and advocates a kind of 'self-loss'. For a thoughtful, trenchant internal critique along these lines, see Fraser, 'Jesus' Humanity and Ours', pp. 187–90.

190. Migliore, 'Sin and Self-Loss', p. 148. Migliore continues: 'Defining sin as also taking the form of passive accommodation to evil does not give us license to say to the unemployed, "You are lazy and lack ambition,"...Barth's analysis of sin as sloth must be carefully nuanced and concretized.' Migliore's point is well-taken, though the importance of encounter must be stressed again. Sin as sloth does not invite us to label *carte blanche* an unemployed person lazy. But in a face-to-face encounter with a particular person who is unemployed for sinful reasons, it may be entirely appropriate! What is called for here is compassion, certainly, but even more, it is true relationship in the context of which a particular truth may be spoken.

191. 'The express intention is to indicate that the experienced reality of oppression is one in which the victims are personally active as subjects, even whilst that subjectivity is significantly and adversely affected. What is being claimed here is that oppression has an internal aspect....Feminist ideological critique makes it clear that women *situate themselves in* at the same time as *being situated by* "patriarchy"' (McFadyen, *Bound to Sin*, pp. 142, 146). Outka makes the same point in writing that the slothful person need not be viewed 'as sheerly a victim. She remains a responsible agent; she is complicit in her self-evacuation. Judgment is then appropriate' (Outka, 'Universal Love and Impartiality', p. 54).

192. McFadyen, *Bound to Sin*, p. 150.

be a self on either end of the relationship. Indeed, an eccentric model presupposes all of this and is twisted if read in any other way. The feminist claim that women must first 'come to themselves' before they can love another seems wise. But too often in feminist discourse the coming to oneself becomes the entire shape of a woman's life. Rather than a means pastorally aimed towards the healing of women *that* they might love others well, we see an endless self-actualization project. This is the other disastrous flaw, of course, that an over-dependence on human relationships will be counteracted by an attempt to extricate oneself from *all* dependence – whether human or divine. The sad irony is that this leads to isolation, not relation. And in many writers, Hampson being a prime example, it bankrupts theological terms. Sin is simply no longer sin, and salvation is mere self-acceptance. That is fine if there is no real objective *problem*. But the Christian witness has always been that salvation involves a real setting-right of wrongs, a real reconciliation of parties and a real transformation of broken and lost sinners. Such sinners (men *and* women) do not need self-acceptance; they need to be made new.

Finally, we return to the question of simple descriptive range and accuracy. At the end of the day, can being curved in on oneself effectively describe sloth, particularly when the latter is understood as entailing self-dissipation or self-loss? We have seen in Barth's case that such a description works; but at the same time, it requires certain counter-intuitive moves. When he speaks of sloth and losing oneself in others as the refusal of relationships, is he not evacuating these terms of their common-sense content? It may be. On the other hand, and I take this to be a virtue more often than a vice, Barth's resolutely *theological* way of speaking frequently requires him to spin familiar concepts in new ways. In so doing, he seeks not to confuse but to shock one out of semantic slumber and, more to the point, to speak *faithfully*. It may well be that our sense of self-loss in terms of victimization (which is where Hampson ends up) is corrupt and needs to be reoriented to encompass the real sin (and therefore human agency) involved in losing oneself in relationships. When Barth redefines sloth to include a self-referential component, he complexifies the moral agent and context.[193] His dialectical approach even here (self-loss as self-love) upsets our expectations and reshuffles the categories in the process. In so doing, he embodies McFadyen's concern to attend to the particularities of sin, to ask about the various exigencies that make this particular sin sloth.[194] Such complexity calls for a subtle, layered analysis of the sinner and his sin and resists the easy problem–solution approach of

193. He also confirms my earlier point about the mutually 'edifying' nature of pride and sloth. See pages 120–1 above.

194. He also thereby 'proves' the insufficiency of general anthropology and natural theology, even a natural theology of sin, in that his Christological account of sloth is both a fitting phenomenology of sloth (so that we think, 'Yes, of course, that's right!') while at the same time being an *unexpected* phenomenology. Even as his description resonates with our experience, it accounts for our experience in a way that we do not expect, reminding us of the need for revelation even in hamartiology.

some of the Western tradition (pride – humility) just as must as it does that of
feminist theology (sloth/self-loss – self-assertion/self-acceptance). As Kathryn
Greene-McCreight points out: 'Self-denial...is not simply the opposite of
self-assertion, and cannot be corrected by it.[195] Furthermore, besides denying
the gospel, 'making self-assertion into the goal of sanctification for women
threatens to generate chronic guilt and constant self-assessment which can
lead to disappointment and a sense of failure'.[196] This is not even to mention
the insidious structural as well as what might be called 'diachronic' (the 'sins
of the fathers') components of sin. All of this can lean in a rather pessimistic
direction. Are we so hopelessly caught up in sin that we are unable to notice
and name it, much less combat it? At this point, all we can do is offer a hopeful conviction, which is that the noticing and naming, as well as the living of
a new life free from the power of sin and death *can be done*. It may be done
in starts and stops, with greater and lesser skill, but that it is done and will be
done is the witness of the Church. And that is where it is done – amongst the
people of God, in the process of listening to the Word of truth which is also
the truth about ourselves, in confessing, confronting, repenting and reconciling with one another in the spiritual community for which we were created
and redeemed.

Conclusion

As we have seen, Augustine and Luther share an emphasis on *incurvatus in
se* as pride or egoism. Luther radicalizes this by applying it to *homo religiosus*, and he provides a critique of all forms of self-love that calls Augustine's
doctrine of the *ordo amoris* which speaks of a proper self-love into question.
Barth severs *incurvatus in se* from its too-strict tie to pride, or he restricts
pride to one amongst many sins. Not that he backs down from Luther's critique of anthropocentrism. Rather, he sees anthropocentrism as the problem,
indeed as the form of sin, which finds manifestation in various sins, amongst
which are pride, sloth and falsehood. Indeed, sin's being seen to take the form
of a curve inward is a function of Barth's theocentrism.

Despite our revitalization of the language of incurvature as an appropriately
broad umbrella concept for understanding sin, the application of this language
requires care. What feminist theologies of sin have made eminently clear is
the vicious implication of a misunderstanding or misapplication of sin. If we
are to speak of *homo incurvatus in se*, an immediate clarification is called for
– this is *not* to be identified without remainder with pride. We may not say less
than that sin catapults one into the wrong orbit – oneself – and represents this
kind of stultifying, isolating, self-aggrandizing *and* self-diminishing posture.
While we are wary of adopting a gendered account of sin due to its descriptive poverty and extra-biblical grammar, we must listen carefully to feminist

195. Greene-McCreight, 'Gender, Sin and Grace', p. 424.
196. Greene-McCreight, 'Gender, Sin and Grace', pp. 431–2.

accounts of the ways in which pride-based hamartiologies have served to lock women into structures of oppression and even insinuate slothful postures among women. In other words, if we are not careful, the way we speak about sin can quickly become itself sinful in its underwriting and even prescribing of certain forms of sin.

I argued in the introduction that personhood has its own logic apart from the grammar of sin. To speak of persons in the first light of sin, even to speak of them as that which sin is not, is to circumscribe humanity within boundaries inappropriate to creatures of God. What's more, if Christ is (among so many other things) the most exemplary, but even more the most real, the most true person, and if we confess his sinless obedience to the Father as axiomatic, then to take sin as the primary locus for understanding personhood is to disqualify Christology (and, therefore, anthropology) from the discussion from the start.

That being said, it is unquestionable that, unless we lapse into a strange idealism, to speak about human persons is to speak immediately about sin. Whether we understand *simul iustus et peccator* along the lines of a way (Augustine) or a dialectic (Luther and Barth), we continue to confess the status of humanity as *peccator* this side of the eschaton. So, while sin is to be defined *a posteriori*, after the establishment of Christology and anthropology, it remains a necessary category in describing human personhood. And while it may only admit of a secondary reality or even describe a fundamentally negative move with a non-ontological status, sin's effects and the human person *as* the sinner who lives in, with and under those effects remain somehow constitutive for humanity in a world on the way to new creation, even a world in which new creation has dawned in the resurrection of Jesus.

Thus, while sin does not give us our initial bearings as we map the human person, it does give a secondary set of coordinates which mark out boundaries and limits. As the refusal to be that for which God created us, sin does afford a glimpse from below of personhood. While never sufficient, definitions of what a thing is *not* are often telling.

What, then, does it mean to be a person? It means, of course, so many things. But a properly theological definition requires us to say at least two of these things: To be a person means to be (1) created (2) for a specific purpose. Theological anthropology requires us to speak of the triune source of personhood. It is not a *bruta facta*, but something which continually has reference to its source in the free, self-giving love of the triune creator. But second, humanity was created for a specific purpose. We are teleological creatures, and to speak without reference to the goal of creation is to speak nonsense. Most simply put, to be human is to be *created* and to be *created for*.

We can, and indeed must, expand on this second point. All of God's creating is in some sense purposeful, but we do not generally refer to rhubarb as personal. My secondary argument throughout these pages has been that the *specific* purpose for which humanity was created is, as John Zizioulas has so powerfully reminded us, communion – communion with the Father in the Son by the Spirit, communion with one another and communion with ourselves. It may be, as Barth continually admits throughout *Church Dogmatics* III/2, that animals and plants have their own, appropriate form of relating with God. But one thing is certain: to be human, to live in the *imago Dei* is to be drawn continuously out of ourselves into communion with God and one another.

But to return to the twofold definition of humanity, to speak in terms of personhood in terms of a being *created* and *created for* allows the Christian theologian to affirm two things. First, every human is by definition a person.[1] Second, personhood is something only fully realized ecclesially and eschatologically in Christ by the Spirit. The notion of the ecclesial mediation of personhood is controversial for its exclusivism. Surely God works outside the Church! Indeed he does. Does this limit the Church to the status of one among many media/locales of God's redemptive work? Or do we follow Cyprian's dictum (*extra ecclesia nulla salus*) and confess that salvation is found in no other house? Maybe we can say salvation is found primarily in the Church. Or should we answer with a vigorous 'exclusively'? Remembering that salvation is itself an eschatological category, and that God creates and saves a people as well as persons, we must at least say that salvation is *finally* located in the Church, understood as the people of God.

This guards against a triumphalist account which would tempt Christians with a vision of completed personhood coupled with an 'us-versus-them' mindset. But it also ensures that true personhood is only fully realized (just as, of course, it only originates) in a Trinitarian context. This is not to deny that those who have no interest in such a context may live more humanly than committed churchgoers. Nor is it to presume (according to the triumphalist account) that churchgoers exemplify what it means to be human. Rather does our ecclesial identity involve us existing 'not as that which [we are] but as that which [we] will be'.[2] It is simply to affirm that we do not become who we are apart from the Father who draws us out of our self-enclosure in Christ by the power and presence of his Spirit. But the scandal of this Trinitarian context is not a late arrival on the scene, a problem of redemption with which to wrestle. It stands just as squarely centre stage in creation, and so we can truly say that personhood comes from and moves to a Trinitarian context.

The space and time between the 'from' and the 'to' is marked by a struggle to live from and to the Father, through the Son, in the Spirit. It is marked by sin. So we are marked, indelibly marked, by sin. Humanity *is* curved in on itself. This is true. 'But it is even more true that there is said to [humanity] with overriding definiteness and all the power of a once-for-all act of God:

---

1.   A point disallowed by Peter Singer, the Princeton ethicist, who wants to define personhood in terms of rationality and self-consciousness (see his discussion of personhood in Peter Singer, *Personal Ethics* [Cambridge: Cambridge University Press, 1993], p. 87) and, to my shame, by me at an earlier stage in writing this book.

2.   Zizioulas, *Being as Communion*, p. 59.

"The Lord is at hand. Be careful for nothing".[3] The final word is not sin. The final word is the Word, which is Christ.

How does this understanding of human sin and personhood inform the dogmatic task? We will look at two, brief implications of this account, one methodological, the other material. The methodological implication is really a statement by way of negation and affirmation. Theology, viewed ecstatically, is open to God and the world, but not in the same way. To speak of the radical freedom and hospitality which characterizes truly *Christian* theology is not to move away from the insight that human talk of God is only possible in light of God's prior speech in God's Word. It is common to criticize theologies which privilege revelation for their insular character. These theologies, so goes the critique, are curved in on themselves.[4] Indeed they may be, but not simply as a function of their revelatory starting point. Might it not be that it is precisely the particularity of the Christological starting point that calls for a radical openness to the world? For all its chequered history, the Church has continued to confess a gospel which is inherently translatable, one which makes a home in each intellectual, cultural and temporal setting it enters. And this gospel engages in a *duplex opus*, at once undermining and establishing the cultures it encounters.[5] Of course, the gospel works like this in religious cultures as well, including the 'culture' of Christian theology. It is the very logic of the gospel which both judges and justifies Christian theology and then compels and frees it to engage widely and deeply with and in the world.

The material implication can be seen in ecclesiology. To be the church, the *ekklesia*, is to be that body of people who have been 'called out' – out of the world, yes, but also out of ourselves. It is to be those who live *excurvatus ex se*, finding our lives, ourselves in Christ and in one another. A relational account of ecclesiology, particularly one with an ecstatic dynamic, will yield a doctrine of the Church that emphasizes its missional, eschatological and, above all, doxological character.[6] This is a Church open *to* the world, the future and God; but even more it is a Church open *for* the world, the future and God. Living in and as the Church is not living self-satisfied in the possession of eternal life but is instead living ecstatically in a continual outreach which hopes for an ever-widening 'inner circle' and lives towards the vision of Revelation 7 in which people from every tongue, tribe and nation bow in worship before the Lamb of God.

***

3.   CD IV/2, p. 478.
4.   Natalie Watson describes Jüngel's theology as a theology curved in on itself. See Watson, 'Theologia Incurvata In Se Ipse?', *Reviews in Religion and Theology* 9 (2002), pp. 201–5. Of Barth's theology, Roberts writes that it is 'ensnared in its own comprehensive and consistent logic, the logic of self-isolation' (Roberts, *A Theology on Its Way?*, p. 79).
5.   See Lamin Sanneh, *Translating the Message* (Maryknoll, NY: Orbis, 1989).
6.   For a richly missional and eschatological vision of the Church, see Newbigin, *The Household of God*.

In the introduction, a couple of hundred pages ago, we noted Jüngel's remark that the sinner is 'a person without relations'. Since then, we have traced the outlines of a relational understanding of sin in Augustine's account of the beginnings of sin in the *City of God*, found these affirmed, deepened and extended in Luther's withering attack on human pride in the lectures on Romans, heard the forceful objection of Hampson to a reductivistically 'manly' tradition of hamartiology and tested the metaphor of incurvature against Barth's threefold description of sin in the doctrine of reconciliation. Many questions have been asked, and Jüngel's comment still retains much of its force. To be a sinner is to be relationless. And yet, after Barth, this must be qualified. The sinner is a person who *tries to live* without relations, who *lives as though* she had no relations. That is, curved in on herself, the sinner is one who lives as if reality were other than it is. In so doing, she sits under judgment, but it is a judgment oriented towards hope, the hope (and trust) that reality is *not* as she thinks and hopes. In this sense, it is hope against hope, hope that the sinner's cause has been taken up (like it or not) by one who will not let her fall out of relationship with him.

BIBLIOGRAPHY

'Hospitality, Justice and Responsibility: A Dialogue with Jacques Derrida', in Richard Kearney and Mark Dooley (eds.), *Questioning in Ethics: Contemporary Debates in Philosophy* (London: Routledge, 1999), pp. 65–83.

Melanchthon on Christian Doctrine: Loci communes 1555 (trans. Clyde L. Manschreck; Grand Rapids: Baker, 1982).

The Theologia Germanica of Martin Luther (trans. Bengt Hoffman; London: SPCK, 1980).

Althaus, Paul, *The Theology of Martin Luther* (trans. Robert C. Schultz; Philadelphia: Fortress Press, 1966).

American Center for Disease Control. 'Suicide Fact-Sheet'. http://www.cdc.gov/ncipc/factsheets/suifacts.htm (11 October 2004).

Arendt, Hannah, *Love and St. Augustine* (London: The University of Chicago Press, 1996).

Armstrong, H., 'Salvation, Plotinian and Christian', *The Downside Review* 75 (1957), pp. 126–39.

St Augustine, 'Exposition 2 of Psalm 18', in *Expositions of the Psalms 1-32*, Vol. 1 (trans. Maria Boulding; Hyde Park, NY: New City Press, 2000).

—*City of God* (trans. Henry Bettenson; New York: Penguin Books, 1984).

—*Confessions* (trans. Henry Chadwick; Oxford: Oxford University Press, 1998).

—*The Trinity* (trans. Edmund Hill; Brooklyn, NY: New City Press, 1991).

Ayres, Lewis, 'Between Athens and Jerusalem: Prolegomena to Anthropology in *De Trinitate*', *Modern Theology* 8 (1992), pp. 53–73.

Babcock, William S., 'Augustine on Sin and Moral Agency', *The Journal of Religious Ethics* 16 (1988), pp. 28–55.

Bainton, Roland H., *Here I Stand: A Life of Martin Luther* (London: Hodder & Stoughton, 1951).

Barth, Karl, *Anselm: Fides Quaerens Intellectum. Anselm's Proof of the Existence of God in the Context of his Theological Scheme* (trans. Ian W. Robertson; London: SCM Press, 2nd edn, 1960).

—*Christ and Adam: Man and Humanity in Romans 5* (trans. T. A. Smail; New York: Harper & Brothers, 1956).

—*The Christian Life: Church Dogmatics IV/4, Lecture Fragments* (trans. Geoffrey W. Bromiley; Grand Rapids: Eerdmans, 1981).

—*Church Dogmatics* (ed. and trans. Geoffrey W. Bromiley *et al.*; 13 vols.; Edinburgh: T&T Clark, 1956–75).

—*The Epistle to the Romans* (trans. Edwyn C. Hoskyns; Oxford: Oxford University Press, 6th edn, 1933).

—'An Introductory Essay' (trans. James Luther Adams), in Ludwig Feuerbach, *The Essence of Christianity* (trans. George Eliot; New York: Harper & Row, 1957), pp. x–xxxii.

—*The Theology of the Reformed Confessions* (trans. Darrell L. Guder and Judith J. Guder; London: Westminster/John Knox Press, 2002).

Bayer, Oswald, 'The Modern Narcissus', *Lutheran Quarterly* 9 (1995), pp. 301–13.

Baylor, Michael G., *Action and Person: Conscience in Late Scholasticism and the Young Luther* (Leiden: E. J. Brill, 1977).

Bender, Kimlyn J., *Karl Barth's Christological Ecclesiology* (Aldershot: Ashgate, 2005).

Biggar, Nigel, *The Hastening that Waits: Karl Barth's Ethics* (Oxford: Clarendon Press, 1993).

Bonhoeffer, Dietrich, *Christology* (trans. John Bowden; London: Collins, 1968).

—*Creation and Fall: A Theological Exposition of Genesis 1-3* (trans. Douglas Stephen Bax; Minneapolis: Fortress Press, 1997).

Bonner, Gerald, 'Augustine's Conception of Deification', *Journal of Theological Studies* N.S. 37 (1986), pp. 369–86.

Booth, Edward, *Saint Augustine and the Western Tradition of Self-Knowing* (Villanova, PA: Villanova University Press, 1989).

Bouyer, Louis, *The Spirit and Forms of Protestantism* (trans. A. V. Littledale; London: Collins, 1963).

Braaten, Carl E. and Robert W. Jenson (eds.), *Union with Christ: The New Finnish Interpretation of Luther* (Grand Rapids: Eerdmans, 1998).

Brown, Peter, *Augustine of Hippo: A Biography* (London: Faber & Faber, 2000).

Burnaby, John, *Amor Dei: A Study of the Religion of St. Augustine* (London: Hodder & Stoughton, 1938).

Busch, Eberhard, *The Great Passion: An Introduction to Karl Barth's Theology* (ed. Darrell L. Guder and Judith J. Guder; trans. Geoffrey W. Bromiley; Grand Rapids: Eerdmans, 2004).

—*Karl Barth and the Pietists: The Young Karl Barth's Critique of Pietism and Its Response* (trans. Daniel W. Bloesch; Downers Grove, IL: InterVarsity Press, 2004).

Cahoy, William J., 'One Species or Two? Kierkegaard's Anthropology and the Feminist Critique of the Concept of Sin', *Modern Theology* 11 (1995), pp. 429–54.

Cary, Phillip. *Augustine's Invention of the Inner Self: The Legacy of a Christian Platonist* (Oxford: Oxford University Press, 2000).

—'Book Seven: Inner Vision as the Goal of Augustine's Life', in Kim Paffenroth and Robert P. Kennedy (eds.), *A Reader's Companion to Augustine's Confessions* (London: Westminster/John Knox Press, 2003), pp. 107–26.

Casiday, Augustine, 'St. Augustine on Deification: His Homily on Psalm 81', *Sobornost* 23 (2001), pp. 23–44.

Cavadini, John, 'The Structure and Intention of Augustine's *De trinitate*', *Augustinian Studies* 23 (1992), pp. 103–23.

Cavanaugh, William T., *Theopolitical Imagination: Christian Practices of Space and Time* (Edinburgh: T&T Clark, 2002).

Chua, Daniel K. L., *Absolute Music and the Construction of Meaning* (Cambridge: Cambridge University Press, 1999).

Clark, Mary T., *Augustinian Personalism* (Villanova, PA: Villanova University Press, 1970).

Clements, Keith, 'Introduction', in Keith Clements (ed.), *Friedrich Schleiermacher: Pioneer of Modern Theology* (Minneapolis: Fortress Press, 1987), pp. 7–65.

Coakley, Sarah, *Powers and Submissions: Spirituality, Philosophy and Gender* (Oxford: Blackwell, 2002).

Cress, Donald A., 'Augustine's Privation Account of Evil: A Defense', *Augustinian Studies* 20 (1989), pp. 109–28.

Crouse, Robert, '*Paucis Mutatis Verbis*: St. Augustine's Platonism', in Robert Dodaro and George Lawless (eds.), *Augustine and His Critics: Essays in Honour of Gerald Bonner* (London: Routledge, 2000), pp. 37–50.

Cushman, Robert E., 'Barth's Attack upon Cartesianism and the Future in Theology', in *Faith Seeking Understanding* (Durham, NC: Duke University Press, 1981).

Daley, Brian E., 'A Humble Mediator: The Distinctive Elements in Saint Augustine's Christology', *Word and Spirit* 9 (1987), pp. 100–17.

Dalferth, Ingolf U., 'Karl Barth's Eschatological Realism', in S. W. Sykes (ed.), *Karl Barth: Centenary Essays* (Cambridge: Cambridge University Press, 1989), pp. 14–45.

Delbanco, Andrew, *The Death of Satan: How Americans Have Lost the Sense of Evil* (New York: Farrar, Straus and Giroux, 1995).

Derrida, Jacques, *On Cosmopolitanism and Forgiveness* (trans. Mark Dooley and Michael Hughes; London: Routledge, 2001).

—'Plato's Pharmacy', in *Dissemination* (Chicago: University of Chicago Press, 1983), pp. 61–172.

Dunfee, Susan Nelson, 'The Sin of Hiding: A Feminist Critique of Reinhold Niebuhr's Account of the Sin of Pride', *Soundings* 65 (1982), pp. 316–27.

Durkin, Eugene F., *The Theological Distinction of Sins in the Writings of St. Augustine* (Mundelein, IL: Saint Mary of the Lake Seminary, 1952).

Dyrness, William A., *Reformed Theology and Visual Culture: The Protestant Imagination from Calvin to Edwards* (Cambridge: Cambridge University Press, 2004).

Ebeling, Gerhard, 'On the Doctrine of the *Triplex Usus Legis* in the Theology of the Reformation', in *Word and Faith* (London: SCM Press, 1963), pp. 62–78.

Edwards, Jonathan, 'Charity and Its Fruits, Sermon 7', in *The Works of Jonathan Edwards*, Vol. 8: *Ethical Writings* (ed. Paul Ramsey; New Haven: Yale University Press, 1989).

Farrow, Douglas, *Ascension and Ecclesia: On the Significance of the Doctrine of the Ascension for Ecclesiology and Christian Cosmology* (Grand Rapids: Eerdmans, 1999).

Fraser, Elouise Renich, 'Jesus' Humanity and Ours in the Theology of Karl Barth', in Marguerite Shuster and Richard Muller (eds.), *Perspectives on Christology: Essays in Honor of Paul K. Jewett* (Grand Rapids: Zondervan, 1991), pp. 179–96.

Gaebler, Mary, 'Luther on the Self', *Journal of the Society of Christian Ethics* 22 (2002), pp. 115–32.

Gerrish, B. A., '"To the Unknown God": Luther and Calvin on the Hiddenness of God' *Journal of Religion* 53 (1973), pp. 263–92.

Gilligan, Carol, *In a Different Voice: Psychological Theory and Women's Development* (London: Harvard University Press, 1993).

Greene-McCreight, Kathryn, 'Feminist Theology and a Generous Orthodoxy', *Scottish Journal of Theology* 57 (2004), pp. 95–108.

—'Gender, Sin and Grace: Feminist Theologies Meet Karl Barth's Hamartiology', *Scottish Journal of Theology* 50 (1997), pp. 415–32.

Guthrie, Steven R., 'A Love Supreme: Creation and Kenosis', Unpublished manuscript.

Haddorff, David W., 'The Postmodern Realism of Barth's Ethics', *Scottish Journal of Theology* 57 (2004), pp. 269–86.

Hampson, Daphne, *After Christianity* (London: SCM Press, 1996).

—'The Challenge of Feminism to Christianity', *Theology* 88 (1985), pp. 341–50.

—*Christian Contradictions: The Structures of Lutheran and Catholic Thought*, (Cambridge: Cambridge University Press, 2001).

—'Feminism: Its Nature and Implications', *The Month* 19 (2nd series) (1986), pp. 96–9.

—'Luther on the Self: A Feminist Critique', *Word & World* 8 (1988), pp. 334–42.

—'On Autonomy and Heteronomy', in Daphne Hampson (ed.), *Swallowing a Fishbone? Feminist Theologians Debate Christianity* (London: SPCK, 1996), pp. 1–16.

—'On Power and Gender', *Modern Theology* 4 (1988), pp. 234–50.

—'Reinhold Niebuhr on Sin: A Critique', in Richard Harries (ed.), *Reinhold Niebuhr and the Issues of Our Time* (Grand Rapids: Eerdmans, 1986), pp. 46–60.

—'A Reply to Angela West', *Scottish Journal of Theology* 51 (1998), pp. 116–21.

—'Reply to Laurence Hemming', *New Blackfriars* 86 (2005), pp. 24–47.

—'Sources and the Relationship to Tradition: What Daphne Hampson is Supposed to Hold (and What She in Fact Holds)', *Feminist Theology* 3 (May 1993), pp. 23–37.

—*Theology and Feminism* (Oxford: Basil Blackwell, 1990).

Hanby, Michael, *Augustine and Modernity* (London: Routledge, 2003).

Harris, Harriet A., 'Should We Say that Personhood is Relational?', *Scottish Journal of Theology* (1998), pp. 214–34.

Harrison, Carol, *Augustine: Christian Truth and Fractured Humanity* (Oxford: Oxford University Press, 2000).

Hart, Trevor, *Regarding Karl Barth: Essays Toward a Reading of His Theology* (Carlisle: Paternoster Press, 1999).

Hauerwas, Stanley, '"Salvation even in Sin": Learning to Speak Truthfully about Ourselves', in *Sanctify Them in the Truth: Holiness Exemplified* (Nashville: Abingdon Press, 1988), pp. 61–74.

Hauerwas, Stanley and Charles Pinches, *Christians among the Virtues: Theological Conversations with Ancient and Modern Ethics* (Notre Dame, IN: University of Notre Dame Press, 1997).

Healy, Nicholas M., 'Karl Barth's Ecclesiology Reconsidered', *Scottish Journal of Theology* 57 (2004), pp. 287–99.

Hemming, Laurence Paul, 'A Contradiction: The Structure of Christian Thought', *New Blackfriars* 86 (2005), pp. 3–23.

Highfield, Ron, *Barth and Rahner in Dialogue: Toward an Ecumenical Understanding of Sin and Evil* (New York: Peter Lang, 1989).

Hunsinger, George, *Disruptive Grace: Studies in the Theology of Karl Barth* (Grand Rapids: Eerdmans, 2000).

—*How to Read Karl Barth: The Shape of His Theology* (Oxford: Oxford University Press, 1991).

Inge, W. R., *The Philosophy of Plotinus: The Gifford Lectures at St. Andrews, 1917-1918.* (2 vols.; London: Longmans, Green and Co., 1918).

Janz, Denis R., *Luther and Late Medieval Thomism: A Study in Theological Anthropology* (Waterloo, Ontario: Wilfrid Laurier University Press, 1983).

Jenson, Robert W., 'The Doctrine of Justification and the Practice of Counseling', in *Essays in Theology of Culture* (Grand Rapids: Eerdmans, 1995), pp. 105–16.

—*Systematic Theology 1: The Triune God* (Oxford: Oxford University Press, 1997).

Joest, Wilfred, *Ontologie der Person bei Luther* (Göttingen: Vandenhoeck and Ruprecht, 1967).

St John of the Cross, *Poems of St. John of the Cross* (trans. Roy Campbell; London: Pantheon Books, 1951).

Johnson, Mark, *The Body in the Mind: The Bodily Basis of Meaning, Imagination, and Reason* (Chicago: The University of Chicago Press, 1987).

Johnson, Wayne G., *Theological Method in Luther and Tillich: Law-Gospel and Correlation* (Washington, DC: University Press of America, 1981).

Johnson, William Stacy, *The Mystery of God: Karl Barth and the Postmodern Foundations of Theology* (Louisville, KY: Westminster/John Knox Press, 1997).

Jorgenson, Allen, 'Karl Barth's Christological Treatment of Sin', *Scottish Journal of Theology* 54 (2001), pp. 437–62.

Jüngel, Eberhard, 'Humanity in Correspondence to God: Remarks on the image of God as a basic concept in theological anthropology', in *Theological Essays* (ed. and trans. J. B. Webster; Edinburgh: T&T Clark, 1989), pp. 124–53.

—*Justification: The Heart of the Christian Faith* (trans. Jeffrey F. Cayzer; Edinburgh: T&T Clark, 2001).

—*Karl Barth, A Theological Legacy* (trans. Garrett E. Paul; Philadelphia: The Westminster Press, 1986).

—'Living Out of Righteousness: God's Action – Human Agency', in *Theological Essays II* (ed. J. B. Webster; trans. Arnold Neufeldt-Fast and J. B. Webster; Edinburgh: T&T Clark, 1995), pp. 241–63.

—'On Becoming Truly Human: The Significance of the Reformation Distinction Between Person and Works for the Self-Understanding of Modern Humanity', in *Theological Essays II* (ed. J. B. Webster; trans. Arnold Neufeldt-Fast and J. B. Webster; Edinburgh: T&T Clark, 1995), pp. 216–40.

—'The World as Possibility and Actuality: The Ontology of the Doctrine of Justification', in *Theological Essays* (ed. and trans. J. B. Webster; Edinburgh: T&T Clark, 1989), pp. 95–123.

Kant, Immanuel, 'An Answer to the Question: What is Enlightenment?', in *Practical Philosophy* (ed. Mary J. Gregor; Cambridge: Cambridge University Press, 1996), pp. 15–22.

—*Groundwork of the Metaphysics of Morals* (trans. Mary Gregor; Cambridge: Cambridge University Press, 1997).

Kärkkäinen, Veli-Matti, '"The Christian as Christ to the Neighbour": On Luther's Theology of Love', *International Journal of Systematic Theology* 6 (2004), pp. 101–17.

Kelsey, David H., 'Whatever Happened to the Doctrine of Sin?', *Theology Today* 50 (1993), pp. 169–78.

Kierkegaard, Søren, *Philosophical Fragments / Johannes Climacus* (ed. and trans. Howard V. Hong and Edna H. Hong; Princeton: Princeton University Press, 1985).

Krötke, Wolf, 'The Humanity of the Human Person in Karl Barth's Anthropology', in John Webster (ed.), *The Cambridge Companion to Karl Barth* (Cambridge: Cambridge University Press, 2000), pp. 159–76.

—*Sin and Nothingness in the Theology of Karl Barth* (ed. and trans. Philip G. Ziegler and Christina-Maria Bammel; Princeton: Princeton Theology Seminary, 2005).

Leclerc, Diane, *Singleness of Heart: Gender, Sin and Holiness in Historical Perspective* (London: Scarecrow Press, 2001).

Lewis, C. S., *The Four Loves* (London: Fount Paperbacks, 1960).

von Loewenich, Walter, *Luther's Theology of the Cross* (trans. Herbert J. A. Bouman; Belfast: Christian Journals Limited, 1976).

—*Martin Luther: The Man and His Work* (trans. Lawrence W. Denef; Minneapolis: Augsburg Publishing House, 1986).

Lohse, Bernard, *A Short History of Christian Doctrine* (trans. F. Ernest Stoeffler; Philadelphia: Fortress Press, 1985).

—*Martin Luther's Theology: Its Historical and Systematic Development* (trans. Roy A. Harrisville; Minneapolis: Fortress Press, 1999).

Long, D. Stephen, 'God is Not Nice', in D. Brent Laytham (ed.), *God is Not...* (Grand Rapids: Eerdmans, 2004), pp. 39–54.

Loughlin, Gerard, *Alien Sex: The Body and Desire in Cinema and Theology* (Oxford: Blackwell, 2004).

Luther, Martin, *Luther's Works* (ed. Jaroslav Pelikan and Helmut T. Lehmann; 55 vols.; St. Louis: Concordia Publishing House and Philadelphia: Muhlenberg Press, 1955–86).

Macken, John, *The Autonomy Theme in the Church Dogmatics: Karl Barth and His Critics* (Cambridge: Cambridge University Press, 1990).

Mackinnon, D. M., '"Substance" in Christology – A Cross-Bench View', in S. W. Sykes and J. P. Clayton (eds.), *Christ, Faith and History: Cambridge Studies in Christology* (London: Cambridge University Press, 1972), pp. 279–300.

Macmurray, John, *Persons in Relation* (London: Faber & Faber, 1961).

Macqueen, D. J., 'Augustine on *Superbia*: The Historical Background and Sources of His Doctrine', *Mélanges de Science Religieuse* 34 (1977), pp. 193–211.

—'*Contemptus Dei*: St Augustine on the Disorder of Pride in Society, and its Remedies', *Recherches Augustiniennes* 9 (1973), pp. 227–93.

Mallard, William, 'The Incarnation in Augustine's Conversion', *Recherches Augustiniennes* 15 (1980), pp. 80–98.

Mangina, Joseph L., *Karl Barth on the Christian Life: The Practical Knowledge of God* (New York: Peter Lang, 2001).

Mannermaa, Tuomo, *Christ Present in Faith: Luther's View of Justification* (ed. Kirsi Stjerna; Minneapolis: Fortress Press, 2005).

—'Why Is Luther So Fascinating?', in Braaten and Jenson (eds.), *Union with Christ*, pp. 1–20.

Marius, Richard, *Martin Luther: The Christian Between God and Death* (London: Belknap Press, 1999).

Markus, R. A., '*De ciuitate dei*: Pride and the Common Good', in Joseph C. Schnaubelt and Frederick Van Fleteren (eds.), *Collectanea Augustiniana*, vol. 1: *Augustine: Second Founder of the Faith* (New York: Peter Lang, 1990), pp. 245–59.

—*Saeculum: History and Society in the Theology of St Augustine* (London: Cambridge University Press, 1970).

Marshall, Ronald F., 'News from the Graveyard: Kierkegaard's Analysis of Christian Self-Hatred', *Pro Ecclesia* 9 (2000), pp. 19–42.

Mathewes, Charles T., 'Augustinian Anthropology: *Interior intimo meo*', *Journal of Religious Ethics* 27 (1999), pp. 195–221.

McCormack, Bruce, 'Grace and Being: The Role of God's Gracious Election in Karl Barth's Theological Ontology', in John Webster (ed.), *The Cambridge Companion to Karl Barth* (Cambridge: Cambridge University Press, 2000), pp. 92–110.

—*Karl Barth's Critically Realistic Dialectical Theology: Its Genesis and Development, 1909-36* (Oxford: Oxford University Press, 1997).

McCue, James F., '*Simul iustus et peccator* in Augustine, Aquinas, and Luther: Toward Putting the Debate in Context', *Journal of the American Academy of Religion* 48 (1947), pp. 81–96.

McDonnell, Kilian, 'Jesus' Baptism in the Jordan', *Theological Studies* 56 (1995), pp. 209–36.

McDonough, Thomas M., *The Law and the Gospel in Luther: A Study of Martin Luther's Confessional Writings* (Oxford: Oxford University Press, 1963).

McFadyen, Alistair, *Bound to Sin: Abuse, Holocaust and the Christian Doctrine of Sin* (Cambridge: Cambridge University Press, 2000).

—*The Call to Personhood: A Christian Theory of the Individual in Social Relationships* (Cambridge: Cambridge University Press, 1990).

—'Sins of Praise: The Assault on God's Freedom', in Colin E. Gunton (ed.), *God and Freedom: Essays in Historical and Systematic Theology* (Edinburgh: T&T Clark, 1995), pp. 32–56.

McGrath, Alister E., *Iustitia Dei: A History of the Christian Doctrine of Justification* (Cambridge: Cambridge University Press, 2nd edn, 1998).

McLean, Stuart D., 'Creation and Anthropology', in John Thompson (ed.), *Theology Beyond Christendom: Essays on the Centenary of the Birth of Karl Barth, May 10, 1886* (Allison Park, PA: Pickwick Publications, 1986), pp. 111–42.

—*Humanity in the Thought of Karl Barth* (Edinburgh: T&T Clark, 1981).

Meagher, Robert (ed.), *Augustine: On the Inner Life of the Mind* (Cambridge: Hackett Publishing Company, 1998).

Meconi, David Vincent, 'The Incarnation and the Role of Participation in St. Augustine's *Confessions*', *Augustinian Studies* 29 (1998), pp. 61–75.

Metzger, Paul Louis, 'Mystical Union with Christ: An Alternative to Blood Transfusions and Legal Fictions', *Westminster Theological Journal* 65 (2003), pp. 201–13.

Migliore, D. L., 'Sin and Self-Loss: Karl Barth and the Feminist Critique of Traditional Doctrines of Sin', in Walter Brueggemann and George W. Stroup (eds.), *Many Voices, One God: Being Faithful in a Pluralistic World* (Louisville: Westminster/John Knox Press, 1998), pp. 139–54.

Milbank, John, 'Sacred Triads: Augustine and the Indo-European Soul', in Robert Dodaro and George Lawless (eds.), *Augustine and His Critics: Essays in Honour of Gerald Bonner* (London: Routledge, 2000), pp. 77–102.

Miles, Margaret, 'Vision: The Eye of the Body and the Eye of the Mind in Saint Augustine's *De trinitate* and *Confessions*', *Journal of Religion* 63 (1983), pp. 125–42.

Moltmann, Jürgen, *Theology of Hope: On the Ground and the Implications of a Christian Eschatology* (trans. James W. Leitch; Minneapolis: Fortress Press, 1993).

—*The Trinity and the Kingdom of God: The doctrine of God* (trans. Margaret Kohl; London: SCM Press, 1981).

Moltmann-Wendel, Elisabeth, and Jürgen Moltmann, *God – His and Hers* (trans. John Bowden; New York: Crossroad, 1991).

Morelli, Elizabeth A., 'The Question of Woman's Experience of God', in Alvin F. Kimel Jr (ed.), *Speaking the Christian God: The Holy Trinity and the Challenge of Feminism* (Leominster: Gracewing, 1992), pp. 222–36.

Newbigin, Lesslie, *The Household of God: Lectures on the Nature of the Church* (London: SCM Press, 1953).

Niebuhr, Reinhold, *The Nature and Destiny of Man: A Christian Interpretation*. vol. 1: *Human Nature* (New York: Charles Scribner's Sons, 1964).

Nygren, Anders, *Agape and Eros* (trans. Philip S. Watson; New York: Harper & Row, 1969).

—*Meaning and Method: Prolegomena to a Scientific Philosophy of Religion and a Scientific Theology* (trans. P. S. Watson; London: Epworth, 1972).

Oberman, Heiko A., '*Facientibus quod in se est deus non denegat gratiam*: Robert Holcot O.P. and the Beginnings of Luther's Theology', in *The Dawn of the Reformation: Essays in Late Medieval and Early Reformation Thought* (Grand Rapids: Eerdmans, 1986), pp. 84–103.

—'Gabriel Biel and Late Medieval Mysticism', *Church History* 30 (1961), pp. 259–87.

—*Luther: Man Between God and the Devil* (trans. Eileen Walliser-Schwarzbart; London: Image Books, 1992).

—'*Simul Gemitus et Raptus*: Luther and Mysticism', in *The Dawn of the Reformation: Essays in Late Medieval and Early Reformation Thought* (Grand Rapids: Eerdmans, 1992), pp. 126–54.

—'Wir sein pettler. Hoc est verum. Covenant and Grace in the Theology of the Middle Ages and Reformation', in *The Reformation: Roots and Ramifications* (Grand Rapids: Eerdmans, 1994), pp. 91–115.

O'Connell, Robert J., 'Augustine's Exegetical Use of Ecclesiasticus 10:9-14', in Frederick Van Fleteren and Joseph C. Schnaubelt (eds.), *Augustine: Biblical Exegete* (Oxford: Peter Lang, 2001), pp. 233–52.

O'Donovan, Oliver, *The Problem of Self-Love in St. Augustine* (London: Yale University Press, 1980).

—'*Usus* and *Fruitio* in Augustine, *De Doctrina Christiana I*', *Journal of Theological Studies*, N.S. 33 (1982), pp. 361–97.

Outka, Gene, 'Universal Love and Impartiality', in Edmund N. Santurri and William Werpehowski (eds.), *The Love Commandments: Essays in Christian Ethics and Moral Philosophy* (Washington, DC: Georgetown University Press, 1992), pp. 1–103.

Ozment, Steven, 'The Mental World of Martin Luther', in *The Age of Reform (1250-1550): An Intellectual and Religious History of Late Medieval and Reformation Europe* (London: Yale University Press, 1980), pp. 223–44.

—*Homo Spiritualis: A Comparative Study of the Anthropology of Johannes Tauler, Jean Gerson and Martin Luther (1509-16) in the Context of Their Theological Thought* (Leiden: E. J. Brill, 1969).

Padgett, Alan G., *God, Eternity and the Nature of Time* (New York: St. Martin's Press, 1992).

Pannenberg, Wolfhart, *Anthropology in Theological Perspective* (trans. Matthew J. O'Connell; Edinburgh: T&T Clark, 1985).

Plaskow, Judith, *Sex, Sin and Grace: Women's Experience and the Theologies of Reinhold Niebuhr and Paul Tillich* (London: University Press of America, 1980).

Plotinus, *Enneads* (trans. A. H. Armstrong; London: Heinemann, 1966–88).

Prenter, Regin, 'Holiness in the Lutheran Tradition', in Marina Chavchavadze (ed.), *Man's Concern with Holiness* (London: Hodder & Stoughton, 1970), pp. 121–44.

—*Spiritus Creator: Luther's Concept of the Holy Spirit* (trans. John M. Jensen; Philadelphia: Muhlenberg Press, 1953).

Raven, Susan, *Rome in Africa* (London: Routledge, 3rd edn, 1993).

Reno, R. R., *In the Ruins of the Church: Sustaining Faith in an Age of Diminished Christianity* (Grand Rapids: Brazos Press, 2002).

Rist, John M., *Augustine: Ancient Thought Baptized* (Cambridge: Cambridge University Press, 1994).

Roberts, Richard H., *A Theology on Its Way? Essays on Karl Barth* (Edinburgh: T&T Clark, 1991).

Rogers, Eugene, 'The Stranger: The Stranger as Blessing', in James J. Buckley and David S. Yeago (eds.), *Knowing the Triune God: The Work of the Spirit in the Practices of the Church* (Grand Rapids: Eerdmans, 2001), pp. 265–83.

Rupp, Gordon, *Luther's Progress to the Diet of Worms: 1521* (London: SCM Press, 1951).

—*The Righteousness of God: Luther Studies* (London: Hodder & Stoughton, 1953).

Russell, Edward, 'Reconsidering Relational Anthropology: A Critical Assessment of John Zizioulas's Theological Anthropology', *International Journal of Systematic Theology* 5 (2003), pp. 168–86.

Saarnivaara, Uuras, 'The Growth of Luther's Teaching of Justification: A Re-Examination of the Development of Luther's Teaching of Justification from a Roman Catholic to an Evangelical Understanding' (doctoral dissertation, University of Chicago, 1945).

Saiving Goldstein, Valerie, 'The Human Situation: A Feminine View', *Journal of Religion* 40 (1960), pp. 100–12.

Sanneh, Lamin, *Translating the Message: The Missionary Impact on Culture* (Maryknoll, NY: Orbis, 1989).

Schleiermacher, Friedrich, *Christmas Eve: Dialogue on the Incarnation* (trans. Terrence N. Tice; San Francisco: The Edwin Mellen Press, 1990).

Schneewind, J. B., 'Autonomy, Obligation, and Virtue: An Overview of Kant's Moral Philosophy', in Paul Guyer (ed.), *The Cambridge Companion to Kant* (Cambridge: Cambridge University Press, 1992), pp. 309–41.

—*The Invention of Autonomy: A History of Modern Moral Philosophy* (Cambridge: Cambridge University Press, 1998).

Selinger, Suzanne, *Charlotte von Kirschbaum and Karl Barth: A Study in Biography and the History of Theology* (University Park, PA: The Pennsylvania State University Press, 1998).

Shults, F. LeRon, *Reforming Theological Anthropology: After the Philosophical Turn to Relationality* (Grand Rapids: Eerdmans, 2003).

Siggins, Ian D. Kingston, *Martin Luther's Doctrine of Christ* (London: Yale University Press, 1970).

Singer, Peter, *Personal Ethics* (Cambridge: Cambridge University Press, 1993).

Smail, Tom, *The Giving Gift: The Holy Spirit in Person* (London: Hodder & Stoughton, 1988).

Smith, James K. A., *Speech and Theology: Language and the Logic of Incarnation* (London: Routledge, 2002).

Sponheim, Paul R., 'On Being and Becoming before God: A Response to Daphne Hampson', *Word & World* 15 (1995), pp. 332–41.

Starnes, Colin, *Augustine's Conversion: A Guide to the Argument of Confessions I–IX* (Waterloo, Ontario: Wilfrid Laurier University Press, 1990).

Steinmetz, David C., *Luther and Staupitz: An Essay in the Intellectual Origins of the Protestant Reformation* (Durham, NC: Duke University Press, 1980).

—*Luther in Context* (Grand Rapids: Baker Academic, 2nd edn, 2002).

Stiver, Dan R., *Theology After Ricoeur: New Directions in Hermeneutical Theology* (Louisville: Westminster/John Knox Press, 2001).

Studer, Basil, *The Grace of Christ and the Grace of God in Augustine of Hippo: Christocentrism or Theocentrism?* (trans. Matthew J. O'Connell; Collegeville, MN: The Liturgical Press, 1997).

Tanner, Kathryn, *God and Creation in Christian Theology: Tyranny or Empowerment?* (Oxford: Basil Blackwell, 1988).

—*Jesus, Humanity and the Trinity: A Brief Systematic Theology* (Edinburgh: T&T Clark, 2001).

—'re: non-competitiveness and research' (personal e-mail, 28 April 2003).

Taylor, Charles, *Sources of the Self: The Making of the Modern Identity* (Cambridge: Cambridge University Press, 1989).

Tennant, F. R., *The Sources of the Doctrines of the Fall and Original Sin* (New York: Schocken Books, 1968 [originally published in 1903]).

Thandeka, 'Schleiermacher's Dialektik: The Discovery of the Self That Kant Lost', *Harvard Theological Review* 85 (1992), pp. 433–52.

Thistlethwaite, Susan Brooks, *Sex, Race, and God: Christian Feminism in Black and White* (New York: Crossroad, 1989).

Torrance, Alan J., 'The Self-Relation, Narcissism and the Gospel of Grace', *Scottish Journal of Theology* 40 (1987), pp. 481–510.

Torrance, J. B., 'Covenant or Contract? A Study of the Theological Background of Worship in Seventeenth-Century Scotland', *Scottish Journal of Theology* 23 (1970), pp. 51–76.

Torrance, T. F., 'The Eschatology of Faith: Martin Luther', in George Yule (ed.), *Luther: Theologian for Catholics and Protestants* (Edinburgh: T&T Clark, 1985), pp. 145–213.

Trench, Richard Chenevix, *Exposition of the Sermon on the Mount Drawn from the Writings of St. Augustine with observations and an introductory essay on his merits as an interpreter of holy scripture* (London: Macmillan and Co., 3rd edn, 1869).

Trible, Phyllis, 'Eve and Adam: Genesis 2-3 Reread', *Andover Newton Quarterly* 13 (1973), pp. 251–8.

Turner, Denys, *The Darkness of God: Negativity in Christian Mysticism* (Cambridge: Cambridge University Press, 1995).

Volf, Miroslav, *Exclusion and Embrace: A Theological Exploration of Identity, Otherness and Reconciliation* (Nashville: Abingdon Press, 1996).

Watson, Natalie K., '*Theologia Incurvata In Se Ipse?*: One Feminist Theologian's Reading of Eberhard Jüngel's Theology', *Reviews in Religion and Theology* 9 (2002), pp. 201–5.

Watson, Philip, 'Luther and Sanctification', *Concordia Theological Monthly* 30 (1959), pp. 243–59.

—*Let God Be God! An Interpretation of the Theology of Martin Luther* (Philadelphia: Muhlenberg Press, 1947).

Webster, John, *Barth's Moral Theology: Human Action in Barth's Thought* (Grand Rapids: Eerdmans, 1998).

—'Rescuing the Subject: Barth and Postmodern Anthropology', in Geoff Thompson and Christiaan Mostert (eds.), *Karl Barth: A Future for Postmodern Theology?* (Hindmarsh: Australian Theological Forum, 2000), pp. 49–69.

West, Angela, *Deadly Innocence: Feminism and the Mythology of Sin* (London: Mowbray, 1995).

—'Justification by Gender – Daphne Hampson's *After Christianity*', *Scottish Journal of Theology* 51 (1998), pp. 99–115.

Whittaker, John H., '"Agape" and Self-Love', in Edmund N. Santurri and William Werpehowski (eds.), *The Love Commandments: Essays in Christian Ethics and Moral Philosophy* (Washington, DC: Georgetown University Press, 1992), pp. 221–39.

Wiley, Tatha, *Original Sin: Origins, Developments, Contemporary Meanings* (New York: Paulist Press, 2002).

Williams, Robert R., 'Sin and Evil', in Peter Hodgson and Robert King (eds.), *Christian Theology: An Introduction to Its Traditions and Tasks* (Minneapolis: Fortress Press, 1994), pp. 168–95.

Williams, Rowan, 'Insubstantial Evil', in Robert Dodaro and George Lawless (eds.), *Augustine and His Critics: Essays in Honour of Gerald Bonner* (London: Routledge, 2000), pp. 105–23.

Wingren, Gustaf, *Luther on Vocation* (trans. Carl C. Rasmussen; Philadelphia: Muhlenberg Press, 1957).

Wolff, Robert Paul, *The Autonomy of Reason: A Commentary on Kant's Groundwork of the Metaphysic of Morals* (Gloucester, MA: Peter Smith, 1986).

Wood, A. Skevington, 'The Theology of Luther's Lectures on Romans - Part I', *Scottish Journal of Theology* 3 (1950), pp. 1–18.

World Health Organization. 'Self-Directed Violence'. http://www.who.int/violence_injury_prevention/violence/global_campaign/en/selfdirectedviolfacts.pdf (11 October 2004).

Wright, N. T., *What Saint Paul Really Said: Was Paul of Tarsus the Real Founder of Christianity?* (Grand Rapids: Eerdmans, 1997).

Yeago, David S., 'The Catholic Luther', *First Things* 61 (1996), pp. 37–41.

—'The New Testament and the Nicene Dogma: A Contribution to the Recovery of Theological Exegesis', in Stephen E. Fowl (ed.), *The Theological Interpretation of Scripture: Classic and Contemporary Readings* (London: Blackwell Publishers, 1997), pp. 87–100.

Zizioulas, John D., *Being as Communion: Studies in Personhood and the Church* (Crestwood, NY: St. Vladimir's Seminary Press, 1985).